Chicken Soup
to Inspire a Woman's Soul

CHICKEN SOUP TO INSPIRE A WOMAN'S SOUL

Stories Celebrating the Wisdom, Fun and Freedom of Midlife

Jack Canfield
Mark Victor Hansen
Stephanie Marston

Health Communications, Inc.
Deerfield Beach, Florida

www.hcibooks.com
www.chickensoup.com

We would like to acknowledge the many publishers and individuals who granted us permission to reprint the cited material. (Note: The stories that are in the public domain or that were written by Jack Canfield, Mark Victor Hansen or Stephanie Marston are not included in this listing.)

Dare To . . . and *It's Never Too Late To . . .* Reprinted by permission of Meiji Stewart. ©2001 Meiji Stewart.

Wild Waters Run Deep. Reprinted by permission of Benita Tobin. ©2003 Benita Tobin.

Babes on Blades. Reprinted by permission of Suzan Davis. ©2002 Suzan Davis.

Paper Suits Me. Reprinted by permission of Mary Clare Lockman. ©1998 Mary Clare Lockman.

Change Is Synonymous with Hope. From *Fifty on Fifty* by Bonnie Miller Rubin. ©1998 by Bonnie Miller Rubin. Reprinted by permission of Warner Books, Inc.

(continued on page 347)

Library of Congress Cataloging-in-Publication Data

Chicken soup to inspire a woman's soul : stories to ignite more meaning, passion, and joy in the prime of your life / [edited by] Jack Canfield, Mark Victor Hansen, Stephanie Marston.
    p. cm.
ISBN 0-7573-0210-6 (tp)
    1. Women—Psychology. 2. Self-realization in women. 3. Women—Conduct of life. I. Canfield, Jack, 1944– II. Hansen, Mark Victor.
III. Marston, Stephanie.

HQ1206.C515 2004
158.1'28'082—dc22

2004047566

Publisher: Health Communications, Inc.
           3201 S.W. 15th Street
           Deerfield Beach, FL 33442–8190

R-10-04

Cover design by Larissa Hise Henoch
Inside formatting by Dawn Von Strolley Grove

This book is dedicated to the millions of midlife women who dare to take time to nurture their souls and open their hearts fully to life.

Contents

3. LETTING GO

4. TAKING TIME FOR LOVE

5. ON PARENTING

X

CONTENTS

Acknowledgments

The path to *Chicken Soup to Inspire a Woman's Soul* has been made all the more beautiful by the many companions who have been there with us along the way. Our heartfelt gratitude to:

Our families, who have been chicken soup for our souls.

Inga, Christopher, Oran and Kyle Canfield, and Travis and Riley Mahoney for all their love and support.

Patty, Elisabeth and Melanie Hansen, for once again sharing and lovingly supporting us in creating yet another book.

Ama Marston, for being a joy and an inspiration.

Our publisher, Peter Vegso, for his vision and commitment to bringing *Chicken Soup for the Soul* to the world.

Patty Aubery and Russ Kalmaski, for being there every step of the journey, with love, laughter and endless creativity.

Tasha Boucher, for producing our final manuscript with magnificent ease, finesse and care. Thanks for making the final stages of production such a breeze!

Leslie Riskin, for her care and loving determination to secure our permissions and get everything just right.

Nancy Autio, Barbara Lomonaco and Gretchen Stadnik, for nourishing us with truly wonderful stories and cartoons.

D'ette Corona, for being there to answer any questions along the way.

Lisa Drucker, for taking the time to carefully line edit the final manuscript.

Patty Hansen, for her thorough and competent handling of the legal and licensing aspects of the *Chicken Soup for the Soul* books. You are magnificent at the challenge!

Laurie Hartman, for being a precious guardian of the Chicken Soup brand.

Veronica Romero, Teresa Esparza, Robin Yerian, Stephanie Thatcher, Jody Emme, Trudy Marschall, Michelle Adams, Dee Dee Romanello, Shanna Vieyra, Lisa Williams, Gina Romanello, Brittany Shaw, Dena Jacobson, Tanya Jones, Mary McKay and David Coleman, who support Jack's and Mark's businesses with skill and love.

Bret Witter, Allison Janse, Elisabeth Rinaldi and Kathy Grant, the editorial department at Health Communications, Inc., for their devotion to excellence.

Terry Burke, Tom Sand, Lori Golden, Kelly Johnson Maragni, Randee Feldman, Patricia McConnell, Kim Weiss, Paola Fernandez-Rana, the marketing, sales and PR departments at Health Communications, Inc., for doing such an incredible job supporting our books.

Tom Sand, Claude Choquette and Luc Jutras, who manage year after year to get our books translated into thirty-six languages around the world.

The art department at Health Communications, Inc., for their talent, creativity and unrelenting patience in producing book covers and inside designs that capture the essence of *Chicken Soup*: Larissa Hise Henoch, Lawna Patterson Oldfield, Andrea Perrine Brower, Anthony Clausi and Dawn Von Strolley Grove.

The *Chicken Soup for the Soul* coauthors, all of whom make it such a joy to be part of this *Chicken Soup* family.

Our glorious panel of readers who helped us make the

final selections and made invaluable suggestions on how to improve the book: Valarie Bechtol, Krisit Boylan, Karen Briggs, Pam Burnham, Sharon Castiglione, June Cerza Kolf, Heather Cook, Don Cummings, Maureen Cummings, Chris Dahl, Celeste Fremon, Renee King, Terry LePine, Ruth Lethrop, Irene Michon, Linda Mitchell, Karen Rivera, Anne Scholder, Shari Shields, Marian Small, Betty Stockton, Nancy Toney, Denene Van Hecker, Cathy Warren, Jeanie Winstrom, Judy Westrich and Suzanne Zoglio.

And, most of all, everyone who submitted their heartfelt stories, poems, quotes and cartoons for possible inclusion in this book. While we were not able to use everything you sent in, we know that each word came from a magical place flourishing within your soul. May the spirit of nature carry you gently toward peace!

Because of the size of this project, we might have left out the names of some people who contributed along the way. If so, we are sorry, but please know that we really do appreciate you.

We are truly grateful and love you all!

Introduction

This book is a gift to you, the midlife women of the world. In writing this book, we wanted to provide support, inspiration and encouragement to any of you who are using this milestone as a time to reclaim your lives and your dreams. As we read through the thousands of stories that we considered for *Chicken Soup to Inspire a Woman's Soul,* we found a depth, a strength, a resilience, a generosity and a resourcefulness that were truly inspiring.

One of our reasons for writing this book is that women in our culture often struggle to focus on themselves, their needs and their dreams. Let's face it, much of women's value comes from the ability to know what other people's needs are and to fulfill them. Yet, deep within, each woman longs to reinstate herself at the center of her own life.

Don't panic: We're not suggesting that you abandon your family, career or loved ones. We're simply suggesting that you bring yourself back into the equation, that you make your needs part of the overall picture.

Let us let you in on a little secret: If you use this time to reevaluate your life—to question anything you've been doing on autopilot for a long time, be it in your career, family or relationships—then you can begin to unearth the secret wishes that will take you back to a more authentic sense of yourself.

Now's the time to take your neglected dreams off of the back burner. Whatever you've been longing to do, whatever you've been yearning to reclaim, now's the time.

This book was created to inspire you to cast off old constraints and become who you truly are at the core of your being. We hope that you will see yourself in the stories of these women—women who at times have struggled yet have successfully reclaimed their lives. As you immerse yourself in these stories, we hope that you will explore your own quest for greater satisfaction and fulfillment.

The question remains: How can you make this time of your life rich in self-discovery, growth and transformation? To start, you can honor where you have been and what you've done; you can acknowledge the challenges you have endured, the strengths you have accumulated, and the knowledge you have extracted from your experiences. In other words, you can celebrate all that you are and all that you are becoming.

It is with this in mind that we offer you *Chicken Soup to Inspire a Woman's Soul.* May you experience the inspiration, support and encouragement you need to discover greater passion, joy and fulfillment, and to make this time one of the best times of your life.

Share with Us

We would love to hear your reactions to the stories in this book. Please let us know what your favorite stories were and how they affected you.

We also invite you to send us stories you would like to see published in future editions of *Chicken Soup for the Soul.* Please send submissions to:

Chicken Soup for the Soul
P.O. Box 30880
Santa Barbara, CA 93130
fax: 805-563-2945

You can also visit or access e-mail at the *Chicken Soup for the Soul* site:

www.chickensoup.com

We hope you enjoy reading this book as much as we enjoyed compiling, editing and writing it.

Dare To . . .

Ask for what you want.
Believe in yourself.
Change your mind.
Do what you love.
Enjoy each and every day.
Follow your heart's desire.
Give more than you receive.
Have a sense of humor.
Insist on being yourself.
Join in more.
Kiss and make up.
Love and be loved.
Make new friends.
Nurture your spirit.
Overcome adversity.
Play more.
Question conformity.
Reach for the stars.
Speak your truth.
Take personal responsibility.
Understand more, judge less.
Volunteer your time.
Walk through fear.
Xperience the moment.
Yearn for grace.
be Zany.

Meiji Stewart

1

IT'S MY TURN NOW

Follow your dreams, for as you dream, so you shall become.

James Allen

Wild Waters Run Deep

If we wait for our hands to stop shaking, we will never open the door.

Naomi Newman

No doubt about it, a fortieth birthday requires a spectacular celebration. So I did what I thought a self-respecting, bold woman who has learned that she is responsible for her happiness might do—I decided to make my own party and take it with me! That my celebration took place in a foreign country, where I was alone, surrounded by a group of strangers and involved a near-death experience that coincided with my birthday was grist for the mill.

I decided to go white-water rafting because it was something new and wild and adventurous that would push the fear envelope. As Eleanor Roosevelt said, "You must do the thing you think you cannot do." White-water rafting through class IV and class V rapids down the Rio Pacuare in the Costa Rican rain forest seemed like just the ticket! So, I packed my Spanish tape, water bottle, bathing suit, sandals and sunscreen, and set off for my "Fortieth Birthday White-Water Rafting Adventure of a Lifetime." Little did I know, wild waters run deep.

I should have taken it as a premonition when our bus made a pit stop along the road to the river where a vendor was selling "I survived Rio Pacuare" T-shirts. I bought one and put it on; people on the bus with me all laughed! Maybe I should have thought better of getting in a raft with a group of total strangers, most who had never rafted before, and going down a river with such potential danger. And, it probably is not the best thing to be with guides who speak limited English and give only cursory lessons in rafting, which mostly included telling us to hold on, *a lot*. And, maybe there is something to the proliferative liability laws that we have in the United States, at least as far as the safety protection they may offer toward the assumption of risk.

Well, you probably guessed it. Not too long into the experience, I was knocked out of the raft, went over a small waterfall into a whirlpool (they call it a "hydraulic"; I call it "hell") and got sucked to the bottom of the river in a swirling confusion of water. And that was just the beginning of the ride. Fortunately, I did have on a helmet and life jacket. I can't imagine what I would have done without them. Nevertheless, I did get quite an exfoliation from the numerous rocks I hit, not to mention all the water I swallowed.

While I was busy getting more than I bargained for, I had an epiphany about life. While being tossed about by those wonderful, wild waters and flopping in and out of submersion like a rag doll, my mind took me to another place. Somehow, I got my feet pointed downstream like you're supposed to. And, I did my best to keep my head above water as much as possible, which, actually, was nearly impossible. It was horrible trying to breathe and not being able to get enough air. But, I became incredibly calm, despite the sheer terror of the situation and the possibility that I might die.

I thought, *Oh wow. I fell into the river in the middle of a rapid. Boy, this really hurts my lungs to try to breathe. Hmmm. Wow. Hey, I might die!* I actually felt pretty neutral about the whole thing, living or dying, that is, and I had a strange sort of peacefulness and the ability to watch myself almost from the outside. Maybe all those Buddhist meditation exercises and books about "mindfulness" had paid off!

They tell me that the primary reason I survived that day is precisely because I did not fight the river, because I did not try to swim against the almighty power of rushing water, because I did, in a sense, surrender to the experience. I let the river take me where it would. I actually went through three whirlpools, and each time it got easier.

The drama that day was high magnitude. All the other rafters pulled over to the shore. People were crying and praying and most just looked on with terror at what was unfolding. There were several ropes across the river and three experienced kayakers went in for my rescue. It was quite a scene.

Later, the guides talked about how amazingly polite I was during my rescue. I don't remember that at all. Inside, I am pretty sure I felt like grabbing some guy by the shirt and growling, "Get me out of here, *now!*" But, in reality, they say that when a kayak came toward me, I simply held out my hand and arm and meekly said, "Could you please help me?" Please? I said that? I learned that oftentimes a rescuer is nearly drowned by someone who desperately wants *out* of the river.

I was dragged to shore and given medical attention and lots of people cheered and some pretty cute Costa Rican guys were all giving me high-fives. I enjoyed the moment and the attention I was getting, *until* they told me I had to get back in the raft and continue down the river. I really did not want to do that at all, but I found out I had no choice. Also, I could tell everyone's morale seemed to be hanging on my getting back in that raft and going on.

Not feeling very brave, I did go on. I got through the whole course of the river and lived to tell about it. I do have to admit to hunkering down in the middle of the raft a few times when I was supposed to be paddling, but I was scared, and that was the best I could do.

One thing I learned that day is that your best is all you can do and that is exactly what you should do—and your best is very often good enough. Sometimes you fall out of the raft and have to get back in and continue on down the river. And sometimes the best way to get through a difficulty is to just let it be! Don't fight it. Let it be difficult. Know that that is what is happening and that your reaction to it, is what it is. Surrender doesn't mean doing nothing, being passive. Or being perfect. On the contrary, it is a very active thing to let yourself have the experience *and not try to control it.*

Certainly, I will always remember how I survived that day and how I handled the challenge—who could forget? Even more important, I will carry with me always and be grateful for the lessons I learned from those "wild waters" about how to live my life.

Benita Tobin

Babes on Blades

I'm not a has-been. I'm a will-be.

Lauren Bacall

The squawking sounds of my children made it difficult for me to hear his soft words. I leaned forward asking him to repeat them. "You ought to do this; it'd be good for you." His finger pointed to an ad in an in-line skating magazine—a publication I had previously ignored because its pages are filled with wildly fit people committing acts that defy gravity. The announcement was for a race from Napa to Calistoga, California—a twenty-seven-mile route—on in-line skates. Everything stopped. The man was Brian Snelson, a representative for K2 Corporation, manufacturer of skis, snowboards and in-line skates. We met after an article appeared in his hometown newspaper about my friends and me discovering the fun of in-line skating and reclaiming our childhoods.

Snelson gave me a free pair of yellow and black K2 Extreme Workout skates with five wheels. He explained that I represented a market that skating manufacturers coveted but could not capture—the over-thirty-five women's market. I had only been on skates for a few months when Brian made that preposterous race suggestion. I could think of dozens of reasons why this mission wouldn't be possible. At nearly forty, I had the weight of mankind's future resting on my shoulders, and quite a bit of that weight had spread around my body.

"The race is next Saturday," Brian said. I had visions of falling. I didn't relish the thought of what would happen after gravity turned the pavement against me. This race was for someone else. No way would I consider it.

Five days later, I was in Napa signing up at 6:00 A.M. with my husband, Dennis, at my side. Doubts about the whole thing, nagging, relentless doubts, whirled in my head. Denied participation to most sports during my highschool years, there I stood in disbelief. Athletes surrounded me. Why did that Snelson character think I could do something "real" athletes do? What did he see in me that I couldn't?

I surveyed the crowd. They were dressed in brightly colored, skintight outfits that had not one wrinkle from neck to knee. I was wearing maternity shorts from three summers before. I put on a shirt depicting a sassy woman on in-line skates boasting, "Caution! Babes on Blades," that I'd designed for my skating girlfriends and me.

Time to skate! A dazzling array of mankind took off. They were in it for speed; I was simply in it. I gathered up my self-doubts and started to plod along. I watched about eighty skaters as they swept around curves on the winding road ahead. Gone! It was now just the "back of the pack" skaters—those along for the "fun" of it.

After a time, I realized I was there with them—a new-to-me breed of people who show up, take risks and participate in sporting events. It was a thrill. My skates fell into a rhythm. The soothing sound of my wheels rose up from the pavement. The distance ahead was overwhelming, so I took notice of the scenery.

The asphalt unfolded smoothly. I was afraid of hills, running out of water, tripping on roadkill, getting hit by a car. You name it—I worried about it. I skated. And skated. And skated some more.

I knew I was skating farther than ever. At times skaters would pass me, other times I would come across one and pass him or her. Spread out but held together by a common bond—we were a team! I continued. My biggest roadblock was not my feet; it was my mind. The fear of the unknown bore more weight than any reality. A long list of anxieties melted as I glided forward.

Suddenly, there was Dennis, up the road, with the old Instamatic camera. He had been driving our van ahead for moral support. Holding up four fingers, he wore a huge smile. I knew what he meant—four more miles! I was going to make it!

"Four miles to go!" I verified, with a victorious shout.

"No. Twenty-three miles to go. You've gone four."

Twenty-three miles later, I crossed the finish line, passing a group of wildly cheering people. I knew they were blown away by my life-affirming accomplishment. They were also glad to finally see the last skaters so they could pack up and join the rest of the group at the park for lunch.

I was ecstatic! I did it! Five days earlier this was deemed impossible. I had put on my skates and conquered the great unknown. I had done Napa to Calistoga. Now I was better, better than ever.

Several of us skated together through the town of Calistoga to reach the park. Townspeople paused to observe us. I was proud to be among these skaters. I was renewed.

Later that evening, glowing with supercharged self-confidence, I skated for another hour in my own neighborhood. I had journeyed beyond my own thinking. I felt like the confident woman on my T-shirt. I indeed was a "Babe on Blades."

Suzan Davis

Paper Suits Me

The big question is whether you are going to be able to say a hearty yes to your adventure.

Joseph Campbell

During the sweltering summer of 1990, my husband, Paul, booked a hotel in Thunder Bay, Canada, that had a giant waterslide in the pool area.

Our four children screamed when they saw it. They got on their swimming suits, walked around the waterslide, and counted the ten twists and turns. I sat happily at a table with four-year-old Colleen on my lap.

"Can Colleen go down the slide with me?" Anne, our oldest at twelve, asked me.

"How can she?"

"On my lap. I'll hang on to her."

Anne took her hand as they headed for the stairs. Clare and Erin, our middle two, followed right behind.

"Be careful," I yelled.

Anne and Colleen had just finished the slide. Anne landed standing up as she lifted her sister into the air.

Since there was no splash, not even a drop of water fell onto our youngest daughter's hair.

I was beginning to wish I hadn't forgotten my swimming suit. It just looked like so much fun. Like Colleen, I had never gone down a waterslide. But unlike the rest of my family, I was afraid of the water.

"Why didn't I bring my swimming suit?" I asked my husband.

"Are you thinking about going down the slide?"

"Maybe."

"Go to the front desk and see if they sell any," Paul said.

I couldn't wonder any longer. I went to the front desk.

"Ma'am, um, this might sound like a weird question, but do you sell any swimming suits?"

"Sure do. They're ten dollars," the woman behind the desk said.

"Great." I couldn't believe my luck.

"One piece or two, Hon?"

"One is fine." My bikini days had gone by the wayside after four pregnancies, stretch marks, and permanent weight gain. "What material are they made of?"

"Paper," the woman said.

Paper? The image I had of myself catapulting down the slide as my suit disintegrated was frightening to say the least. "That's okay," I said as I started walking away from the desk.

"They're very strong, Ma'am."

"Strong enough for a waterslide?"

"Yes. Look." She took the suit and pulled at the seams. The stitches didn't budge.

"Okay, I guess I'll try it," I said, as I handed over a ten-dollar bill.

I went back to the room and changed into my paper suit. I inspected the texture again. It seemed strong, more like a heavy linen than paper. Just in case of any rupture, though, I wore a T-shirt over it.

"I'm ready," I said when I arrived at the pool.

My family was waiting to escort me to the steps going up to the waterslide. There were two girls in front of me and two others bringing up the rear. Paul was in the pool, anticipating my landing.

"How do you slow down?" I kept asking.

No one answered. My children glanced at each other. The eye contact with me was nonexistent.

We made it up the probably fifty steps without mishap. I didn't realize it was so high until I got to the top.

The line moved rapidly.

Anne and Colleen departed.

It was my turn now. No one was in front of me. The pounding in my chest let me know my heart was still beating.

"Do I sit?"

The attendant nodded his head.

I sat waiting for my signal to go. I swallowed the modest amount of saliva left in my mouth.

"How do you slow down?" I asked.

He looked at me strangely and said, "Just sit up straight."

"Okay," I said. I was sitting up straighter already.

"Go." The man motioned to me.

"ME? Right now?"

I was starting to sweat, but it wasn't from the heat. I looked at the long line behind me and decided it would be more embarrassing crawling over strangers and family than drowning in the three feet of water at the end.

"Lady, you can go."

I heard the words as I gingerly pushed myself down the slide.

I approached the first curve. I realized quickly and astutely that I had no control in the curves at all. I thought about swearing and then, luckily, thought again. I knew the words would echo and reverberate throughout the slide. My children would probably be traumatized for life. I was going too fast.

Maybe if I put my legs up along the sides more, I'll slow down, I thought.

I did seem to slow down a fraction of a second. I knew I had to concentrate the entire length of the slide. The man had told me not to put my hands on the sides; I tried to keep them on my thighs, although I needed them for balance.

The bottom of my paper suit seemed to be filling with water but I didn't dare try to get it out. I pictured myself careening to the top of a curve, hanging suspended for a split second, and plopping down on my side. Or worse, I could flip over and land on my face with the water rushing up my nose.

Don't worry about the water, I told myself, as my buttocks swung from side to side.

I was weighing more with each passing second.

Paul said he would be waiting at the end for me. I hoped he planned to catch me and keep me from going under water. I went around the S-shaped curve and saw the opening that signaled the end of the slide. I wanted to land without so much as a ripple, as Anne and Colleen had. I saw my husband standing in the water. That was my last conscious sight before feeling my body fly through the air. I hit the surface, water-filled buttocks first, with a large splash as my face and every other part of me went completely under. I was still trying to stand when my husband grabbed my arm and pulled me up.

"Are you okay?" he said.

There was a mixture of laughter and clapping around the pool.

"I'm okay," I said. "I can't believe how fast it is." I stated this fact loudly, so everyone could hear. "I felt like a rocket on that last curve."

"Mom, are you going again?" little Colleen asked.

There are some experiences in life that truly are "once is not enough." How could I say no to a four-year-old when she was almost jumping up and down?

"I think I'll go again," I said. I went back to the steps, and one of my daughters shielded me while I let out the ten pounds of water collected at the bottom of my suit. First the one side, then the other. I felt lighter already.

When the poor man saw me, he was too polite to let out a groan. And when he said go, I went. The third time I actually landed feet first, toes touching the bottom of the pool.

There was more applause from the bystanders.

After my tenth slide down, I decided to quit. The paper suit was miraculously still intact.

Paul told me later that all the people around the pool agreed that they had never seen a person go down a waterslide so slowly.

Mary Clare Lockman

Change Is Synonymous with Hope

Don't fear the space between your dreams and reality. If you can dream it, you can do it.

Belva Davis

All changes are a risk—and it does get harder as you get older—but change makes you know you're alive. You're exploring, you're stumbling—almost certainly stumbling, if my past is any indication—but there is a certain exhilaration, too. You can't wait to see what happens next.

Of course, there are the changes we choose and then there are the changes that choose us. I chose to leave the network, but breast cancer chose me. What I like most about change is that it's a synonym for "hope." If you are taking a risk, what you are really saying is "I believe in tomorrow, and I will be part of it."

I have trouble understanding the fear people have about change and certainly about aging. Our prospects haven't narrowed just because the years have; if anything, they've never been richer. Oh, I suppose I'll never be a brain surgeon, but there is so much time left for new choices, for new paths. At fifty, you can have another half a century left.

We are already rewriting the definition of "old." My goodness, there are women in their fifties with children under ten. We're hiking, we're writing plays, we're running for office, we're quitting salaried jobs to open our own businesses—and what's so amazing is that we're doing it for the first time at this age.

Our notion of retirement will be totally different than the generation before us. We women in our fifties do not have a lot in common with women in their seventies, and a generation ago, I don't think that was the case.

All I know is that I can take the four flights of stairs in my house better today than I could five years ago. I'm taking active vacations—something I wouldn't have even considered when I was younger. I just returned from white-water canoeing in Montana, and next fall I'm hiking through England by myself. Those are the things that will keep me young . . . that will keep me engaged.

Linda Ellerbee

Gallery of Love

Dreams are renewable. No matter what our age or condition, there are still untapped possibilities within us and new beauty waiting to be born.

Dale Turner

My slightly bruised ego whispers in my ear that it's time for another one-woman show in my private gallery. After yesterday's mail delivered a rejection letter in response to what I considered the best piece of writing I'd ever submitted, I'm feeling too thin-skinned to put up much of an argument with my inner urgings. I trust the gentle voices of my soul. They know when my self-esteem needs replenishment.

I enter the room housing my personal collection of framed treasures. No expensive Picassos in gilded frames adorned with jewels on the walls here. Just an ordinary beige wall with a dozen or so thin black frames hanging in random order. Behind the bordered rectangles of glass lie the riches of my achievements. More valuable than

Rembrandts are certificates and diplomas with shiny gold seals and looping calligraphy detailing each of my hard-earned awards.

The morning sunlight is the lone observer of my sacred ritual. Peeking silently between angled vertical shades, its reflective rays make the simple frames on my wall dazzle as if they were diamonds. A peace lily in an earth-tone pot spreads shiny emerald leaves, absorbing the warmth that permeates the small room. My index finger traces an outline in the gray dust accumulated on a dark frame. It's been a while since my last visit.

My gallery was born with the hanging of a single "plaque of recognition" when I was in my early fifties, soon after entering college as a first-time grandmother. One by one, new frames would decorate the wall and four more grandchildren would arrive before I fulfilled my dream of receiving a college degree. Somehow, during those stressful years of studying and final exams, I managed to find a balance between school and home. I coped with, and survived, hectic holiday celebrations, illness and the deaths of beloved family members.

You've never been a quitter, reminds the voice within. *Don't start now.*

I remember filling with pride when I hung my college diploma in its rightful place of honor, then christened the backdrop of my framed accomplishments the "Love Wall." Ever since that day, I come here to celebrate all that I have been and strive to be.

Gradually, a special magic occurs in my humble gallery. While quietly reviewing tangible tokens of past achievements, the self-inflicted wounds to my ego are soothed, and self-doubting thoughts dissipate in the glow of a new day.

I am happy and proud of me again—just the way I am.

Before I leave, I must ready the wall for my next visit.

Gently I wipe the dust from each frame and pass a cloth over the glass mirroring my reflection, smile lines and all. It may be a while before I return. Dust will surely gather while I am busy working on the next best piece of writing I've ever done.

Diane M. Vanover

Adventure on Mount Hood

Adventures don't begin until you get into the forest. That first step is an act of faith.

Mickey Hart

We call ourselves the "Amazing Graces." We borrowed the idea from Patricia Gaffney's wonderful book about friendship, *Saving Graces*. We altered the name slightly to reflect our faith in God.

In over twenty years of friendship, the four Amazing Graces have seen each other through several weddings, a divorce, various illnesses, the birth of a disabled child, one household fire and several major career changes. With the passage of time, we found ourselves sharing new concerns about weight gain, hot flashes and the almost daily appearance of wrinkles.

The Amazing Graces have stood the test of time despite the fact that we're all so different. I'm the one who advises the others on the latest fashion dos and don'ts. They call me the queen of QVC because I love shoes, jewelry and clothes. Tracy has tireless energy. She has an autistic son, a ranch full of horses and a house full of dogs. Laura is quiet and softhearted. She puts her long hair up in a clip, slips into a well-worn pair of blue jeans and off she goes. After years of living with a husband who made it his life's mission to point out her flaws, it's hardest for her to think of herself as "amazing." But she's coming along. And Vicki's the brave, adventurous one. She's the one who talked us into backpacking around Mount Hood in celebration—or defiance—of middle age. And so, she's the one we alternately blame and thank for all the memories we packed out of Oregon when we left.

We took the first step that would eventually carry us forty miles around the perimeter of this beautiful mountain on a warm summer morning. Tracy and Vicki walked with brisk, sure steps. Laura wandered around smelling flowers and identifying plants. I felt a sense of wonder and excitement that seemed to vanquish my earlier fears. Everything seemed so huge.

The trail led us through woods and coves, over rocks and glaciers, along spectacular waterfalls and deep, cool canyons. Each night we camped in the shadow of Mount Hood, surrounded by vibrant fields of wildflowers and great, towering pines.

It was on the second night that the rain began. Huge bolts of lightning lit the sky. Loud, angry thunder—the likes of which I had never experienced—shook the ground. There was nothing but a thin piece of nylon separating us from nature's fury. Vicki and Tracy slept soundly. Laura and I talked until she dozed off. I lay awake for hours, willing the rain to stop.

Despite my hopes, the rain was still with us the following day. Our backpacks were sodden and heavy and all the equipment inside was wet. We hiked through deep, muddy puddles until our boots were soaked, leaving our feet blistered and sore. We crossed rain-swollen streams that were wide, rushing torrents. We carefully stepped from rock to rock with swirls of angry water circling our ankles.

When the sun finally reappeared, we were dirty and exhausted. But we were also happy. We had just a few more miles and one last stream crossing to go. But, we couldn't believe our eyes when we approached Eliot Creek. A flash flood had swept the large wooden bridge away. There was a huge gulf separating us from our last campsite. The park service had posted a sign that read "Unsafe to Cross." But we had come so far. After a brief discussion, we decided that turning back was not an option.

We gathered our courage and decided on the safest route from the top of the cliff. Vicki was the first to slide down the steep embankment. The rest of us followed. The rocks and branches that lined the mountainside tore at our clothes and scraped our skin. I was last down the slope. The loose rocks that lay on the riverbank gave way as I landed. Even though I dug my hands and feet into the sharp rocks, I still felt myself sliding uncontrollably toward the raging water. Seconds before I would have been swept into the creek, Vicki and Laura grabbed my backpack and pulled me to safety.

We had all gathered on the bank, but we still faced one more obstacle. How were we going to cross the deep, raging creek? The only option seemed to be a huge block of ice that covered the water. The constant flow of water throughout the freezing days of winter had built the block up until it towered six feet in the air. It spanned nearly the entire width of the creek. We climbed to the top and ran toward the opposite bank. But with each step, the ice cracked beneath our feet. Tracy yelled, "The ice is giving way!" Then someone yelled: "JUMP!" In a moment of desperation, the Amazing Graces were airborne. We leapt from the block of ice and dived for the other side. The four of us were clinging to the side of the steep bank as Vicki yelled, "Look at the bridge!" We watched in disbelief as the ice collapsed into the water with a roar. We had only been seconds away from falling into Eliot Creek.

We scrambled up the steep cliff and pulled ourselves to surer footing. We shrugged out of our packs and hugged each other in relief. We had done it. We survived the biting black flies and the mosquitoes. We went on despite rain, the icy glacier crossings and the deep, swollen streams. Even Eliot Creek could not stop us.

When I looked down at the steep cliffs and raging creek that we had just crossed, I had never felt so alive. Mount Hood seemed to symbolize all the things we had accomplished. And all the great things that lay ahead. I had never loved these women more. I stepped forward and yelled toward the sky: "We are the Amazing Graces!"

Joyce Briggs

Realize Your Dreams

I had been working at a job I loved, an attendance coordinator at a high school, for eighteen years when I began to feel the stirrings of discontent. I had always been in a disciplinarian role and it was becoming uncomfortable. I felt as though I wasn't being true to myself in this role. I was ten years away from retirement and had decided to stick it out when the school district sent me to a weekend workshop. One of the classes, "Realizing Your Dreams," sounded intriguing, so I signed up for it.

After being introduced to the presenter, we were asked to close our eyes and think as far back as we could remember. What was it we loved to do most in the world? What had excited us and made us feel alive? We were to allow whatever came to our minds to be there, no matter how bizarre it might seem. The word "rhythm" came to my mind. I had loved it as a youngster. I had played the clarinet since third grade but had always wanted to be the kid behind the drums. However, during the fifties, girls usually played the flute, clarinet or piano. In high school, my dream had been to be in a rock band, but after years of playing the clarinet, learning to play the drums and joining a rock band seemed out of reach.

The presenter then gave us several exercises to take home. He said if we did the exercises religiously our "vision" would crystallize and manifest itself in our lives. At this point, I was thinking that drumming at the age of forty-five was probably a bit "out there," and maybe I should come up with something more suited to my age group. However, we were told to stick with our original idea, and start journaling, visualizing and acting like we had already reached our goal. It didn't matter, he said, that we had no idea at this moment exactly what the goal was . . . just do the exercises. He also said that doors would start opening in our lives, and we would need to recognize them as opportunities and walk through them—even if they felt uncomfortable at the time.

I don't know how many people in the class actually went home, did the exercises and realized a dream, but I decided I would try it. I bought myself a spiral notebook, and every morning I sat quietly and wrote a full page of "I am a drummer . . . I am a drummer . . . I am a drummer." I said this mantra to myself over and over during the day, and started to imagine myself drumming. All this seemed weird at the beginning, but it actually started to feel exciting and "right" after a couple of weeks.

After about two weeks of journaling and visualizing, my sister called to ask me if I knew about the large African drumming community in Seattle. I hadn't known about this, but I imagined that the community consisted of either Africans, which I am not, or hippies, which I am no longer. I did recognize this as a door opening, however, and decided to take a drumming class. The first six months found me in a group of people I judged to be very different from me. They were mostly younger, offbeat, not your mainstream types. Despite my discomfort, I found I loved the heart-pounding rhythms that were being generated. Soon after, I bought my first drum—it called to me; it had an energy that was powerful, yet simple and beautiful.

Several months later, I was at Seattle's Folklife Festival where I saw a group of children performing on African drums. It made the hairs stand up on my arms and brought tears to my eyes . . . this powerful sound coming from children! That was the crystallizing moment for me. I realized then and there that I wanted to take my educational experience and my love of drumming and teach children. I gathered my courage and spoke to the director, Kip, after the performance. He was excited to share his expertise and invited me to come to Port Townsend in the summer to help him teach a summer drumming camp. In August 1999, I boarded the Seattle to Port Townsend Ferry alone for my adventurous weekend. I pampered myself by staying in an old Victorian hotel. I spent my days learning that teaching drumming was not only fairly easy for me but also joyful and fulfilling. Kip was more than willing to let me instruct and give me information on starting my own business, purchasing drums and equipment, and lining up jobs. In the evenings, I walked on the beach, meditated, read, took in a movie and shopped at the local craft shops. I will always remember that weekend as a turning point in my life, spiritually as well as occupationally.

Back at home, I started fine-tuning my journaling: "I am a drumming teacher . . . I am a drumming teacher . . . I am a drumming teacher." My husband started introducing me as a drumming teacher, even though I still worked at the high school and only had one drum. I continued taking lessons and performing with my class; I started feeling a part of the Seattle drumming community. At this point, I knew I had to take this "game" I was playing to a different level, or it would always be just a game.

Just before the turn of the new millennium, at the age of forty-eight, I resigned from nineteen years at the high school, bought ten drums and a basketful of small percussion instruments, printed business cards, got a business license and made flyers describing my goals, spiritual intentions and drumming experience. I started calling parks departments, schools, Boys and Girls Clubs and YMCAs. I named my business "Heartbeats," because I loved with all my heart the journey I was embarking on. I was terrified but I did it. Now, four years later, I have a wonderful business where teaching drumming allows me to play instead of work.

In addition to teaching drumming, I also felt a great need to be a performer in a women's drumming group. I wanted our songs to be original compositions with a spirit-filled agenda. I wanted to be part of a group that played not only drums, but also other instruments to give it an unusual and interesting flavor. I started journaling these intentions and am now a member of OmBili Afro-Cuban Tribal Jazz all-women performing troupe.

I believe that we all can create whatever is in our hearts. We just need to visualize it, journal it, and feel what it is like to have accomplished it. It works for anything in life. Our imaginations are real and vibrant, and can be used to fill our lives with such joy.

Margie Pasero

Full Bloom

To dare is to lose one's footing momentarily. To not dare is to lose oneself.

Soren Kierkegaard

When I was twelve years old, I kept a journal; it was a mixed bag of nurtured dreams and nursed wounds. On the inside cover, I made a list of things I wanted to be when I grew up: the first woman coach in the NFL, an actress and a writer. These were big dreams, but I had time on my side.

Reality quickly pecked away at my plans, and I learned to amend them. Football was the first to go. Having no athletic talent and not much of a competitive drive, I forgot about being a coach and settled for the joy of being able to make many a boy's jaw drop whenever I decided to show off my knowledge of the game. As for dreams of the stage and screen, I soon discovered every school and church I attended had plenty of outlets for would-be performers, and I was satisfied.

But the dream of being a writer was different: It was not

so easily laid to rest. It would seem to vanish, only to pop up again like a backyard plant that can't quite be classified as either weed or flower. Youthful uncertainty meant that I often mistreated this persistent idea instead of listening to its call and nurturing it. You might call me a late bloomer; it was not until midlife that I accepted the identity planted in that childhood notebook of mine.

As a young woman, I felt reality pushing me to prove my use to society, to develop marketable skills, marry and raise a family. These undertakings require feverish energy, and my twenties and thirties provided it, though it often meant plowing under that nagging backyard perennial, the call to write.

When I fell in love at twenty, my desire to finish college took a backseat to my desire to be happily married to the man I loved. After marriage, I went to work as an office manager of a photofinishing company. I wrote policies and training guides at work, and at home wrote poetry and essays. I had two sons and stopped working to care for them full time. This time at home did enable me to nurture my writing, and I published essays and a short play. But at parties, when the dreadful question, "What do you do?" was popped, I chose the awkward title of "stay-at-home mom" rather than risk identifying myself as a writer.

I returned to college and finished my degree then went back to work, this time as a part-time English instructor at the local college. Grading stacks of freshmen essays slowed my writing output considerably, but I kept at it. I won $1,000 for an editorial entered in a contest, and celebrated the news with my students. But I would not allow even this triumphal moment to redefine myself outside a comfortable norm; at thirty, I was still too young to claim an identity as a writer.

Part-time teaching wasn't paying the bills, so I earned a master's degree in counseling while continuing to teach.

I stopped writing; I was "too busy" to tend to such a personal need when I was about to secure a career. I took a job as a K–12 counselor in a rural community near my home. I had a title, but I was not a writer. The dream was withering; it rarely crossed my mind.

My first year as a counselor was a blizzard of new challenges, but I did enjoy it. When I grew tired of coaxing high school seniors to get their college applications in the mail, I went to the elementary school and taught character development to a wide-eyed and eager audience. I told the children that the secret to a happy life is to find things you love and do them with all your heart. I was forty-two. An inner voice told me I'd better take the advice I was giving.

So when my first summer off opened before me, I made space in my life to nurture the growth of my dormant dream. I began writing just for the love of it, putting the need to be understood behind. Midlife brought new freedom. I had a marriage, a family and a good job. Having done all the "right" things, I no longer cared whether or not I measured up to the preconceived notions of others.

Some plants, I am told, spend years saving up enough starch in their roots to produce a full bloom.

Last week a twelve-year-old girl came to see me in the counselor's office. She shared a sad story of living with a verbally abusive father on weekends and with a confused and tired mother during the week. Searching for ways that she could care for herself in such a situation, I asked her what she did for fun. Her brown eyes widened. "I'm a writer," she said. "I have poems and stories all over my room." I took this child into my heart. "I'm a writer, too," I said.

Peggy Haslar

The Odyssey

One frosty Colorado morning, while I sipped coffee, my husband, John, said, "We need a lifestyle change. Let's go cruising." I listened dumbstruck, as he continued, "Leslie, what if all our savings and possessions were in one small briefcase? Imagine standing on a sidewalk with that brief-case dangling in your hand; where would you want to go? What would you do next?" Not taking him too seriously, I replied, "I guess I'd go to the beach, sit in a lounge chair and think about it first!"

John was obviously in the throes of a midlife crisis, and it was scaring me. In the ensuing weeks, I noticed his behavior changing. An avid technical reader, John was now read-ing things like *How to Live Without a Salary* by Charles Long. My husband has always been an upbeat person, able to find new projects to keep himself motivated. Lately, John had been showing little interest in work and hobbies. His can-dle was burning low and dim. At fifty-four, he had enjoyed life as a university professor, but I could see he was ready for a metamorphosis, a new "lifestyle."

John wanted to be captain of his own ship, to sail with me from Florida to South America and back. "Let's rent a boat," I offered. But he insisted that we needed a lifestyle change. If we could come back too easily to our home and possessions, it wouldn't qualify as a true change.

In the back of my mind were the sad stories of two couples who had recently divorced, after years of good marriages. I pictured the ex-husbands, in their mid-fifties, riding new red motorcycles, young girlfriends aboard, off into the sunset. I wanted to blame their failed marriages on those red motorcycles. *Could their wives have been the ones riding on those motorcycles instead?* I wondered.

It was clear that John had to do something about his longings. It was also clear that I wanted to be part of whatever he did. So, I decided to invest in John's midlife-crisis recovery plan. "Okay, I will do this with you, but only for one or two years, max. What's two years in a whole lifetime?" I rationalized.

Weekly planning and budget meetings soon followed that cold January morning. We read about other people living the cruising lifestyle. In May, John requested sabbatical leave. In June it was approved, and I left my job soon after. We took two short trips down the East and West Coasts, shopping for a boat and a launch pad where we would begin our sailing odyssey.

In July our home sold the first hour it was on the market. At that moment, it became utterly real to me that we were really going to do this "lifestyle" change! In a blur of garage sales and donations, we frantically got rid of STUFF that took us ninety-six combined years to accumulate.

Time was money now. For the first time as adults, we were unemployed and living off our savings and retirement monies. Decision making got easier. We needed to buy a boat soon and start sailing before both our time and money dried up.

Homeless now after closing on our house, we put the proceeds into a beautiful near-new, forty-foot sailboat named *Sola Fide*, which means "faithful one" in Latin.

We drove our overstuffed ten-year-old compact car to Ft. Lauderdale, Florida, and rented a studio on a canal. With *Sola Fide* steps away, we began the sweaty process of outfitting her for ocean voyaging. Days turned into months as we hunted for marine gear and installed "homey" additions like a wind generator, a water maker, a bank of batteries, and a freezer cold plate. I was shocked at the costs of all these "necessities" and wondered if we would slip the dock lines before our money ran out.

Our big day finally arrived and we set sail. Our plan was to sail a loop from Florida to Venezuela and back, enjoying all the beautiful islands along the way.

We were novice cruisers with only limited sailing experience from brief chartering in the past. We picked up "just-in-time" cruising skills as we lived aboard our little vessel 24/7. Most of our sailing was during the daylight hours, with an occasional ocean passage in the blackness of night. I learned that you can't just stop your boat and anchor in 6,000 feet of water; you have to keep sailing until you reach a safe harbor.

There were dangers among all the pleasures. Occasionally we were challenged by heavy wind and sea. We met an unfortunate cruiser family that endured the loss of their boat. We also met cruisers who had gotten roughed up by modern pirates. John helped rescue cruisers who had run aground or who were dragging anchors.

Somehow our marriage survived this dramatic change of lifestyle. John took out a big "marriage-insurance policy": Thirty days into our trip, stressed-out over the steep learning curve, and getting a full dose of my ranting and wailing, John looked me in the eye and said, "Leslie, if you want to turn around at anytime, we can quit. Our marriage means more to me than this odyssey." Those were the most loving words I had ever heard. Knowing I had a parachute to safely escape with my husband, not without him, helped me endure the discomforts of this pioneerlike life. Curiosity also kept me going. I wanted to know everything this new way of life could teach me.

As we sailed the islands, we took time to enjoy the companionship of the locals and other cruisers, some of whom have become close friends. We had new adventures every day. When weather kept us at anchor, we got involved locally and in volunteer work, tutoring and reading with young children. One exciting day, we helped save dozens of beached pilot whales in Trinidad.

As our midlife odyssey approached the end of its second year, we sailed back up the islands to our Florida starting point. It was bittersweet to be home again. We were filled with new understanding and appreciation, and a renewed confidence that we could accomplish anything we set our minds to.

I am glad I responded positively to my husband's passionate desire to break out of our everyday lives. As we sailed, my own midlife voice spoke, having awaited this opportunity to be set free. It helped me rediscover myself. I learned that I am tough and resilient. Sometimes, we must step outside ourselves to learn who we really are. I am glad I experienced this radically different way of life. It was simple and freer than any I had ever known.

So where do you want to go? And what do you want to do now?

Leslie J. Clark

[AUTHOR'S NOTE: *When we returned ashore, it took a while to pick up the fast pace. Without a home, we temporarily lived out of duffel bags in a rental, but I appreciated the earth beneath my feet and the warm welcome of friends. John and I work full-time now, at full throttle. I'm thankful that we unplugged from our hectic lifestyles and set sail. Memories of our shared midlife odyssey fill me with a sense of wonder and accomplishment.*]

Side-Tracked at Silver Plume

*You will do foolish things, but do them with
enthusiasm.*

Colette

Rounding a hairpin curve, I spied a sign for Silver Plume
and exited.

It looked like time had stood still. A one-time mining
community, all that remained were a few short blocks of
sleepy Victorian houses rubbing shoulders on the narrow,
unpaved roads. Quaint and quiet. A little too quiet, nearly
a ghost town.

On the last leg home from my first uneventful
overnight speaking engagement, I conveniently disre-
garded my initial nervousness and was busy congratulat-
ing myself on my recent successes: discovering "life after
kids," trading my stay-at-home-mother title for "Working
Woman," establishing a business in midlife, even traveling
without my husband for the first time.

Tense from the unaccustomed mountain driving, I
stopped in front of a lone, weathered antique store. What

better way to take a break, stretch my legs?

Inside was a sign: "More in basement. Enter at your own risk." A direct challenge to an avid antique buff! I ducked down the rough wooden stairs. They weren't kidding.

Loose planks of plywood blanketed the floor, sagging with each step I took. I peered into dim corners, peeked at chair frames tangled in skeletal heaps and prowled the maze of timeworn clutter. Working my way back upstairs, I paused in front of a copper-lined humidor. *I wonder how much it costs? And where is the sales clerk?*

I wandered to the back of the store and snooped around the corner, startled to discover a starkly modern kitchen, empty. At a lone door (the restroom?), I waited a decent amount of time for someone to exit, and finally knocked. No answer. *That's odd. But I've dawdled long enough.*

I headed to the front door and opened it. Only it didn't. Open, that is. *What?* It was true. The building was empty, the door was bolted, and I was locked inside. Alone.

Once more I rattled the old door. *Do I laugh or do I cry? And what kind of place closes in the middle of the afternoon, anyway?* Suspiciously, I looked around more closely. *Am I on* Candid Camera?

And I smiled—just in case.

I did another once-over of the store. I called out. I raced to the front door again and pried at the handle. *Front door. Could there be a* back *door? Yes!* More important, it was unlocked. But it opened onto a stairless fretwork sill with a sheer drop down the side of the mountain.

Okay. Stay calm.

After all, what better place to be locked in? There was a tidy row of antique books; I could read to my heart's content. There was a kitchen; I wouldn't starve. There was a bathroom; I wouldn't disgrace myself. Why, there was even a musty fainting couch and a worn, hand-stitched quilt; I could bed down for the night if it came to that.

Spend the night? This place is too spooky!
Pressing my face pancake-flat against the glass pane, I turned my eyes to the left, slapping the window with both palms to get attention. Then I rolled my eyes as far as I could to the right. The graveled street was completely empty of life. And no amount of shaking, rattling, banging, yelling or rapping made the least bit of difference. But I tried them all again, anyway. Especially the yelling. Nervous perspiration beaded on my upper lip.

This was not funny. *If only I could call someone.* Wait! A brand-new cell phone nestled inside my purse. Why didn't I think of that sooner? Punching in the familiar numbers, I phoned home. Nothing. The teeny monitor read: "searching." After all, Silver Plume was nestled in the cavernous Colorado Rockies.

This is a place of business. Shouldn't it have a phone? I hated to snoop, but . . . nope, none that I could find.

This is nuts! Picking up an antique iron cannonball, I speculated on its hefty weight as I contemplated the storefront. What was that old saying? Desperate times call for desperate measures. And I *was* beginning to feel pretty desperate. It would break my heart (which would mend) to ruin the ancient plateglass window (which was probably irreplaceable), but panic was setting in.

Drawing my arm back, I squinted, gauged the distance and took careful aim.

Then I opened my eyes wide. There, on the other side—the *out*side—of the bolted door, stood an equally wide-eyed proprietor. We stared at each other in shock.

I don't know what gave me away—wild, glazed look? pounding heart?—but that door was unlocked in record time. Amidst my profuse apologies and unintelligible explanations, she showered me with comforting hugs and hot tea. Lots of hot tea.

All I knew was the afternoon I had spent in that

deserted store was the longest year of my life.

"What? What's that you say? I was only here *one hour?*" Well, hmmm.

Anyway, I was cured. I drove the final miles with nary a stop. Why, each and every time the car veered toward a sign boasting "Antiques," I jerked it back on the road, gave it a piece of my mind, and kept on pedaling. Straight-arrow home. Where I belonged.

On the other hand . . . there *was* the cutest little walnut humidor at that Silver Plume Antique Shop. Somehow, I completely forgot to ask the price. I wonder if it's still there? It's probably worth a trip back.

Carol McAdoo Rehme

No More Babies

There is no greater power in the world than the zest of a postmenopausal woman.

Margaret Mead

None of the things I have accomplished in my life ever consumed my imagination or yielded the intense gratification that having babies did. And I say this having written books and baked pies, grown vegetables, fixed up houses, rafted rivers, organized political campaigns, acted in plays and built enduring friendships. None of them came close.

This makes things tricky. If what you love best is playing the flute, you can (with luck) play the flute until your dying day. Same with gardening, reading, bird-watching and golfing. What I happen to love best is a game you can play for only so many years. Then you turn in your jersey, clean out your locker and retire from the sport, knowing you're never again going to play it. I will always be the mother of my three children, but the particular thrill (as well as the terror, exhaustion, frustration and loss of self) that comes with conceiving, giving birth and launching a new human being into the world is one I will not know again. There is a measure of relief in that, but regret, too.

Fertility is a great and mysterious gift—our blessing and, as we occasionally call it, our curse. I remember the precise moment I learned my ovaries contained all the eggs I would ever possess—my lifetime's store of potential children. And I remember the moment when I first got my period and realized my body could make a baby. To a thirteen-year-old, it was an awe-inspiring and more-than-slightly terrifying thought. It's been thirty years since that day, but I've never ceased to be amazed by it.

From the time I was very young, I pictured myself a mother. At twenty-four, I became one. I had another baby four years later, and a third, two years after that. Even then I didn't say I would never have another. Five years later, when I was thirty-five, my marriage ended, but I continued to imagine I might have another child with another man. It's embarrassing to admit, but every time I found a man who possessed life-partner potential, my thinking turned toward babies. For me, loving someone was nearly always accompanied by an interest in procreation—and a longing to know one more child of mine. I was forty-three years old when it came to me that the person I needed to know better, after a couple of decades of motherhood, was me.

My moment of closing the door to the baby dream came relatively late. But whether a woman bids good-bye to having babies at menopause or at age twenty-five, because of biology or conscious choice, happily or with great sadness, it is a rite of passage none of us can avoid. It is a moment that ranks—with first menstruation, loss of virginity, marriage, childbirth, death of a parent and divorce—among the landmarks of life.

Throughout adulthood, my fertility symbolized possibility

to me. I obviously didn't take advantage of my childbearing potential more than a few times, but I still loved knowing it was there. It's as if I had been carrying an airplane ticket in my purse, destination anyplace. I might not have gotten on the plane, but over the years I took enormous pleasure in thinking about all the places I could go.

Of the adjectives I'd use to describe myself, fertile would be only one, and probably not in the first fifty I'd mention. I was the same me before I had children, and I will be the same me now that I'm done. It was never difficult, even a decade back, to see why the time had come to close the door on the idea of more babies, starting with the fact that I'd had three already. My children have made huge demands on my time, energy and concentration for close to two decades. Without them, I would have written more books, contributed more to my community and planet, cooked more elaborate meals, had a more beautiful home, kept a lusher garden, maintained a flatter stomach. Without children, I would have had more time for friends, more money for trips—and more freedom to take them. Without children, I might now play the piano, run in marathons, dance the tango.

Or not. Because I've also learned over the many years I haven't been doing those things (and occasionally using my children as the excuse) that sometimes it's only when an obstacle prevents you from accomplishing a goal that you acquire the drive to reach it. Before I had children— back when I had all the time and concentration in the world for my own concerns—I wasted a lot of time on very little. I had to lose the freedom of my time to value it sufficiently.

I've finally realized I've been carrying more than one airplane ticket in my purse all these years. One would have taken me back to the land of parenthood. If I had gone there, I would have taken in amazing sights and met

unforgettable people—or one, anyway: the child I would
have had. If I had gone on that trip, it's doubtful I ever
would have said, "I wish I had stayed home."

But there's another trip a woman can take—the one I'm
opting for now. This one will take me somewhere I've
never been before. Because of that, it's scarier for me than
the other journey. It's not an ending, though, for as much
as the ability to procreate signals possibilities, the choice
to put that aside also signals possibilities—just different
ones. Like tango lessons and the freedom to stay out late
or sleep in the next morning. And the possibility of having
sex on the kitchen floor in the middle of the day or the
financial freedom to go on safari in Tanzania.

It's easy to see what a person gives up when she finally
acknowledges the hard truth that not one of those remain-
ing eggs in her ovaries is ever going to turn into a person.
The rest of that truth is this: Whichever route a woman
chooses—to have a child or not—represents both the loss
of one gift and the discovery of another. When a woman
relinquishes the dream of babies, what she gets, if she is
wise enough to recognize it, is her own self back. Maybe a
person has to have lost that for a while to recognize how
precious it is.

I thought I would feel very old when the day finally
came that I knew I was done having babies. That day has
come, all right. The funny thing is, it's making me feel very
young again. I'm not finished; I'm starting.

Joyce Maynard

The Piranha

My mother told me never to rock the boat or challenge a male authority figure.

"Men need to save face," she explained. "Conflict isn't worth it."

I took after my father. Opinionated, fearless, ready to crusade for justice.

I struggled with my natural gift of courage versus my desire to please Mom and never be pushy. As a result, I was always conflicted and guilt-ridden if I spoke up.

When my husband and I packed our few possessions and headed west to pursue our dreams of music, I would receive a lesson in assertiveness that would change me forever. Back in the Midwest, I sang local TV commercials. The prospect of finding work in Hollywood was frightening to say the least. For eight months, I mailed out demo tapes, called producers, dropped by studios and basically struck out. One day, I mailed my demo to a new production company.

They called me the very next day.

"We loved your tape!" the producer gushed. "Come to the studio Friday. There's a national TV commercial I want you to sing."

"Wow, that's great," I said.

"We can't pay you regular union rates, and you won't get future royalties, but I can guarantee one day of work a week at one hundred dollars an hour."

So that Friday, I sang the commercial, met the studio musicians and became a national "jingle singer."

Within weeks, I was their regular soloist and even sang backup with the other singers. The fact that we were grossly underpaid and signed agreements to waive all our royalties was okay with me. The hourly rate was more than I had ever earned in my life, and I was doing what I loved, so what did it matter?

Then reality hit.

My paycheck came in the mail every two weeks, and I kept perfect records about every recording session, but somehow the paychecks and my records would never coincide. The checks were always smaller than the amounts I showed being due. I kept "fluffing" it off thinking maybe I hadn't worked as many hours as I thought, figuring it must be my fault. Every two weeks, a check would arrive that was too small, my heart would sink and the same frustration would rise up in me. Finally, I called the accountant and asked her to check it.

"Thanks," I said weakly, "I'm sure it's my mistake, but . . ."

"No, those are the right amounts," she said.

"But I have down that I worked these days and these hours."

"You did," she said. "What's the problem?"

"At one hundred dollars an hour, that's not right."

"Oh," she laughed. "Well, you're figuring this up at the wrong rate. Why do you think you get a hundred dollars an hour? You make seventy. All the singers do."

"What? Trent guaranteed me one hundred dollars an hour with no future royalties."

"He would never pay a singer that much." She smirked.

"He told me to pay you seventy dollars an hour like all the other girls get."

The way she said "girls" made me feel small and stupid. I didn't like that feeling.

"I need to talk to Trent," I said, my heart racing.

She transferred me and he picked up the phone. If I hadn't felt so angry and used, I would never have found the courage to even phone him. I kindly reminded him how much he had promised to pay me. When he laughed, I felt worse.

"Look," he said, "you're scheduled to sing Friday afternoon. Why don't you come over to the business office—we'll straighten out this misunderstanding."

Misunderstanding? That's what he called it?

Friday, I walked into the office complex and saw a new Jaguar parked in Trent's space. The atrium lobby was filled with waterfalls and tropical fish. I had no idea it would be so palatial. I grew more upset as I thought about my small, inaccurate paychecks.

"Trent will see you now," his secretary said.

"Hi! Come on in," he smiled.

I took the seat in front of him. Just then, he reached under his desk and pressed a button. The drapes closed electronically. He pressed another button and the door locked.

"There, that's better," he smiled. "Hold all my calls," he said, leaning into his speakerphone.

The "good girl" who never confronted a man in authority was ready to take this guy on.

"What's the next button you're going to push?" I said folding my arms.

"Does the floor open up and the piranha appear?"

He laughed in a phony sort way and I leaned forward, shouting in my mind not to be intimidated. I came to the point and reminded him what he promised to pay me when he hired me.

"Wow, I just don't remember saying that," he said evasively. "You see, none of the other singers get that and I just don't know why I ever would have promised you that much. Hey, even if I agree now to give you that, how would it look to them? What would I tell them?"

"What you pay other singers is none of my business," I said quickly. "I only know what I need to be paid and I can't work for less than the one hundred an hour you promised me."

"Hope, this is a tough business. You have no idea how much it costs to do this kind of production," he said, staring at me.

Tough business? I thought. *Jaguar? Waterfalls?*

I felt myself weakening. The old guilt rose up again. What others needed came before what I needed. I didn't count. I shouldn't inconvenience people.

I was lucky to even have a job. I was just a "woman."

Suddenly, I "woke up."

"I'm an experienced, talented singer," I proclaimed. "Whether you remember or not, we did agree on one hundred dollars an hour. It's way below what other national singers make with royalties, but I chose to work with you in this arrangement. This isn't about what you pay everyone else, it's about what you and I agreed upon."

"I just don't think that would be fair," he repeated.

"I sang those TV station tags." I began. "The ones going to every city."

"So?"

"I've only sung half of them. If you want me to finish them, I will—at one hundred dollars an hour."

Trent put his hands behind his head. "Oh, I get it." He laughed.

Suddenly, he reached under his desk. The door clicked open. The drapes started moving.

"No problem," he said. "A hundred an hour it is, I just thought we should chat a bit."

I walked outside, put on my sunglasses and shouted, "Yes!"

Every two weeks my checks arrived for the right amounts, and I continued an enjoyable career there until I moved to another city.

I had been willing to lose everything in that meeting because I was finally tired of losing myself. I wasn't driving a Jaguar or going to a house filled with waterfalls. But as I drove my little Toyota down the freeway, I felt richer than I had ever felt in my life. I found something I had given up so many times, I thought it was gone forever: my self-respect. And I was never going to lose it again.

Hope Faith

Trophy Girl

*It is the soul's duty to be loyal to its own desires.
It must abandon itself to its master, passion.*

Rebecca West

Trophy Girl has beautiful perky bosoms, sinewy legs, muscular arms and a ponytail flying behind her as she dunks basketballs, hits home runs and surges across a finish line. If you have girls in sports, you've seen this mass-produced golden girl perched atop a faux marble platform, performing her amazing athletic stunts.

My daughters have boxes of dusty Trophy Girls from their years of softball, basketball, tennis and dance competitions. Every team they've ever played for includes the obligatory self-esteem-building trophy at the end of the season. Win or lose, they all get the same award. As a result, the trophies mean very little to them. There's no sense of accomplishment when everyone gets one. It's like getting a slice of the cookie cake—everyone who shows up gets a piece.

I don't know if it's the trophy manufacturers or parents

who perpetuate the notion, "It doesn't matter who wins or loses, we all get trophies anyway," but the kids are not fooled. They know that all that glitters is not really gold. They don't care about the trinkets the team mother spends hours selecting, collecting money for, having engraved and then distributing at the team party. After the last softball party, I had three trophies left behind with the debris from the picnic. They remain in my garage waiting to be reclaimed by their owners.

But I'm not like them; I don't have the luxury of their indifference. I've never, in my whole life, won a trophy. I was a Girl Scout and earned cloth badges. I collected plaster busts of Bach and Beethoven after piano recitals, but never a shiny monument to an athletic achievement. I was never on a team, never won an award, and never competed for a title. Every time I pack up one of my daughter's new Trophy Girls, I spend a wistful moment envying her graceful, athletic accomplishments.

But I'm finally going to do something about it. I have decided to take a year and train to run a marathon. I know—you can't up and decide to run a marathon, especially when you are a nonrunner and forty-three years old. Since I'm not one to take up new things on impulse, this venture was a shock to everyone, including myself. But the main reason I decided to go for it? In Chicago during the Chicago Marathon, I saw the shiny bronze medal marathoners wear around their neck after completing the race. I want that medal for myself, and intend to get one.

So I started a running program, and entered a 5K race two months after my first run around the block. As the start of the race approached, I immersed myself in the experience. The more jaded runners joked with their companions, stretched and fiddled with their watches. I stood back, tensely watching, waiting for the signal to begin the run. Somehow, and I really don't know how, I ended up in second place for my age division. After the race, I noticed a table of small trophies, each emblazoned with a golden running shoe. A veteran runner noticed my transfixed gaze and casually mentioned that the first-, second- and third-place winner of each age division received a trophy—which was news to me. I never thought about winning anything. My goal in the race was to not be the last one over the finish line.

When they called my name, I floated through the cheering crowd to accept my award. There have been great moments in my life—my wedding, the birth of my children, my first byline—but clutching that trophy and holding it in the air is a moment I'll relive forever. That afternoon I stuck a magnet on my race card and hung it on the refrigerator alongside my daughters' certificates of achievement. Next, I put the first trophy of my new athletic career on the fireplace mantle.

My family of superstars smiled indulgently at my delight. My girls are lucky. They've had the chance to compete on teams where they have won championship titles and all-star status. But their pile of golden trophies will never mean to them what my one means to me.

You go, Trophy Girl.

Carolyn Mason

The Ugly Orchid

The quality of your life is measured by the little things.

Barbara Braham

There it sat, one sad, gangly stem leaning to the left of a plain terra-cotta pot. I peered closer. Tiny brown pods clung weakly to the lackluster plant. I was puzzled. This was the wonderful gift my daughter and son-in-law had sent all the way from their new home in Hanoi?

I picked up the phone, determined not to mention that my new plant looked as forlorn as I felt.

Katie was enthusiastic. "Now, Mom, for a while, you'll have to keep it in a cool, dark place."

No problem there. This plant was not only an eyesore, but it reminded me of what I had lost: family dinners, meeting the school bus, even helping with homework. When my husband, Jim, had died several years ago, I'd gone straight from being Mrs. Jim Ennis to being "Sara and Michael's Nana." That plant with its bare stem reminded me of what I was now: a widow, mother and grandmother with no one left to nurture. It just wasn't fair.

Plunk! I deposited my gift on a junk table in the basement and switched off the light.

Six weeks later, I was lugging boxes to the basement. There it was: the most beautiful flowering plant I'd ever seen! Creamy white petals draped themselves delicately around the cherry red centers. I stretched out my finger but hesitated to touch. The blossoms were fragile, yet so alive. They looked as though they might fly away.

Back up the stairs I crept, cradling the pot in my arms and trying hard not to breathe on the blossoms. Six weeks alone in the basement had been just what this plant needed!

Suddenly it struck me that what had seemed so ugly and useless only weeks before had now shown itself a treasure.

And what a treasure it was! From its wicker stand, my beautiful orchid shined like a beacon of friendship to passersby. The mail carrier and people I had rarely spoken to waved and even came right up onto the porch, always commenting on "the gorgeous orchid."

"Six weeks ago, it was barely alive," I frequently replied, as I passed iced tea and the orange marmalade cake I was making again after three years. Each day my orchid gave birth to new blossoms, and I renewed old friendships and formed new ones.

Then one morning, Katie called. Ted had accepted a position at a nearby college. They were coming home!

Now, I was the one who was blooming. My once-empty life was filled with joy and friendship. Every day was like a precious blossom waiting to unfold. Time without my family had seemed an ugly and useless thing, but without it, would I ever have begun to live again?

I had been wrong about the ugly orchid and I had been wrong about myself. I wasn't useless or ugly. I wasn't just a widow, a mother or grandmother. *I'm all those things and more!* I thought gratefully. *All I needed was time alone in the darkness to recognize my true potential.*

One morning, I grabbed a broom and stepped out onto the front porch. Dried orchid blossoms littered the floor. Why, my orchid was as bare as it was the day it had come! I was still sweeping up when one of my new friends stopped by with an invitation to join her gardening club.

"Oh, dear, it's so sad!" she exclaimed upon seeing the bare stem.

"It'll be okay," I said. "You should have seen *me* six weeks ago!"

Shelah Brewer Ogletree

2

ON FRIENDSHIP

Each friend represents a world in us, a world possibly not born until they arrive, and it is only by this meeting that a new world is born.

Anaïs Nin

No Old Friends

A friend doesn't go on a diet because you are fat. A friend never defends a husband who gets his wife an electric skillet for her birthday. A friend will tell you she saw your old boyfriend— and he's a priest.

Erma Bombeck

I've decided to not have any old friends. Old cars break down and are sold for scrap. Old shoes are tossed out and replaced. You want that to happen to a friend?

Becoming a bit touchy as we edged past forty, my buddy Linda and I agreed that it was time to stop gleefully introducing each other as "my oldest friend in the world." We invented a new title: "My Friend of Longest Duration." We felt it honored the roots of our relationship which started in grade school, while not immediately directing people's focus to those other roots—the ones we try to rinse away every six weeks.

For a while, I believed that the blessing of having friends of long duration was primarily based on eyesight. As I age, so do my friends. As my wrinkles set in, their visual acuity diminishes. So, when we meet for lunch and one says, "Wow, you look great. You haven't changed at all," I know she means it. Of course, she can't read the small print on the menu either, but I choose not to make the correlation.

Lately, though, I'm noticing other benefits of those long-term connections. For example: Recently, Janey, my best friend during high school, quietly observed, "You know, you're my only friend who remembers my dad." She was an only child and the pride of his life. He was her larger-than-life, silver-haired, soft-spoken hero, and I help her carry his memory.

I'm also the only one of her friends who remembers her as a girl. How she worshiped Andy Williams and Audrey Hepburn. How she sparkled with enthusiasm editing the yearbook and stage-managing the senior play. She was bold enough to have boys as real friends, but timid enough to doubt her ability to catch one romantically. Even today I could go upstairs to a box in my closet and put my hands on one of the notes we passed to each other in history class. (Does the guitar-playing tenth-grader still like her? Will the twelfth-grade basketball star notice me?)

Through college and across miles, we held on to our bond in the same way many friends do. We stood up for each other's weddings. I phoned comfort through her divorces. Together we celebrated pregnancies and parenting; sweated career changes; shared fears and losses, with our souls bare and raw; kept secrets; toasted successes.

We carry more memories of each other—where we've been and who we've been—than anyone else does. So we're the ones who can fully appreciate the women we have become.

Today when I tell Janey, "You look great," it's not because I can't see her wrinkles without my glasses, or even because she is still pretty. When I look at her, I see everything it took to grow this woman. I see a formerly pampered princess who single-handedly takes her daughter camping; a formerly uncertain academic, who first became a college professor and is now a knowledgeable and respected businesswoman. No stranger to sadness, she's a person who revels in the beauty she finds in life. I see the loyalty of her friendship. She has become a formidable person.

And when she tells me I'm terrific, she's seeing me whole-cloth. A newer acquaintance may compliment me for a current professional coup, healthy kids or thirty-plus years of marriage, assuming I'm "lucky" and it has all come easily. A friend who's been along for the whole ride knows that nothing in life is easy, remembers my false steps along the way, and pats me on the back for what I've learned and how hard I've worked to grow.

As "friends of long duration," we carry each other's memories, not to sit and page through, but to frame the present with the distance we've come, to help us appreciate all that we are at this present moment.

Upon reflection, that "new" way of introducing each other is over a decade old, and may need freshening. It sounds a bit like, "Meet my durable friend." Durable—like rubber tires ready to be recycled.

So what should we choose as a suitable accolade to introduce such valuable guardians? "I'd like you to meet my archivist, my cheerleader, my therapist?" Currently I'm torn between "my oh-so-deeply-valued-and-treasured associate" and "my bud."

I suppose what we tell the rest of the world matters little compared with what we tell each other. When we look at each other, we know that the real value of an old friend is, in fact, a deeper connection with life. Come to think of it, I'm not going trade my "old friends"—my good old friends—for anything.

Anne Merle

The Warm Waters of Friendship

*When you care about a person . . . you accept
that this person is in your life, and for me that's
it . . . this person is a permanent part of me.*

Lynn Sharon Schwartz

I don't remember why I called. We never talked much
on the phone. Since the fourth grade, when our families
moved to different towns, Susan and I had been pen pals.
Over thirty years, our letters dwindled. Yet, they still held
the intensity of a friendship based not on proximity or
shared experiences, but on a bond that's deeply chosen. I
learned that her family was planning a vacation to a lake
in the mountains of Oregon. I lived eleven hours away.

"Can I come?" I asked, letting go of my uncertainty that
I would be welcome. Although friends for a lifetime, we
traveled on different tracks. Their lifestyle focused on
higher education and financial success; my husband and I
squeaked by with part-time jobs so we could pursue our
love of hiking, biking and skiing. They purchased an elegant new home in the suburbs of Ohio. We chose a tiny,

old cabin in the woods of Idaho. They had four bright, beautiful daughters. We had two bright, beautiful dogs.

Still, I wanted to see her. Maybe it was the way she used to hug me from behind, her arms squeezing me into the round belly of her Brownie uniform. Maybe it was the imaginary pet we shared, a string on a stick we named "Nothing At All." Whether joined coincidentally by the arrangement of our names on the kindergarten roster (my last name started with the letter H, hers with the letter K) or something fated, the results were the same. In boxes of letters, faded and dated over three decades, we'd sworn we'd always be best friends.

She agreed that a day of vacation was mine if I'd drive out to see them. The two older girls, seven and nine, could barely have remembered me. It had been three years since I'd held the third daughter, my godchild, in my arms, her body wriggling against the itchy, white baptismal dress. Within minutes of our reunion, the girls took me in.

"Aunt Marian!" "AUNT MARIAN!" they screamed to me across the parking lot, as if I were their own lost best friend. Their mother must have prompted them. "Aunt Marian's the one who sent that birthday package to you girls. Aunt Marian has been my friend since we were your age," she must have said.

Children don't allow time or circumstance to sway their relationships. They don't worry that we may not have anything in common anymore. Susan and I were more reserved. What stories had we told each other? Would our friendship still fit in? We skirted around topics that were sensitive: husbands, money, children and our seemingly opposing goals.

None of this mattered to the girls. They knew that I was there because I loved them. The proof was in an eight-dollar inner tube. It was stuffed in the back of my trunk, still partially inflated from a trip on the river. I blew it up and invited the girls along.

Even though it was summer and the air was hot, the water didn't know it. "They're not used to swimming in such freezing water," their mother said. "They're used to swimming pools."

I knew a few things about mountain water, how its icy grip refreshed the soul. As long as you keep the sun on your back, you don't notice your toes growing cold. So we sat on the edge of the huge purple tube, our feet sticking through the center. Together we rocked. We paddled with our hands, we laughed and we splashed to the floating platform. It was a musty wooden raft anchored in the middle of the lake. Like a good friend, it served its purpose well. We took turns slithering out of the inner tube and onto the solid deck, warming ourselves in the light.

"Your bathing suit looks good on you," one said. "Yeah, you look pretty," said the other. They didn't notice how my thighs had grown since my last visit. They didn't know I didn't have those lines before around my eyes and nose.

Looking at their grinning faces, I wondered what it is that makes me love these girls as if they were my own. Sure, they are uncommonly cute, their dark eyes sensitive and expressive. But there is something more. They are my best friend's children. They embody all that I have loved in her for so long. I see their mother in the way they show they care. In their tight hugs, I feel their unwavering loyalty, despite my absence from their lives. They are our history made tangible somehow.

I want to know my best friend's children, who grow up much too quickly and so sweetly. I want their greetings squealing, "Aunt Marian's here!" I long to hear their voices say again, "I'm sad you're leaving. Why can't you stay?"

I didn't say that to my friend, my almost-sister friend, although I felt it from the bottom of my bones. I never asked, "Why don't we spend more time together? Why don't we make our visits a priority?"

Susan and I walked alone along the lake that night, agreeing that the sunset came too soon. Taking the lessons of her girls, we picked up where we left off years before, sharing disappointments, fears and goals.

"It means so much to me that you love my girls," she said at our visit's end. "Even more than you loving me, which I probably take for granted."

After our reunion, Susan packed up her family and moved to Switzerland to help further her husband's career. I stayed in Idaho, leaving the vast Atlantic churning between us.

Our letters continue, now via e-mail. Sometimes when I cannot sleep, we connect online at the same moment, her early morning meeting my late night. I see that time and setting matter nothing to our friendship when it borders on the sacred. Although we swim in separate waters, love will warm us and unite us, if we let it.

Marian Wilson

The Friend Who Listened

If you want to be listened to, you should put in time listening.

Marge Piercy

I placed the peony on June's grave. Looking at her name on the stone brought back memories of the special lilt in her voice.

"Joan, this is June. How about meeting me for lunch today?" I hadn't been interested in leaving the house for some time and started to give her my list of rehearsed excuses. But I liked June, even though I didn't know her well, and I was touched that she'd called with the invitation. We made arrangements to meet.

As I put down the receiver, I felt panic. What had I done? Small talk held no appeal, and I certainly didn't feel like eating. Then I remembered what my ten-year-old son said the evening before, "Mom, you don't smile anymore."

"That's silly," I told him, "of course I do." I gave him a large toothy grin. Then I went into the bathroom and looked in the mirror. I smiled at that face, but my mouth felt stretched and strange. I locked the door and sat on the edge of the bathtub and let the tears have their way.

Bill, our oldest son, had been killed in an accident six months before, and I thought I had been presenting a healed person to my family. I was a fake.

I brought armloads of books home from the library, looking for a word or sentence that might help explain or comfort. The faith that had been a part of me no longer held answers. I realized my beliefs seemed childlike. Although our minister, family, neighbors and friends had been there for my husband and me, the emptiness and longing for an end to the pain continued. I realized that perhaps June's telephone call would herald a new beginning. It was probably what I needed—to get away and just visit for a while.

But while June and I sat at the table in the restaurant waiting for our order, it was obvious that chatting was not what she had in mind. "I've been wanting to talk to you," she started, "to see if you are all right and to let you know I'm hurting right along with you. You see, years ago my son died." I asked her questions about his death, wanting to hear her feelings and reactions, how she coped. Talking about that time in her life, reliving it, she cried—and I cried with her. She placed her hand on mine, "It was a long time ago, but I can feel it as though it were yesterday."

I don't remember if I ate my lunch that day but I do remember sitting there, finally pouring out my despair; and she listened. It was the first time anyone had allowed me to do this. I had wanted so much to talk about Bill, but whenever those with me heard me say his name or saw tears in my eyes, they were uncomfortable. It seemed a signal to leave or to immediately change the subject to some lighthearted topic. Now, at last, I could get rid of some of the feelings and questions I'd not been able to come to terms with. I told her how I missed my son, his presence in my life, his smile, his voice. I told her I wondered if I would ever have any enthusiasm for the things I needed to do, and about my constant concern for the safety of my two other sons. I told her how differently my husband and I were dealing with his death and about my struggle with God and the thought that, perhaps, I had somehow failed and not been a good mother. She confided she had worked through some of the same questions. We talked and talked and hugged, and I went home.

I realized I felt a sense of relief I could not explain, a relief I had been searching for. Perhaps, I thought, God speaks to us through our friends.

Our friendship deepened and we planned outings that included our husbands. We had pleasant times in each others' homes, eating out or sharing activities. June had a lively sense of fun and a wonderful laugh, but that was only one part of her. The woman I knew and loved was the questioning June, pondering on something she'd read or giving the details of a concern—even if tears and hurt were involved.

We enjoyed this comfortable relationship for many years and always, when I answered the phone and heard, "Joan, this is June," I felt pleasure. During one Christmas season, I told her I had read that the greatest gifts were not ones we buy. We discussed the gift we would give each other, that of complete acceptance.

One fall day she asked if I could drop over. When I got there she seemed upset. "Something just isn't right," she explained, "I don't feel like myself lately." We talked about getting older, about our needs. But when I got up to leave, I could see her face reflected a worry we had not been able to touch upon or identify. She gained no peace of mind from our conversation. I left feeling inadequate, as though I'd somehow failed her.

Before the end of the year, she was diagnosed as having

a brain tumor. On New Year's Eve after her surgery, my husband and I visited June in the hospital. Seeing her that night, with memories of the New Year's Eve we spent together the year before, was an agony. The surgery was not successful. She went through treatment and therapy but made little progress. Her condition worsened, and she was confined to a wheelchair, unable to return home. I visited almost daily, stopping in for a few minutes. I watched her month after month, praying for her recovery and, if that wasn't to be, praying for the peace of mind she sought.

I'd promised to accept her that Christmas, just as she was, and I found it very difficult to keep my promise. I had to face the realization that I would never be able to give her the wonderful relief, the help, she had given me when I needed it.

June died that August. I realize now, many years later as I stand looking at her grave, that I still grieve. My wonderful friend, June. She taught me what a friend really is: one who listens.

Joan Downey

Eulogizing a Friend

Your friend is . . . your field which you sow with love and reap with thanksgiving.

Kahlil Gibran

Too many blinking lights on the answering machine on a Sunday.

Too many veiled messages from anxious voices asking that we call—as soon as possible.

And then the horrible, unfathomable news: our friend Jan had died. He was gone in an instant, his old enemy— a damaged heart—finally blindsiding him.

This very public man—a beloved judge—had died alone by the water on Long Beach Island at the New Jersey shore.

There is no way to predict one's reaction to awful news, no way to know what mode the body and spirit will adopt. In our case, the grief came instantly, in a great flood. My husband and I stood in our kitchen holding on to one another for dear life. The news, quite literally, took our breath away.

And then the surreal ride to the familiar home of our old friends, the walk past the glorious deck and yard so carefully cultivated, and through the doorway of a house forever altered. The furniture was the same—the pictures on the wall were, too—but everything felt different, even in that first moment. As we reached out our arms to enclose Ruth Ann, there was the weird expectation that Jan himself would come bounding out to greet us, looking bemused at our arrival on a Sunday night.

But Jan did not come out. And there we stood, dear old friends who had known one another through every life passage, dealing with a new reality: Death had swept into our lives at the midpoint and had edged out our complacency, our smug sense of invincibility and our foolish hope that the good are rewarded with long years.

Three days later, my husband and I faced our most formidable task. Each of us was to deliver a eulogy at Jan's funeral, where hundreds of mourners filled the Cherry Hill, New Jersey, funeral home to overflowing, our collective grief seeming to saturate the very air of the chapel.

The day before, a day when rain poured out of the skies as if on cue, my husband and I had sat at opposite ends of our house, each of us working on our remarks. It was strangely silent, almost eerie, as we searched vainly for words too small for the feelings.

Neither of us had ever done this terrible/ennobling/painful/humbling work before. Neither of us could have guessed how it would feel.

All day and all night, we searched for words that would do justice to a brilliant, funny, kind, generous, irreverent man we had loved, a public man we had known so privately and personally.

Three times I ripped up the pages my printer had spit out. As many times, my husband crumpled the lined yellow pages of his legal tablet. But standing at the podium the next day, looking out at the faces of Jan's widow, his children, his colleagues and his friends, I suddenly understood what a privilege my husband and I had been given. Not one we would have sought, surely. Not one we could have imagined.

But a eulogy is a special way, a final gift—an offering—a chance to fortify the grieving with treasured, loving, even silly memories. And my husband and I had so many of them.

As our words tumbled out, I understood that we were all living an experience for which we had not yet found a name. The death of a friend is a wild new territory, and there are few road maps to guide us.

But my husband and I understood, as we eulogized our beloved friend Jan, that at the heart of every relationship that matters is risk. And nothing teaches more piercingly than delivering a eulogy that, yes, caring can cost a lot, but not caring can cost even more.

Sally Friedman

The Blessing of Old Age

My coworkers and I had lunch together every day. As with any group of women, our conversation ranged from our families and work to our female problems. One day, the conversation centered on our litany of complaints over getting older.

One coworker described her hot flashes in detail, how in the middle of the night she got out of bed, got naked and lay on the cool tile floor in her bathroom to calm her night sweats. Another described dressing and undressing constantly depending on her body temperature. One woman commented that between her mood swings and arthritis, her family compared her to Dr. Jekyll and Mr. Hyde, never knowing what personality was going to show up next. They all bemoaned the fact that their behinds had spread and that they seemed to work harder to try to maintain a decent weight. Then there was the existential question: "My life is half over and what have I done with it?"

Throughout this entire conversation, I remained silent, listening to their complaints. Finally, one woman turned to me. "You're going to be fifty this year. You must have some complaints."

I smiled and sipped my tea. "Well, I guess I look at age differently. Sure, I wish I was twenty pounds lighter, and I have hot flashes and bursitis in my shoulder, but I can live with those things. But you know what? I can't wait to turn fifty. I'm finally starting my writing career and I feel great. I'm looking forward to getting my AARP card and never paying full price for anything anymore."

Everyone laughed, but I could tell by their curious looks that they thought I was just a little strange.

"My mother died of cancer when she was forty-eight years old. She never got to experience what I'm experiencing now," I said. My coworkers suddenly became quiet. "So I welcome old age with all its aches and pains. Old age is a blessing, and that's just how I'm going to treat it."

"You know, I never thought of it that way," one woman said. "I guess you're right."

Suddenly, the conversation changed from the aches and pains of old age to older persons they knew who were still active, and how they hoped to be like them. Old age, they agreed, might have its aches and pains, but it was indeed a blessing. A blessing to be embraced with an open heart and mind.

Sharon M. Stanford

Rules for Paging, Rules for Aging

After fifty most of the bullshit is gone.

Isabel Allende

We didn't intend to come up with rules when the three of us decided to share our writing. We were all over fifty and thought we could be free of rules. We'd followed them all. Now we wanted to shed them, like we'd shed girdles in the sixties.

So, when we started our writer's group, we decided to work without constricting guidelines. We'd have free-form meetings. But after floundering around for a while, we gave up this anarchy, realizing some rules were needed if we were to take our writing seriously.

Only later did we come to see that these rules worked in other areas of our lives, as well. We're learning to navigate a new stage of life, just the three of us, meeting every other Monday with short stories, plays, mysteries and memoirs—and our rules.

Rule 1: START WITH THE GOOD STUFF

When we critique each other's work, there are frequently

red marks all over the pages. To make this medicine easier to take, we start each critique with what is good about the piece. Then, with the writer basking in the glow of hearing how skillful her writing is, the not-so-positive stuff can be discussed.

If there is any rule that applies to aging, this is it. The papers and television news are full of the problems of aging—fading memories, fatal illnesses, scams to cheat the trusting. But what if we started by thinking about what we gain from getting older, not what we lose? Like a new sense of time. When we were raising our kids, we always looked ahead to each new stage, to when our babies would crawl, talk, walk, feed themselves, get out of diapers, get into school.

Now we know how fast the chipmunk–cheeked face of the nursing baby sharpens into the schoolgirl's studious look. And we realize that, with each change, the special world each face inhabits disappears, too. So, we take the time to value what the world presents to us, through the eyes of our grandchildren and through our own more understanding eyes.

Rule 2: BELIEVE IN THE POSSIBILITIES OF THE PIECE

Writing, like life, is not a goal but a process. And, as in life, it is easy to give up. The excuses are legion. It's too difficult to write; the storyline isn't working; I don't know where it's taking me. But if we don't trust the possibility that it will work out, we'll never get it written. And if those who read our work don't look for the possibilities, their doubts can discourage us from finishing it. So, we look for the possibilities of each idea, each piece of work.

Just as we look for the potential in aging. Not that growing older in our society is easy. The emphasis on staying young—no matter what it takes or costs—is strong. It's sometimes hard to find the upside of getting old.

But as mature women we have endless possibilities,

from the sublime to the silly: never wearing panty hose again; wearing big, dangling rhinestone earrings with jeans; eating dessert first—or eating dessert only; going back to graduate school for the sheer joy of learning; taking up glassblowing—or skydiving. We can do what we want. It's all possible.

Rule 3: PRESENT YOUR WORK WITHOUT EXPLANATIONS OR APOLOGIES

What has been written in solitude is not easily presented to a group. There is a temptation to explain it away, to discount our work as unimportant. This rule means never saying we're sorry for what we've written.

It's harder to do sometimes, with our lives. We look back, rethink decisions. *Should I have married him? Should I have gone back to school? Why didn't I take that job in Duluth? Why did (or didn't) I have children?*

But who we are is the sum of all our life decisions. Change one decision and the whole thing falls apart like the plot of a story unravels when a character is changed. Perhaps the story of our life isn't what we started out to write. It doesn't matter. It is special because it's ours. We present our lives—and our work—as we've written them, without excuses or explanations.

Rule 4: IT'S YOUR STORY AND YOU CAN DO ANYTHING WITH IT YOU LIKE

Often when our work is seen through another's eyes, we see the holes in our thinking, the mistakes in our grammar, the confusion in our explanations. But sometimes it's hard to understand why the group doesn't get it. This rule reminds us that even though we solicited the advice, we don't have to take it.

Women of our generation have frequently led their lives listening to voices other than their own. Following the guidance of parents, teachers or spouses, they let their own dreams sleep quietly in their hearts. Now, as we get older, we can listen to our own voices, still hearing the viewpoints of others, but doing with our lives what we want to do. To write, to sing, to dance, to gain control of our time and talents, in spite of and without regard to—sometimes even contrary to—what others expect of us. It's our story and we'll write the second half the way we want to.

Rule 5: LISTENING CAN BE AS IMPORTANT AS PROBLEM SOLVING

Sometimes a writer just needs a listener. For example, one of us needed to vent her frustration when a hoped-for mentor showed no interest in her writing. It was enough that we listened to her and read her unsent venomous letters. And when one of us faced a public reading of her story about red lingerie and sex on the kitchen floor, talking about her feelings let her go forth with confidence. We've come to realize that a writing-associated problem may come up time after time—the ongoing revisions of a play, the problem of finding time to write—precisely because there are no easy or uniform solutions.

Just like in our lives. We provide a shoulder but not a solution for frustrations with kids, husbands, grandchildren and computer programs, as well as writing. But then, we've always known about the listening rule. Women are good at it.

Rule 6: END WITH THE GOOD STUFF

We begin critiques with good stuff, and we end them positively, too, not wanting to leave critical words hanging in the air. And as we close our notebooks at the end of our meetings, we always express how glad we are to have been together.

Frequently we exchange e-mails after our meetings about how helpful a critique was, or how inspiring someone's hard work was or how the group's support helped one of us keep going with her writing.

The longer we live, the more we know about hurts and sadness in our own lives and in the world. But we know more, too, about the joys and beauty. Why not end each day, then, with a recounting of what went right that day? And each time we leave those we care about, we can leave them a positive word, a gift of the good stuff, until we see them again.

Jane Mozena, Ginny Foster and Peggy Bird

Friendship That Endured the Years

Yes'm, old friends is always best, 'less you can catch a new one that's fit to make an old one out of.

Sarah Orne Jewett

Jane and I met in a suburban neighborhood many years ago when our children were very young. A close friendship developed—one that endured throughout the years, even when she moved out of the area. Through telephone calls, social evenings and frequent visits, we kept our special bond.

Jane was unique—taking on such varied jobs as registered nurse, wife, mother, community volunteer and art appraiser. She was articulate when expressing thoughts, even when they were not popular, and often motivated me to take new directions in career choices and to speak out, when I was used to listening and not participating.

Four women, including Jane and myself, met every Thursday at a weekly "traveling" bridge game. The card game was good, but the conversation was worth a grand slam. Over lunch we discussed world events as well as literature, art and family. When election time rolled around, we would argue for our candidates—Jane usually taking a different view from the rest of us. These discussions were always lively and stimulating.

Our weekly card games were in their thirtieth year when, one Thursday, Jane asked the three of us to come to her home early. She and her husband wanted to talk to us. I had a feeling in the pit of my stomach that I wasn't going to like what they had to say. I wanted to say, "No, I think I'll stay home today." Not to be! We arrived at her home and went into the cozy kitchen. There was an air of gloom all around, and my usual smile felt as if it were painted on my face.

Her husband started to speak—hedging, while trying to get to the point. Jane's eyes were bright and glistening. We all knew she had been to Mayo Clinic and were waiting and praying for a good prognosis.

Jane said, "I have been diagnosed with ALS, Lou Gehrig's disease." I can't remember any more of the hour-long conversation. We played our usual game of bridge that afternoon, hiding the ache we all felt.

That was five years ago. During that time, her physical condition deteriorated. Although she traveled a hundred miles for experimental injections once a month, she eventually had to have daily help in her home.

We continued our Thursday bridge games, but now had them exclusively at her house. I talked to her every day, not about her illness, but about other things—our kids, husbands, and subjects that would stimulate her mind. I visited her several times a week, bringing with me a flower, a bit of conversation, an egg-salad sandwich and, most of all, my love.

The four of us kept playing bridge. When Jane lost a lot

of mobility of her hands, I fashioned a shoebox for her into which she could fit the cards. Not once did she complain or talk of her illness. Her caregiver kept her hair coiffed and nails manicured. Small things certainly, but would I have done this? I think not.

Jane grew steadily weaker, and the card games ceased. I continued to visit her every Thursday, often for only twenty minutes, until she became too ill to receive visitors.

She died ten days after my last visit.

I think of her daily—her smile, her outlook on life and her dignity. I'm glad I said to her often, "Jane, I love you." These words remain in my heart to this day. Jane was a woman of great courage and a friend to cherish.

Lois Schmidt

Hangin' with the Fast Girls

Friends are people who help you be more your-self, more the person you are intended to be.

Merle Shain

When I went to high school in the late fifties, girls were divided into two groups: the good girls and the fast girls. Since the rigid rules didn't make allowances for gray areas, I fell solidly in the legions of the good girls. Scrawny, full of nervous energy and insecure, I raced from my college-preparatory classes to working on the high-school newspaper, the yearbook and any other activity that took my mind off feeling I was probably a dork.

The fast girls were those senior girls who were pretty, dated and flirted with boys, reigned as prom queens or attendants, and were cheerleaders. What cemented their bad-girl reputations were their occasional displays of affection in dark corners of the school hallways or the backseats of cars with said boys. Oh, and they wore eye makeup and clothes that were actually flattering. I, on the other hand, wore pleated skirts and sweaters that were

two sizes too big for me lest I appear to be "forward."
They dated; I only wrote about it. "There's plenty of
chemistry between Jeanette and Owen and not just in the
lab, ha ha," was one of the exceedingly clever items I
added to my high-school gossip column in those rare
moments when I wasn't rushing around being compul-
sively nice to everyone.

In fact, while they did the things one is supposed to do
during high school, I dreamed about the perfect man and
tried to smile constantly, even though I was sure they saw
me as a nerd.

During college, graduate school and through much of a
twenty-plus career at a financial magazine in New York, I
managed to repress this pathetic self-image. In fact, days
went by when I was working like a dog and enjoying life
in the city when I never gave high school a thought. But
each time I got an announcement of a class reunion, my
dork image resurfaced.

It didn't matter that I had lunched in private dining
rooms on Wall Street, dressed in my dark business suit
and round-toed pumps or that I had learned all about
power politics by ignoring the self-serving arrogance of
Wall Street hotshots. Any reunion invitation made me
edgy with nervousness about fitting in with my old
classmates.

However, each reunion I felt a little more comfortable
about who I'd become. I made little inroads in getting to
know my classmates better by telling them I'd started
writing love stories that were published in a tabloid. I
shared some of my travel stories to weird places like
Yemen. I looked at their pictures of kids, dogs, boats, RVs
and grandchildren.

After sharing a few laughs over the class Romeo, who
had wound up as a petty criminal, Sally, one of the petti-
est and most outgoing of the gang, began e-mailing me,

and I e-mailed back. I was flattered to receive an invitation from her to spend some time with her and the other girls at the 2001 reunion.

Despite my newfound confidence, I was still nervous. Waiting outside the motel for them to pick me up for the reunion dinner, I paced in my black pants, silk top and three-inch black slides. There would be eight of us (none of their husbands came with them) sitting together at the dinner. In the car, we made awkward conversation about who was attending, who had a Mercedes and who was thought to be obnoxious.

At the banquet hall, I was assigned a seat with the girls. And I was proud to be at a table of women who knew everyone at the reunion. Never for a moment did I feel out of place as we retold the old story of Kenny cutting the legs off the coach's chair in history class and Ruthann taking out a gas pump during driving class.

Still, it wasn't until the next day when we rode in two cars of four each through the summer green rolling hills of Ohio, stopping for soft drinks, shopping in antique stores and strolling through the Amish tourist sites that we really talked.

Dressed in our shorts or crop pants, our waists discreetly covered with overblouses, we sat in outdoor cafes and talked of hot flashes, diets, high cholesterol, dealing with sick parents, relationships with men and what we hoped the future held.

There were joyous tales of long marriages, winning lottery tickets, healthy children and grandchildren, and second marriages. And, of course, there were disappointments—divorces, affairs, relationships that didn't make it, babies who were never born, illness, widowhood and children who had problems.

But somehow we'd all survived and become middle-aged. And despite our various paths, we were linked by having been influenced by the same set of emotional values and economic constraints. You married the man you slept with. You had four vocational choices: nurse, teacher, secretary or housewife. You put up with photocopying, fetching coffee and being called "honey." And in 1956 you didn't know any better.

And now, fifty years later, comfortable and satisfied with ourselves, the eight of us sat for two hours talking, laughing and gorging ourselves on fried chicken, mashed potatoes, biscuits, iced tea, homemade coleslaw and berry cobbler. When you come down to it, we're all just women.

Perhaps when our guidance counselor taught us "human nature never changes," she knew that when you come right down to it, we're all just human. How silly to have wasted so much time focusing on our differences when, all the time, we were in the same class.

Barbara Bent

$\overline{\underline{3}}$

LETTING GO

Courage is the power to let go of the familiar.

Mary Bryant

Building a Home for an Autumn Butterfly

I rolled the unfamiliar key in the palm of my hand and stuck it in the deadbolt lock. With a deep breath, I pushed open the heavy door and stepped inside my new two-bedroom world. The smells of pine disinfectant and carpet cleaner wafted up as I scuffed across the carpeting that looked like a beige, well-groomed lawn. The freshly painted cream-cheese–colored walls added to the aroma, and the blandness of it all seemed to taunt me and say, "Come on, I dare you—show me your true colors!"

After years of fighting, months of a bitter divorce and forty-eight hours of a court-ordered eviction from a home I'd known over twenty years, I was battle weary. So when I packed to begin a new life, I took little. My clothes, a portable TV, a couple of lawn chairs and enough kitchen, bath and bedroom things to start again. I didn't want any of the furniture because my ex had never sanctioned good furniture purchases, and what was left was worn and dirty. I decided I could sleep on the floor and sit in the lawn chairs until I found the right pieces at the right prices to turn this sterile dwelling into a comfortable place.

As I listened to the emptiness around me, I felt strangely calm. Alone, but not lonely. Safe. At home. The feeling was comforting. I tried to remember if there ever was another time in my life when I felt what I was feeling now. I smiled when my thoughts brought me to vigils at the bedside of my sleeping babies so many years ago.

I drew open the beige vertical blinds that covered the living-room patio door and opened the room to the crisp southern breezes of that Indian summer afternoon. I drifted back to that bright September day when my lawyer and I walked down the steps of the courthouse after the divorce was final. "You know, Barbara, you've lived in a cocoon for most of your life, and this divorce has set you free. It's up to you what you do with the freedom. I think you should take a little time to pick your way out of that cocoon and let your wings dry. Then I want you to fly. Fly as high as you can, because you have everything it takes to be successful." She gave me a precious gift that day, because every time I felt afraid or too old to be reborn, I thought of butterflies and rebirth.

The fresh air helped dilute the chemical smells in the apartment; I pushed up my sweatshirt sleeves and got to work. I walked into the one-woman, dark galley kitchen that was so different from the sun-filled country kitchen I had enjoyed for most of my adult life. I ripped open a box marked "Cleaning Stuff," took out a bottle of Lysol and began washing. It probably was silly to clean again with the heavy disinfectant smells in the air, but there was a part of me that needed to make sure my life here was a fresh start in every way. When the cupboards were dry, I pulled out the bright yellow shelf paper from the dollar store that my ex would have hated, but now I reminded myself I didn't have to worry about such things anymore.

I put the silverware, wooden spoons, whisks, spatulas, tongs and other gadgets that I had used for over two decades in the drawer nearest the stove. Potholders, dishrags and kitchen towels in the drawer below the gadgets. Somehow, touching these things helped to ground me. I began to believe I could really do this.

Afternoon tea gave me energy to tackle the bathroom. I clicked on the light and was blinded by the bright white ceramic tile walls and the cold tile floor. I dug through the box marked "Bathroom Stuff" and pulled out the maroon-and-gold shower curtain and towels I had found on a sale table at Target the day before. Hanging the curtain and towels and laying the fluffy, soft maroon throw rugs on the floor was like posting a warning to the vanilla landlord, "Caution! Butterfly at Work!"

The ring of the telephone interrupted the silence. I couldn't imagine who'd be calling me today.

"Barb, this is Cathy. How're you doing in your new place?" That was just like Cathy. She had been my friend since kindergarten, and I always could count on her.

"Right now, I'm wondering why I rented such a big apartment," I laughed.

"Well, maybe I can help you fill it up a little. Jim and I wondered whether you'd like a king-size waterbed for your bedroom."

"You're kidding, right?"

"No. We bought the bed years ago, and when Jim hurt his back, he could never sleep on it again, so it's just been sitting in the basement."

"I'd love it!" I blurted like an excited teenager. "But I don't know anything about waterbeds."

"Don't worry about a thing. Jim and I will bring it over on Saturday, set it up and fill it so you can sleep on it that night. I'll have to warn you, though, it takes a couple of days for waterbeds to warm up so you'll probably have to sleep on top of the blanket."

"I guess I'd better go out and buy a blanket, then, shouldn't I?"

"No. Don't do that! You can have the sheets, blankets,

comforter and the mattress pad that we bought for the bed. We sleep on a queen-size bed now, so this stuff is just sitting there, too—we want you to have all of it."

"Cathy you're a gift from God."

"Oh, now, don't get dramatic. We're just glad we can help."

I felt a lump forming in my throat, "I'm so lucky to have had you in my life all of these years."

"That's just the way we feel about you, too, Barb. You hang in there, and we'll see you on Saturday."

I said good-bye and hung up the phone. Tears filled my eyes as I realized how blessed I was. I panned from my new kitchen, to the card table and the silly dangling chandelier, to the living room with two lawn chairs that looked ready for a lazy picnic and the TV with the "rabbit ear" antennae, and for some odd reason, everything was okay. Cathy's phone call reminded me I wasn't alone. God was walking with me through the people he put in my life. And I owed it to him and myself to be the best butterfly I could be.

Barbara McCloskey

Key Words to Survival

In order to gain my life I had to lose it.

Carol Collopy

As a young mother, I thought having four children under the age of four was a challenge. That challenge pales, however, when compared with having two weddings, a mastectomy, and serving as hostess for my husband's business conference—all in two weeks.

Survival became the key word, followed in swift order by *hurry* and *secrecy*, along with *support* and *humor*.

In February 1980, two of our sons announced that they each wanted to be married in early June. They agreed on the first and third Saturdays. One wedding would be in Michigan, the other in Colorado.

Delighted that they had made happy commitments, we chorused, "Wonderful! It's fine with us."

"It even works well for the conference," added my husband. "We can stay in Colorado after the second wedding."

As president of the American Bankers' Association, he had major responsibilities in Colorado the third week of

June. "I'll just take two suitcases," I added, thinking about my responsibilities as his hostess.

All went well until I discovered a small lump in my left breast three days before the first wedding. I hurried to my doctor who hurried me to X ray. From the moment he saw the X ray, *hurry* became a key word.

The doctors rushed me into surgery for a biopsy. As I came out from the anesthesia, the wavering lines of a shape formed into the young surgeon who had done the biopsy. Groggy, I barely comprehended his words. "Remove the breast tomorrow." I tried to shout, but it was just a whisper. "No! Not now! The weddings!"

The older doctor, a friend, explained the percentages of survival based on treatment, and how long it took to recover. Everyone hastened to tell me what I must do *immediately.*

Finally, I announced in what I hoped was a normal voice, "This is Thursday. I will not ruin the wedding. I will come home Sunday and you can operate on Monday."

Secrecy was added to the key-word list. Had I known my daughter-in-law as well then as I do now, I might have told her. But at the time, I would not announce such frightening news to her in the midst of such joy.

Although our son, the groom-to-be, was very worried, my husband and I swore him to secrecy. "Let's wait until after the celebration," we said. Then we drove to Michigan, held the rehearsal dinner, cried and smiled during the wedding and danced at the reception. Our insistence on leaving at dawn the next day, missing the special breakfast, caused some raised eyebrows, but it could not be helped.

I went to the hospital that evening, had surgery the following morning and awoke minus a breast—but free from cancer. No chemotherapy or radiation required.

Prayers and thanksgiving were very important to us at

this time, but *hurry* became vital again. Rapid recovery was essential. The next wedding was in twelve days, and we had to drive to Colorado.

Support joined the key-word list. Friends and family supported me vigorously. They brought food and sent get-well cards. The just-married couple called from their honeymoon in Florida to thank us for not spoiling their wedding. The about-to-be-married couple in Colorado offered to change the date. But the conference could not be canceled. All had to proceed as planned.

With more prayers, thanks and all the fine support, I did begin the recovery process quickly. But other worries arose that, in retrospect, now seem trivial. How would I look? Unable to wear a prosthesis immediately, I worried about my appearance at this next wedding. How could I look like a mother of the groom? My dress would not fit properly.

Again, *support.* A friend who'd had a mastectomy the year before showed me how she'd used cotton and Kleenex to fill out and look balanced during the time before she could start wearing her prosthesis.

It is easy now to look back and laugh at this and the other little strategies we devised, but at the time, conquering each problem caused pain and seemed traumatic. I had not had time to grieve about my loss in private before events pressed me into the public eye at a major occasion of my life: our second son's marriage.

However, slowly, *humor* began to help us cope. My left arm could not reach my back. The first time my husband awkwardly worked at the fastener of my brassiere, we exploded with laughter as he commented, "Somehow, this isn't the same as it used to be." Pulling up my panty hose initially caused frustration then giggles then snorts of laughter as I squirmed and he tugged.

In Colorado, the key word from my family continued to

be *support*, shown by their encouragement. While no one expressed pity, all of them built up my confidence. I *could* handle this happy occasion. A hug here, a pat and a smile, a chair conveniently placed nearby relieved fatigue and let me know how much someone cared. Later, I learned they'd promised each other not to pity me.

"We promised to be strong, so you would have to be," one of them told me years later.

The bride glowed with joy and gratitude at not having to change plans. The second son and his friends took over the rehearsal dinner, a relaxed picnic at which I could be a happy guest. I marched up the church aisle proudly, knowing that my dress hung appropriately. My husband and I shared the joy of this second wedding. Our dancing at the reception was limited, but I managed a dance with the groom and another with my husband. No one paid attention to my left arm hanging limply at my side. We all had more fun than I had thought possible.

Despite friends urging me to skip the conference, where my hostess duties might be very tiring, I was determined to go. By then, my husband had become an expert at brassiere fastening and helping with panty hose. I was adept at padding appropriately. And *humor* had become a habitual key word. To this day, I giggle when I squirm my way into a pair of panty hose. A banker's wife with whom I had become acquainted over the years offered to come to our hotel room any time I needed assistance with my hair. When conference duties kept my husband too busy to help me, she arrived energetically to fasten a pearl necklace, put in my pierced earrings or wash my hair. We became close friends, sharing stories of our children and of our fears and dreams. She taught me to relax with breathing techniques and to gain strength through visualization exercises. Our times together helped me survive and enjoy the conference. Most important, she helped me start the necessary grieving process so that I would eventually feel whole again. By the end of the conference, despite the hurry and emotion, I was beginning to put my mastectomy into perspective.

The words, from *survival* to *hurry*, from *secrecy* to *support*, stand out in my memory of those demanding weeks. Family and friends, prayers and thanksgiving, along with a growing sense of *humor* helped me resolve fears and grief. Recognizing and using key words made survival a reality.

Peg Sherry

Forty Years in the Wilderness

For the first time in forty years, I'm not working. I didn't realize it until just recently when, with nothing else to do at my desk one day, I penciled a few numbers on the side of a worksheet. There it was. *Forty* years.

Good grief, I thought. *Isn't that the number of years the children of Israel wandered in the wilderness?*

So I sat with my cup of Darjeeling, watching the rain hit the window, mentally conducting a review of where my life had been and where it might be going.

My forty years of work began when I turned fourteen and took a part-time job at the local Ben Franklin variety store. They knew and I knew that I should have been sixteen, but they needed me and I needed them. It was fun going to work after school . . . even more fun having money in my pocket on payday. During the next four years, I learned how to check inventory, price merchandise, attend the cash register and stock a candy counter. I prided myself on knowing the names of customers, decorating display windows and creating Easter baskets to sell in the springtime. Although I was just a young girl, I was gaining skills that would stay with me forever.

From my days behind a counter at Ben Franklin, I

moved swiftly through a lifetime of employment. I played the role of secretary, worked in schools and hospitals, spent time on the mission field and taught a diversity of classes, including kindergarten, needlework, cooking and drama. I manned phones and wrote payroll, co-owned a graphics business and opened a half-price card and gift shop. All in forty years.

My last job before retirement was difficult to leave behind. A Victorian tearoom in the heart of Duncanville, Texas, was the icing on the cake of my long career. Three years of hard work and pleasure mixed to perfection. It was an unforgettable day when I handed over the keys to the new owner. I took my time saying good-bye to familiar faces, favorite pieces of china and a parlor full of antique furnishings I had grown to love. Reluctantly, I handed over the copies of all my recipes. Then I walked one last time through the parlor, running my fingers along the gold fringe of the velvet drapes on the front window. It was an elegant tribute to four decades of labor.

Now, for the moment, there is nothing pressing in my life. No demands being made. No appointments to keep. No parties to plan. Recently, I finished reading my seventh book since leaving the workforce. Page by page, I fought getting up to go *do* something, but I overcame and read on. I've met new friends and traveled to faraway places, just sitting in my tapestry armchair.

My garden of herbs flourished on the porch this last season. After years of neglect, now there is time. Time to water and cut back, check the soil and feed. I've enjoyed chive blossoms and fresh basil on salad, and stored away rosemary and thyme for winter soups.

Next month my sister and I are taking a trip together to San Antonio. It's her sixtieth birthday and we are celebrating by heading out of town. No rush. No fuss. No hurrying back to dive into stress again. We're planning to stroll down the Riverwalk and talk, sit in rockers at a log cabin bed-and-breakfast and sip on homemade lemonade in the afternoon.

Wandering in the wilderness for forty years has brought me into a new place. Friends often ask me if I will ever work again. "Maybe," I tell them. But for now I am enjoying the beauty of rest. I'm camping in the quiet of the day. Stillness is my neighbor. God is my peace.

Charlotte A. Lanham

To Everything There Is a Season

Life is a succession of lessons which must be lived to be understood.

Helen Keller

I think it was the sign that so unhinged me at first. There it was, that impossible-to-miss sign stuck on our front lawn and announcing to the world that an era had ended: Our house was for sale.

For the first few days, I blinked in disbelief at the mere sight of it. Surely, that sign had been plunked down at the wrong address, because we really weren't ready for this. Not yet.

No matter that it had been over a decade since any child had occupied the house with too many bedrooms and bathrooms, the house that suddenly seemed cavernous, silent and a bit forlorn for two late-middle-aged adults.

No matter that from the start, this house, an imperious English Tudor with a will all its own, had been a bit much to handle. Nothing was ever simple in a house where the architectural plans dated back to 1929.

But the weird floor plan, impractical rooms, wide-open spaces? Instead of being annoying, those very "negatives" seemed enormously appealing. Downright charming.

The first time the Realtor, a lovely, highly professional woman, brought potential buyers to our door, I felt mounting rage. How dare she? The fact that it was her job, her mission, her mandate mattered not at all. The fact that just a few nights before, we had signed on for this, were future partners in this deed—forgotten. What mattered was that this Realtor and the intruders she had in tow were about to judge this place—our place—the house that had enclosed within it everything that had mattered to us for the past twenty-eight years.

Every image of our daughters blowing out birthday candles or going off to proms in pale gauzy dresses, every holiday dinner, every party in the living room, came rushing back as these audacious strangers were overheard remarking that the "flow" was really poor and the kitchen was totally outdated.

I wanted to announce with appropriate disdain and hauteur that the "flow" was just fine for a family that loved every inch of this old place, and that the kitchen had managed to serve up some pretty decent food, to say nothing of joyful memories.

It took a sheer effort of will not to point out the beech tree in the side yard where three daughters had stood as brides on those luminous June days when the concepts "home" and "love" were joined forever.

Instead, I kept my mouth shut and hoped these ingrates wouldn't get to live in our house.

They didn't even make an offer.

Through several very long months, it went on and on, this parade of lookers.

And for that long, I awoke every day with a knot in my stomach. Would there be that phone call announcing that some potential buyers from out-of-state wanted to come in at 2:00 P.M., the precise time I'd planned a finger-painting party with Zay, our gentle four-year-old grandson? Would I have to rush around cleaning and straightening, hiding all evidence that people actually *lived* here, and create, instead, a perfect stage set?

Oh, how I hated that illusion!

Occasionally, I rebelled and deliberately left various "exhibits"—a broom, a newspaper, a pair of shoes, towels piled on the dryer—just to be defiant.

Sometimes I tortured myself by staying around and eavesdropping as men and women I'd never met before flung open our closets and saw my shoes, my cosmetics, our dishes. But mostly, I took deep breaths and wondered where we would go, and how we'd ever find a house with a dogwood tree outside our bedroom window that made waking up in spring a gift, or leaded windows that let the afternoon light filter gently into the little den near the front stairs.

My husband and I started a countdown as the contract with the real estate firm entered its final days. And you can bet that just as the calendar was closing in on "the end," along came the lovely couple from Chicago who didn't want to plunk down wall-to-wall carpeting over our fine old wood floors or paint over the mellow chestnut paneling in the foyer. We liked them immediately.

And on a momentous Wednesday morning, after a flurry of faxes and e-mails, inspections and engineer's reports, the deed was done. I signed on the dotted line then ran into my husband's arms sobbing. That was the morning when we understood fully that a home is so very much more than wood, plaster and stucco. Home is a shel-ter for the soul, a place where hope and memory collide—a sacred place. But when you're ready to leave a home, you know it.

Yes, to everything, there is a season. And ours for parting has come. I'm sure I'll stop weeping soon.

At last, despite the profound attachment to place, my husband and I felt some new stirrings: a sense of optimism that lightened the gloom, the feeling that endings aside, we were in for an adventure as we shifted the center of family gravity from one address to another.

Yes, to everything, there is a season. At last, ours for parting had come.

And on moving day, as we pulled out of the driveway for the last time, neither one of us even looked back.

Sally Friedman

Youthful Promises

We turn not older in years, but new every day.

Emily Dickinson

The water sparkles below me. Breezes blow through my hair. I am feeling young. The titillating promise of excitement, fun and more youthful feelings is only a ski-length away.

While on vacation with my husband and two sons, I wanted to rent a ski boat and make a day of it. I thought it was a grand idea. I was imagining myself actually being an active participant in this family experience instead of the same, tired old cheerleader Mom. Since hitting midlife, I sporadically become delusional. So it was I, who shamed my reluctant husband into renting the boat by calling him a middle-aged grouch with no sense of adventure and precious little time to still assert his male athletic prowess. That seemed to do it.

I was feeling unusually frisky and daring that morning as I tugged on the old swimsuit, *not* standing in front of a mirror, of course. I recalled the young girl of my early twenties. Ah, I was so cute, so tan, so skinny. I had once skied on a clear blue lake in Colorado. The sky so blue, the air so clean as I skimmed effortlessly along the surface of the water. I had the world at my feet. I was in control. I could do anything! The flood of exciting memories was quickly taking hold, smothering that one little nagging doubt. The doubt that whispered, "You only did this *once?*" But who cares for caution when the lure of the ski is calling? I was pumped! I was revved! I was ready! My husband could see the gleam in my eye, the determination to ski toward my youth. He knew there was nothing he could say to dissuade me. He only stood there slowly shaking his head.

The first minor detail to attend to is finding the right size life vest. After rummaging around the boat and trying on three or four, which were, of course, made for big strong men (who know how to ski), I finally found a cute little red vest that I thought looked pretty good on me, especially since it hid most of my body.

Next comes the part where I jump, however awkwardly, off the boat and into the water. This was my only moment of slight hesitation as I remembered the swarm of nasty-looking fish up by the dock. I had more pressing things to think about at the moment though. The boys were throwing skis at me. I began struggling to get those slender, very long skis on my feet, not an easy task when you're in the water with your cute little life vest having swollen up around your neck and continuously making you roll on your back. After accomplishing that unladylike task, I was feeling pretty damn good about myself, feeling a little more empowered—a little more cocky, a little more back-to-the-middle of middle age.

Meanwhile, the guys are circling around me in the boat. Over the hum of the engine I think I hear words. "Row-row!" *Row? Why do they want me to row?* I begin to move my

arms in some sort of circular motion when my son leans
way over the boat and screams "Rope!" *Oh yes! The rope!*
Grab the rope as it comes around. I knew that. All I need
to do is to *find* the rope that is floating out there somewhere in all that water. I don't see it, but the guys are
yelling and pointing so I guess it's out there. I keep searching, searching. Paddling this way, paddling that way,
spinning in circles looking for the rope. "Right *there*, Mom!
Right there!" "Right where—WHERE?" Finally the boys
throw the rope out where I can see it. I'm wondering why
they didn't just do that in the first place.

Rope in hand, skis in a semi-upward direction, I nod my
head like a professional, signaling "Good to go!" I'm sure I
can do this. I did it once before, didn't I? The engine revs
up, the propeller begins spinning. My husband, behind
the wheel, full of trepidation, pulls back on the throttle
and takes the boat slowly forward, his head bowed, in
what I think is prayer.

We start slowly. I feel the rushing of the water against
my skin, surfacing the memories of yesteryear. *Aaah, yes.*
I'm beginning to relax into this when the boat starts
speeding up. I grip the rope a little tighter, remembering
that I still need to get *up* out of the water. Suddenly we
begin going very fast . . . faster . . . and now *way* too fast! I
don't know what happened, but without warning, this
sleek, shiny new ski boat has turned into a rip-roaring
monster, twisting and turning, blazing through the water
at breakneck speed. My mind is a complete blank. *What am
I supposed to do?* There's no time to think. I just keep grip-
ping the rope even as my arms are being ripped apart
from the rest of my body! I do remember I'm supposed to
keep my legs together—but, oh, the water. There's so
much water! I don't remember this much water. Coming
at me with the force of steel. I'm using every single muscle
in these fifty-year-old legs, struggling to keep them

together. Trying to maintain my balance, as well as a little dignity, I begin to come up-up—just a little more—and then . . . in a nano-second I feel it! Oh my God! My legs are actually coming apart—it's happening—it's—it's the splits!

The rope tears itself out of my clutches as if to say, "I've had enough of you," and leaves me to slam face down into what feels like a brick wall. Water immediately rushes up my nose and into my mouth. I think I may be drowning! *Am I drowning? Is this it? Is this what will be in my obituary: "Drowned by splitting"?* But then, I feel myself being buoyed up and rolled over on my back—Oh my dear, dear little red life vest!

Dazed and sputtering, I surface to find my family circling back towards me. They beg me to get back on the boat, which would have been the intelligent thing to do. But I couldn't let go of the dream just yet. After two more attempts, which were exact replicas of the first, I finally succumb to defeat. With resignation weighing heavy in my mind and heavier still in my body, I clumsily climb back on board, hitting my ankle on the propeller—the last humiliation. The monster's final way of saying, "Gotcha!"

While riding back to middle age, I look behind me, knowing I left my youth somewhere out there in the wide expanse of blue water. A tear forms and rolls down my sunburned (slightly wrinkled) cheek. My mind knows it is time to say good-bye. My heart, well, my heart is heavy and sad.

My boys are already scrambling to jump in and begin their amazing acrobatics. As I watch them I feel my sad and heavy heart begin its slow and healing journey. It will take time, but somehow this cushy seat makes it a little more tolerable. I feel my bones relaxing and my skin soaking up the sun. Maybe, just maybe, there are a few perks that come with my much-resisted promotion. I may not have to struggle so hard anymore. Perhaps the hard raw action of youth is giving way to a softer, gentler gesture of age. I am being carried along by the waves of time and with that thought I collapse into an exhausted and most welcomed sleep.

Denise Fleming

Where the Heart Is

My house is gone. Not by fire, flood or act of God. The house I grew up in as a child, where I lived and laughed and learned, the house where magic danced down every hall and angels breathed through every window . . . is gone. In its place, a bigger, roomier, more modern version—a two-story lumbering giant that all the neighbors say just doesn't fit in.

Did the new owners realize that in the process of tearing down my childhood home, they were also tearing down my spirit? Their only thought was to provide more room for their own growing family, and they had every right to do so, you see, for I have not lived in that house for more than twenty years. I left not by choice, but by necessity in the summer of 1974. My father, a geophysicist, was offered a lucrative job on the West Coast. My mother, whose own family had vacated the right coast for the left years before, seconded the upheaval, and Mayflower loaded what was left of my growing years into a truck and we hauled the tow west.

I fought the move tooth and nail, not wanting to leave those years full of luscious summers, thunderstorms and fireflies, flashlight tag and sledding down the neighbor's hilly backyard, fireworks and carnivals and the 7:00 P.M. siren commemorative of a more dangerous time. Men walked on the moon, women marched in the streets, Woodstock rocked only a few miles to the north and the Beatles played on Ed Sullivan—all in that house.

Tromping through the woods behind that house, with my *Field Guide to Birds* in one hand and a pair of cheap binoculars in the other, I tracked animal markings and identified thrushes, larks, robins and wrens. The results of these scientific explorations led me to such rich rewards: feathers and shells of every size and shape, a jarful of fossils I dug up with the help of the neighborhood kids—found beneath our swing set after my scientist father casually remarked, "We were all underwater once."

When I wasn't outside, I was inside reading and writing and learning, devouring books on every subject as I sat on my bed near the window, listening to crickets hum in the woods. I became a spy in that house, sneaking from room to room with my binoculars, peeking out windows at unsuspecting neighbors. I saw the lady next door in her bra, the man up the street in his boxers, and the fat lady across the way fall off her kitchen table while unceremoniously swatting at a fly with a broom handle.

My favorite target was the older boy next door, who would foolishly study at his desk by his window, which just happened to overlook my own. I fancied myself so slick, a femme Bond, if you will, and if any of the neighbors ever caught on, they never showed it. Besides, I was just a kid, and kids do all kinds of crazy, wonderful things. It's only when they grow up that they stop having so much fun.

I heard my first rock-and-roll in that house, read my first Nancy Drew novel, and watched as my body changed from thin and boyish to just a bit more round. My mother enchanted me with fanciful stories in that house, told as we all sat upon the "magic carpet" by the kitchen doorway. My father traveled the world on research trips, returning each time with tales of intrigue and wonderful coins from the Four Corners that I kept safe in a ceramic crocodile bank.

I made friends, real and imaginary, in that house. The imaginary ones included an alligator in a top hat named Peenafurt Franklin and a cadre of triangle-shaped "heater men" that chased me when the furnace kicked in. I dreamed of being an astronaut, jockey, lady cop, president, super spy, scientist, Olympic runner and actress in that house. I spent my adulthood writing, but it was in that house my big dream took hold. I became a writer.

Since I moved away, I've been back to that old neighborhood a few times, always feeling that resurgence of awe and magic. Even without the huge maple in the front yard, even without the hedgerow and the bushes and flower garden, even without all the outer trappings I had known and loved, it was still the same house and just seeing it gave me chills of sweet joy.

But when my mom called to tell me the distressing news—that an old neighbor had called her earlier and filled her in on the demolition of my house and the rising of a new one in its place, it was as though I had just been told a family member had died. It was gone. Really gone. Not just changed, not just different. *Gone.*

My last trip back, I had gotten strep throat and couldn't even hold my head up long enough to see my house as we took our ride down memory lane. I had vowed to go back again soon, maybe even get up the courage to ask the new owners if I could peek inside for "one last look." But that trip never happened. I got busy, in work, life, paying the bills.

Perhaps it wasn't just that house I was missing, but the dreams and hopes and possibilities left behind. I guess when we loaded up that Mayflower truck, we forgot to pack one thing—my childhood spirit, so bold and free and unafraid to live.

And now it's too late. Too late to ever go back and knock on that door and walk through those rooms again. Rooms where I felt so warm, so alive, so at home. Rooms where I came to know who I was.

I cried when my mom told me. For three straight hours. Then I did the only thing I know how to do when faced with life—I wrote. And in my grief and mourning, for far more than just a lost house, serendipity whispered. They say you can't go home again, but I beg to differ. You never really leave. It's always there, that voice, deep inside, calling you to come back home, however quiet and stifled it might be from years of running to safety and away from the risk of our dreams.

The land can cast a spell . . . houses do that, too. It may be too late for me to ever walk those cherished halls, but it's not too late to fulfill the dreams I came to believe were my own, in that house. Because in my grieving of childhood's end, I realized this: that the magical house of my youth isn't really gone at all . . . it lies within.

Marie D. Jones

"Yes, Doctor. But empty nest syndrome
is your diagnosis for everything."

Reprinted with permission of Steve Smeltzer.

Without You

Love knows not its own depth until the hour of separation.

Kahlil Gibran

We were all saddened and angry at losing Daddy, but the hardest hit was our three-year-old son, Patrick. He had established a unique bond with his grandfather from the moment he could hold onto the elder's hand and take his first steps. Then, in those final days, he spent hours playing hide-and-seek around the bedroom door, finally coming to let Grampa hold him tight with a paralyzed arm.

Patrick was the most insistent of our four children when it came to talking about Grampa no longer being in his life. My mother tried to soothe him but couldn't find the words. Following the funeral and returning to the city where we lived, Patrick could speak of nothing else. We were required to repeat the explanation that Grampa's heart got tired and decided to stop working. "Like the ol' tick-tock in Grampa's room?" he asked. The answer was yes. His three-year-old mind still wasn't satisfied, especially when his older sister said that Grampa was gone forever. The confusion and wondering were too much. Together one day, rolling out snickerdoodles on the kitchen table, Patrick blurted out another question, "Will I see Forever someday, like Grampa?" Tears welled up in my eyes as I explained that yes, someday he would join Grampa, but not for a long, long time. "I don't want Grampa in Forever!" Patrick cried out. "I want him here RIGHT NOW!"

I had to admit that I wanted that, too. In desperate prayer, I asked for some kind of wisdom and guidance concerning this dear child's struggle with his grievous loss. There just had to be a way for him to understand the faith I held onto in times of distress.

Groping for words, I reminded Patrick of how very much Grampa had loved him physically; of all the laughs and winks, the hugs and kisses they had shared. Oh, yes, Patrick smiled, remembering them. "Well," I said, "there are times when I can almost feel those hugs he gave and all the love Grampa gave us. Sometimes it seems like his love is still around us, like a blanket on a cold night."

"Like HOW? I wanna feel it, too." He was insistent.

"Okay," I said, "when you ride your trike down the driveway, I stand at the door and wave and say out loud, 'Patrick, I love you.' You hear me and call back to say that you love me, too. You ride farther down the sidewalk, past the Ketelsen's big tree where I can't see you. But I can still say, 'Patrick, I love you.' You can't hear me, but if you think about it, you know that when I go back to the kitchen dishes, I can say it again with you still not hearing, but it's there in the air where I said it. You can go pedaling all the way to the corner, and while you're doing it, you can say ever so softly, 'Mommy, I love you.' And if I think about it, I can feel your loving without hearing you say it.

I can still feel it all around me. Now, I think that's the way Grampa is still around us and with us with his love that didn't stop when his heart did. Even if we can't hear it, we can feel it all the time."

Patrick was very quiet, thinking there in the kitchen with me that day. And I remember that he didn't pester us with questions as much, even when my mother came to spend a few days. When Patrick and I took her to the bus station for her trip home, she couldn't hold back the tears. They flowed freely while Patrick held her hand and watched closely.

"Why you cryin', Gramma?" he asked. When her answer came that she would miss us all so very much, he said something we didn't understand at first. "Don't be lonesome, Gramma. 'Member, I wuv you wiffout YOU."

"Whatever does he mean?" my mother queried, and for a second I had to rack my brain. Suddenly, it dawned on me, recalling our snickerdoodle talk. Patrick really had understood what I'd spoken of and now was putting it into words a three-year-old could understand. A remarkable answer to prayer.

Ever afterward, my mother put at the close of her letters or telephone conversations, "Remember, I love you without you!" That saying has become a family trademark when we are apart from each other, thanks to a little boy's persistence and insight.

Her grandson is now in his midlife, and she nearing 102, but they still end their letters using their "without you" love.

Alice Ann Knisely

A Change of Seasons

I've been so involved with motherhood for most of my life that I hardly noticed when it ended. Oh, there was the year when our first bird left the nest, going to college just an hour away. I thought I'd see her often—my mistake!

For the first few months after she left, each time I passed her bedroom I'd look at the stuffed animals scattered about her colorful bedspread, her band jacket hanging in the closet, little trinkets of memories on her dresser. By the time I'd get to the piano in the living room, the tears were really falling. Then I'd head for the phone and call our daughter, just to hear her voice.

We had two more at home, and we were still actively involved at school, church and in the community. I hardly noticed when our oldest son left, because he lived in the area and he came home for meals. We were still busy and the changes were slight.

Two years later when our youngest son left for college, I packed to go with him! His school was three hours away. On the weekends when my hubby and I could no longer stand it, we would take a drive and go to see him. We would spend a couple of hours visiting, always taking him out to dinner, where he could get a good meal. Then

I'd hug him good-bye and cry all the way home.

He was my baby and it was so hard to let go.

During the week, I'd drive by the ball field where we spent so much time watching the boys play and working at the concession stand with our daughter; my heart ached for a rerun of those years. All around town I'd see other kids walking along, going to all the activities our kids had once done. Who said, "You can never go home again"? I'd welcome them all back in a minute.

But I knew that wasn't how things were to be. Another season passed and our daughter got engaged and was planning her wedding. There were things to do, places to go, bridal showers to plan and many details to attend to. The empty nest was full again as summer came, and then empty as college resumed. In February, a beautiful wedding took place, and I knew things would never be the same. It was a happy day, but hard to believe my first-born was becoming a wife.

It hit me one afternoon when I went into my gynecologist's office for my usual checkup. I looked around the room where mothers-to-be were seated. Their world was just beginning. Mine, I felt, was taking another turn. *Hadn't it just been me sitting in this office, awaiting the birth of our now-married daughter? Then the boys. Where had the years gone?* I headed for the ladies' room, and turned on the water in the sink and started to sob!

I knew this was a mere interruption in the pattern of things, but this was the most important job I'd had in my life. *Why did it hurt so much now?* I had friends who were starting new careers and many had jobs they were still at. But my job had been my husband and children and home. *What would my life be now?*

I splashed some water on my face and wiped my eyes. Then I went to take my seat with the young mothers. *Why couldn't they have a separate room for us menopausal women? Don't they know how hard it is to sit and look and be reminded of the days when our bellies were huge!*

When I got in to see my doctor I made this suggestion openly to him. He prescribed hormone replacement, some brisk walking and instructed me to "Get a life." I told him I'd had one, and always would—my children. I got a lecture, a prescription for estrogen and sample of Prozac tablets.

That was several years ago. Today, I'm doing the work I enjoyed before my children came along—the work I placed on hold during those wonderful years. I also have two darling rewards in our grand-gals. What a blessing they are to me, and what a blessing to watch as our children continue growing into happy, responsible adults.

Maybe the seasons change too quickly, but each one is a wonder of beauty. And God gives us the strength to make changes in our own lives when needed. Our children are priceless. But so are those memories we've made, and each one will last a lifetime. Wherever we go, our memories remain, movies replayed in slow motion, ours to watch whenever we desire and to treasure deep within our hearts.

Diane White

Taking It in Stride

Don't compromise yourself. You are all you've got.

Janis Joplin

As we grow older, life's embarrassing moments don't seem to send us into a tizzy like they did when we were seventeen. Remember how we used to fret and cry over the silliest things? Having a pimple at the end of our nose was a major crisis, charged with great drama and hysteria. Stumbling on the stairs during assembly was enough to keep us home for days, while eye contact with cute boys in the hall could easily send us bumping into walls. Nowadays, let's hope we can simply laugh about those little mishaps and chalk them up to experience.

Take for example, what recently happened to me at a business conference in Salt Lake City. It's one of "those moments" that I'd like to forget but, unfortunately, is etched in my brain forever.

My flight arrived at the airport just thirty minutes before the first session in the afternoon. Luckily, the shuttle bus was at the curb and got me to the hotel in time to dash into the meeting room. I plopped my suitcase in the corner, grabbed my three-ring binder from it, and began mingling with other attendees as I found my way to a seat.

To my surprise and horror, the entire time I had been circulating around the room, a pair of my purple under-pants was hooked onto the end of my notebook, clinging ever so nicely to my forearm for all to see. Let's just say I'll never be a size two, and my undies aren't lacey little snippets from the Victoria's Secret catalog. No, I get my practical cotton underwear at Sears in the full-figure department next to lawn chairs and power tools.

As I approached the table and noticed my faux pas, my undies did additional damage by falling smack-dab into the teacup of the gentleman seated in the next chair. The weight and bulk of the fabric tipped the cup over, spilling hot water across the tablecloth onto the poor man's lap. What could I do but scoop the panties up and offer him another cup of tea? (I can't remember, but I hope I didn't wring them out—that would have been so tacky.) Meekly, he declined, but to his credit and courage, he stayed right there for the rest of the session, turning out to be a good sport about the entire fiasco.

Everyone had a good laugh, me included. If I had been seventeen, I would have had to drop out of school and move to another town, but at age forty-five I could laugh along with everyone else. What else could I do, especially when many at the conference asked about next year's encore? Perhaps I'll do something in pink!

Cappy Tosetti

4

TAKING TIME
FOR LOVE

Lovers don't finally meet somewhere. They're in each other all along.

Rumi

Love: A Novel Approach

Quite a few women told me, one way or another, that they thought it was sex, not youth, that's wasted on the young.

Janet Harris

It was reading romance novels that let me know—my relationship with David is fizzling rather than sizzling. David is sweet, sensitive and reliable, but he's also becoming way too rational for my taste. He folds his underwear before climbing into bed, sits in an easy chair instead of snuggled next to me on the sofa and is too busy doing yardwork to slip away for an afternoon tryst. I decide to be brave and find out how bad things really are.

"Darling," I say to David, as I hand him a dish of chopped onions for the stir-fry he is making, "do you ever have to suppress a sexually charged groan when you step close to me?"

"Huh?" he asks.

"Does the passion rise so fiercely that you have to groan

to keep yourself from tearing off all my clothes and ravishing me?"

"No," he says and adds broccoli to the frying pan.

My worst fears are confirmed. In the romances, the handsome heroes frequently have to suppress passionate groans. And that's just from being in the same room with the long-legged, tousle-haired, full-bosomed heroine.

While David and I eat dinner, he tells me about his out-of-town client from Nebraska. I'm discouraged to note he does not suddenly shove away his half-eaten dinner and impetuously pull me toward him for a rousing embrace. In fact, he goes back for seconds.

"Do you ever longingly look at the hollows of my knees?" I ask, as we clear the dishes.

"No," he says. "But I did notice you seem to be biting your fingernails again." He smiles as if this observation should win him a sensitivity award.

"How come you never cry out my name in a hoarse, impassioned whisper?" I ask.

"You mean like this?" He lowers his voice and hisses "Deborah" like he is a spy about to be caught.

"Well, with more of a sense of sexual urgency," I coach.

He pants a couple times, flexes his jaw muscles and says my name like a steam engine with laryngitis.

In the books, the guys emit these throaty unrequited whispers all the time. What's wrong with David? Why is he causing me to miss out on love as it's truly supposed to be?

Maybe David needs a little more assistance in transforming himself into my romantic ideal. Accordingly, I make a list of gestures that will enhance and strengthen our relationship.

At dinner the next evening, I read David the list:

1. Gaze longingly at me.

2. Crush me in your impassioned embrace.
3. Watch me hungrily when I enter a room.
4. Push back my tousled hair and smile into my eyes.
5. Groan with the impossible task of suppressing your surging sexual urges for even a second more.

David frowns. "I thought we had a great sexual relationship," he says. "I thought you were happy."

"I am," I tell him, "but more romance will deepen our relationship."

He stares at me with a stricken look.

"What's wrong?" I say, as the silence stiffens.

He keeps looking, his mouth turned down, his eyes in pools of agony.

"David," I put my hand on his. "Darling, what's wrong?"

"Nothing," he says blithely, "I'm staring longingly at you." And he continues his mournful gaze. I feel as though a basset hound has developed a huge crush on me.

He follows me into the kitchen and lurks about as I clean up the dishes. Suddenly he seizes my arms, pulls me to him and envelops me in a huge bear hug. I can barely breathe.

"You're crushing me," I tell him, pulling loose.

"Exactly. Isn't that what you've been yearning for?"

I don't know whether to kiss him or kick him.

The next day, I worry that my romantic ideas are being misconstrued. Maybe I should start with something simpler, like a loving missive tucked under my pillow or slipped into my briefcase.

I intend to discuss the nature of such a missive at dinner, but David stops me by plunking down a pile of paperbacks on the table.

"I've been doing some reading," he says. "How come your nipples never strain against the gauzy fabric of your enticing summer frock? How come you never moan out my name and bite your full, fleshy lower lip in a beguiling profusion of confused sensuality? Why don't you shudder with ecstasy at my merest touch? What is it with you— don't you love me anymore?"

He reaches out to me. I do feel a little row of goose bumps when he touches my arm. Not quite enough for a full-blown shudder but plenty for a gentle little shiver.

I look at David and smile. I pick up one of the books and open it toward the end, wanting to get to the "good" part. David begins to read and I move closer, hanging on to him and his every word. Neither one of us can wait to see what will happen next.

Deborah Shouse

Freedom

My husband and I pull away from the curb, and I look tearfully through the back window as my youngest child disappears into the yawning abyss of a college campus. How can I let her go? My baby, only eighteen years old, alone, halfway across the country. She tosses a wave in our direction and is gone.

My life is over. First, my son, Zack, left for school and now Nora. My nest is empty.

About fifty miles down the road, on the spur of the moment (a new concept!) my husband and I change our route and wind through the glorious Green Mountains of Vermont. We spend the rest of the day hiking and sleep that night in a charming bed-and-breakfast.

We do it without consulting our children. And we do it without the promise of a nearby amusement park, shopping mall or movie theater. (And we do it without the fear of anyone walking in!)

Et voilà! The end of my much-dreaded empty nest syndrome.

Now I'm convinced it's all a myth. A joke. A lie. If parents knew beforehand how delightful an empty nest really is, they'd be tossing teenagers out of their houses right and left.

I am a good mom, loving and nurturing. Sort of. I have to admit I wasn't wild about Candy Land or Suzuki violin, but I did it, and I did it well. And having devoted myself to my kids for so many years, I do occasionally have great moments of longing for those good old days.

But those moments pass the second I glance down at my car's odometer, only fifty miles added each week instead of 354. Miles of driving to and from and back and forth to every game, dance, practice, lesson or meet. And the car insurance! Without teenagers on your insurance policy, you can save enough for a trek through Nepal or a Las Vegas vacation, losses included.

Yet another bonus: When I reach for my car keys, lo and behold, they're on the hook where I last left them. In fact, all my possessions are where I last left them: my brush, my tennis racquet, my yellow sweater, my books.

I do laundry only once a week now. I watch whatever I want on TV (the remote isn't lost), and last but not least, I listen to my own music! I sleep at night not worrying about where my children are or when they might come rolling in.

Everything changes, especially your relationships. If you're married, you can rediscover why you came together in the first place. You're less judgmental, less cautious, less concerned with what you say and do since it no longer affects the children.

If you want to begin a relationship now, you might just find it easier to start one without the demands of your children coming (where else?) first. You might just discover a date prefers you with perfume instead of eau de peanut butter, and you will, I promise, discover the delight of finishing a sentence uninterrupted.

There is, as with everything, a downside to an empty nest. Those little fledglings have to fly and land somewhere, so you might need a second job to help furnish their landing pad, or to refurnish yours. Why? Because they will have carried off dishes, mops and the occasional table or chair. And if they're off to college, the cost is a killer—but the money saved on Froot Loops alone practically pays the tuition.

Since you no longer have to keep the household organized around the kids, your house can become an adult home, strewn with your own favorite toys and treasure. Oh, and if you've ever longed to sit for hours in meditation or dreamed of reading an entire book in one sitting, go for it right now.

Enjoy the freedom. It won't be long before that front door bursts open and newly hatched chicks fly in calling, "Grandma!"

Bonnie West

Life's Short

Spirituality is seeded, germinates, sprouts and blossoms in the mundane. It is to be found and nurtured in the smallest of daily activities.

Thomas Moore

It always happens suddenly, doesn't it? That first time you realize life really is short and you don't have forever.

I was in Los Angeles when I got the call from my husband. He calmly explained the pain radiating down his left arm, the trip to the cardiologist and the time of his scheduled angiogram. I paid an exorbitant amount of money to be able to take the earliest possible flight home.

In the days before the procedure, I maintained only an imitation of calmness. I remember explaining to family and friends how we trusted God, we weren't worried and what would be would be. We had had a good life—long and happy. I didn't think I needed a friend with me on that day, but thankfully, God provided one anyway.

Becky insisted on being with me in the hospital, and oh, how I needed her there. My brave front cracked as they wheeled my husband of thirty-two years out of his room. It finally became clear to me, that this kiss might, indeed, be our last. Becky held me as I sobbed and then spent hours waiting with me until we heard from the doctor.

The news wasn't the best—but it wasn't the worst. No operation or bypass would be possible. Several arteries were already blocked, but "collateral arteries" had developed around the many blockages. The only things we could try now were prayer, diet and drugs.

At first I was overcome with worry. All of my "what if" thoughts took control of me. What if Bill died? What if he had a heart attack? What if he had chronic pain? What if we couldn't do the wonderful things we had planned for retirement? My list went on and on. It wasn't until I began to appreciate the "now," that I was able to let go of the future.

One morning I turned to see if Bill was still breathing. It was then that I knew what I had to do. I had to thank God for this moment and this day. It was his gift to me and I was to be glad and use it to love my husband like never before. It was then that those kisses good-bye as I ran off to shop or see a friend meant so much. It was then that eye contact when he was talking became so important. It was then that his ideas, goals and desires took on new meaning in my life. And it was then that I began living just for today!

It's been that way for almost a year now. Our days spent together are better than ever because we know we only have this moment, this day.

Patricia A. Hoyt

His Hands

*To mature is in part to realize that while com-
plete intimacy and omniscience and power cannot be had, self-transcendence, growth and
closeness to others are nevertheless within one's
reach.*

Sissela Bok

I didn't think much about his hands when we were
young. As a new bride, I had other things on my mind.

The first year of our marriage was a time of getting to
know one another.

But a year is such a short time. As I look back now, I can
see how hard his hands worked. I never noticed them
then, though.

It's been thirty-four years since those hands became a
part of my life. I have so much to reflect on.

There was a big difference in his hands compared to my
father's. My father's hands were hard and rough. His were
rugged yet still smooth.

When our first daughter was born, I noticed the

hardness in his hands seemed to mellow. As I watched him hold her and play with her, I saw a gentleness that I had never seen in him before. Was this how it started? Did it take a baby to soften those hands?

But he was a construction pipe fitter and his hands toiled so hard. They had to withstand all of the elements and continue to serve him. They were the hands of a provider.

When we bought our first home, I saw how his hands worked. There was never a weed in the lawn. The gutters were always clean and the trees in the yard trimmed. It was about this time that he built his first wood project, a doghouse. He was so proud, even though it was big enough to be a playhouse for the children. They were becoming the hands of a gardener and carpenter.

In the summer, he would go fishing. I watched him scale the fish with a skill that I never learned. His hands worked so hard to clean two dozen ducks after hunting all day. They were the hands of a fisherman and hunter.

Yet, I also saw those hands go into the field across from our house and pick mushrooms, never breaking a single one. His hands discovered wild strawberries in a matter of minutes amid all the weeds in the field. He would bring home enough for pancakes for breakfast. They were becoming the hands of a harvester.

As our family grew, so did our need for a bigger house. With the new house came a lot of work. The first year there, his hands stripped the paint from all of the windows. Through the years his hands have painted the outside of our home at least three times. They were the hands of a painter.

Because our house was very old, the walls had cracked from settling. He plastered and repaired the cracks. They were the hands of a plasterer.

The mortar in the chimney needed to be pointed. His

hands became the hands of a mason.

He has always loved music, and one year he received a guitar for Christmas. Though the tips of his fingers ached because they were too soft to play the guitar strings, he never gave up. Now he plays the guitar beautifully. They were the hands of a musician.

When our daughters were in high school, he would help build the floats and chaperone dances. He danced with his daughters. His hands were helpers for school projects, and also the hands of a special date.

A few years ago, when one of our daughters was married, he walked her down the aisle. His arm in hers and his hand touching hers, he gave her away. His hands had become the hands of a happy yet sad father.

As our grandchildren began to arrive, he was there to receive them in his arms. His hands picked them up and cradled them to his chest to begin a bonding process that continues to this day. They had become the hands of a grandfather.

Through the years, his yearning for working with wood could no longer be kept at bay. He built many beautiful things for our home. He made keepsakes for his grandchildren, including a cradle for his firstborn grandchild. Our family will forever have the memory of his wonderful hands and the care they gave.

As he and I grew older, we chose to do some traveling. He has always enjoyed driving. His hands continue to chauffeur and guide.

A few years ago, my health started to fail, and he began to spend more time taking care of me. His hands color my hair. They massage my legs. They help me in and out of bed. His hands bring me my medicine when I am unable to get it myself. His hands make dinner and then clean up the mess. He raises his hands in prayer as he pleads with God to relieve my pain. They are the hands of a hairdresser. They are the hands of a masseur. They are the hands of a nurse. They are the hands of a cook and home-maker. They are the hands of a full-time caretaker. They are the hands of an intercessor.

They are the hands that always serve.

Through the years, his hands have taken on many roles. They are older and are hard to the touch. But those hands have also become more and more gentle. They are so ten-der when handling me or playing with the grandchildren. They are the hands that have worked and given through his whole life.

They are the hands I love to hold. They are the hands of love.

Laurel A. Pilon-Weick

How I Stopped Looking for Mr. Right

I'll never forget that Christmas season of 1986. It was the year I went into a full-fledged panic. It happened after hearing a panel of experts on the subject of single women declare on a TV talk show: "Any woman, not married by the age of forty, has a better chance of being shot by a terrorist than she has of finding her 'Mr. Right.'"

I was forty-four years old and hadn't married. Obviously, the experts were talking about me. Their words hit me like a lightning bolt, jolting me into the reality of my bleak future. A silent scream choked in my throat.

My imagination soared. Who and what was waiting for me in my future . . . spinsterhood . . . the man of my dreams . . . or a terrorist? That night, I found it impossible to sleep. Visions of terrorists and lonely spinsterhood invaded my thoughts. The next morning, I reluctantly but bravely walked to work, looking over my shoulder every step of the way.

At the office, my coworker Mable noticed my depressed state of mind and quickly attributed it to my advanced age. She suggested that I was probably going through "the change," and advised me to drink a glass of vinegar and water spiked with a clove of garlic to set me right.

Change? I bristled to myself. What sort of change was Mable talking about? Was I suddenly going to sprout fangs and furry knuckles and commence baying at the full moon? Nothing less would induce me to indulge in a diet of garlic and vinegar.

Mable went on to compare my plight with that of her aged Aunt Agatha who, at my age, had begun taking daily doses of the concoction. The potent mixture had sustained the old woman well into her nineties.

Mable's story made me feel worse. The following day, I launched a frantic campaign to find my Mr. Right. I begged for advice from all the married women I knew. Mable was quick to tell me I was too old to be particular. She said I should hang around singles bars, where she found her Benji.

My friend Jane told me her aunt had actually found her husband several years ago by reading books on "how to find a man." There was a long list of these books available, some that guaranteed the reader a husband in one month's time: where to go, how to look, walk and talk—all the important nuances for finding a husband. I was so desperate to find a Mr. Right before Christmas, I scoured the bookstores and immediately went on a reading binge.

I feverishly read each paragraph and page. One book suggested I hang around the frozen-food sections of my local supermarkets. The book assured me that single men were sure to be there buying their dinners. But after two weeks of buying frozen dinners, all I had to show for it was a freezer full of frozen foods, and the only people I had met were young housewives and old married couples. I also spent long, frantic hours loitering in sporting-goods shops where, the books promised, I'd find a treasure trove of rich, handsome bachelors buying sporting equipment. But the only shoppers I found turned out to be young athletic women, soccer moms and little boys in the peewee league. After weeks of lingering and loitering at these shops, the only thing I got was some strange looks from the store security. In desperation, I followed the books' advice and took night classes in carpentry and automotive repair; these classes were supposed to be full of men. The books were several years old and so were their statistics. The classes were filled with women. Even the teacher was a woman. I tried beauty treatments and a whole new wardrobe, but still no luck. After months of following every instruction to the letter, the only bachelors I met were boys barely old enough to shave and men my grandpa's age.

Finally, I surrendered to defeat. I couldn't fight the Fates any longer. If I was going to end up an old maid, or worse, then so be it. I conceded that the experts were right and with a sense of freedom and relief, I chucked every one of books in the office Dumpster.

That night was Christmas Eve. Every year after work, the staff gave an office party for the workers. I decided to stay after work and have a cup of eggnog with the girls. The lights of the office were dimmed for atmosphere; the glow of flickering candles cast dark shadows in every corner of the room. About twenty minutes into the party, I was bored and decided to leave.

As I started down the long, darkened office corridor to the exit elevators, I was aware of someone in the shadows—a tall silhouette of a man in a dim corner of the hallway. The sinewy figure sprang toward me from the darkness. A glimmer of light reflected off a black shiny object he held at his side.

Was it the barrel of a gun? Was this the deadly terrorist the experts had warned me about? Was I about to meet my fate? I wasn't going to wait around to find out. In sheer panic, I bolted for the exits, running as fast as my shaky legs could carry me. Down the dark corridor I ran. The tall figure followed me in quick pursuit, catching up with me at the elevator.

"Hey, wait up," his voice shot through the darkness.

I spun around, my back pinned against the elevator door. With nowhere else to go, I faced him straight on: "Take one more step closer, and I'll scream!" I heard my voice cry out.

A complete look of bewilderment crossed over my handsome pursuer's face. "What did you say?" He asked quizzically, while holding in his right hand a large black umbrella.

Just then the elevator doors pulled open, putting some light on the subject. I soon realized that my overactive imagination had gotten the best of me. This very attractive man was no more a terrorist than I was. Trying to cover up my stupidity, I quickly introduced myself. "Hello, my name is Rosalie. What's yours?" I asked, trying to change the subject.

"I'm Dan," he answered. "I've been trying to meet you all month, but you always have your head buried in a book!"

That was me, all right, so preoccupied with my frantic search for Mr. Right, I'd overlooked what was right in front of me all along.

I wasted no time that night digging up some information on this handsome hunk. I couldn't believe my ears when the girls in the office told me his name was actually Dan Wright—Mr. Wright! All the time I'd had my head buried in those books, he was working just across the hall from me. And he was single. I would have learned all these facts if I hadn't stopped taking coffee breaks with the office girls to read those darn books.

It never dawned on me, all the while I was looking so

hard for Mr. Right, that Mr. Wright was trying equally hard to find me.

We were married the following year and marked the occasion with a grand wedding celebration. Finding Mr. Wright, and marrying for the very first time at age forty-five, was a small miracle in itself. But more than that, it proved that even experts on finding true love can be wrong. And we should hang on to our hopes and dreams no matter the odds against them. And a little advice, just from me to you: If you're looking for something, or someone, don't look so hard for it that you don't see what's been right there in front of you all along.

Rosalie Wright

"Please call me Herb. I only go
by 'The Bod' when I'm online."

The Change

My sweetheart just turned forty-five,
And I love her, oh, so dearly.
But I'm a little mystified,
Since she's acting, oh, so queerly.

"Oh, it's nothing that you've said or done,"
She assures me, ever-sweetly.
"My Change of Life has now begun,"
She smiles and winks discreetly.

Smiling back, I take her hand,
Reassuring and placating.
In truth, I didn't understand
A thing that she was stating!

Just what she meant by "Change of Life,"
I didn't have a clue.
And when I asked my darling wife,
Into a rage she flew!

"Well, I'm always tired! I'm hot! I'm cold!
I didn't sleep last night!
I'm fat! I'm ugly! I'm getting old!
My clothes don't fit me right!

"I think I'd like to KILL you,
And I'd love to run away!
But I know how that would thrill you,
So, for spite, I think I'll stay!

"My body's turned against me,
And I want to SCREAM again!
My hormones have convinced me
That this "Change" is caused by MEN!

"Yes, you just sit there smiling
While I'm going through pure hell!
You think you're so beguiling?
You think I couldn't tell?

"This is some cruel joke you play!
It's all your fault, no doubt!
You never loved me anyway
You selfish, brutish lout!"

Yes, my sweetheart just turned forty-five,
And she changes by the hour.
Like Dr. Jekyll and Mrs. Hyde
She goes from sweet to sour.

But I've been told, "This is a phase."
They say, "This, too, shall pass."
So, I'll remember better days,
Till they come again at last!

Paul Weller

Bonfire of the Tampons

The thermostat is off, and I overheat like a stalled car.

Judith Bishop

As luck would have it, just before I had been told I was menopausal, my husband, Gerald, and I had taken a weekend drive to one of those enormous suburban wholesale price clubs. As is typical of many city dwellers overwhelmed by the great discounts and enormous selection, we temporarily forgot how small our apartment was, and we stuffed the car to overflowing with far too many purchases. Included in that haul were several giant-sized boxes of tampons, enough to carry me for half a year or more. Now they were stacked next to the sink in the bathroom, staring at me as though mocking my foolishness in stocking up as though a run on tampons was imminent.

When I told Gerald it appeared I was really done with my period, and how I felt, he understood exactly. "Congratulations," was his first word. His ability to often say precisely the right thing is one of the things I most love about him, and I could not have hoped for better than that single word.

Then I reminded him about all the tampons we had recently bought, expecting him to grimace in disapproval, since he often chides me for overstocking. The receipts were long ago thrown out, so we couldn't return them. And they aren't the types of things you give girlfriends as a gift. There was, of course, the easy route of just tossing them into the garbage room, but Gerald had a better idea. "Let's have a celebration," he said. He wouldn't tell me what he had in mind, but I know that when he is determined to do something, it is tough to dissuade him.

Two days later, we packed an overnight bag; he told me we were going to a hotel for the night. I watched with amusement as he energetically stuffed all the tampons into a separate suitcase.

"What the hell are you up to?"

"Just wait and see," he said. He had a devilish grin. "You'll like it, I promise."

I wasn't sure what was going on but knew it was worth being patient to find out. After a five-block taxi ride, we pulled in front of a charming neighborhood hotel I knew well. It was a European-boutique–style town house, and Gerald had booked a suite on the top floor. When we got settled in, I turned to him.

"Look, this is great as a treat, but what's the purpose? I've been patient, and it's driving me nuts, so you've got to tell me now, or I'll start screaming," I teased him.

Gerald just smiled and pointed to the corner of the room where there was a large stone fireplace.

"I found the nicest hotel near us with a real wood-burning fireplace," he said. "How many times have you told me that you'd love to burn those things?" He glanced toward the suitcase stuffed with the tampons. "Let's order a fabulous meal to the room and then have a bonfire."

I couldn't stop laughing. I am sure a lot of paper products are used to start fires, but I don't know if a several-foot stack of tampons has ever been used for that purpose. It was the perfect way to celebrate my most visible marker of menopause. On that night, with a wonderful fire roaring in the background, even my dormant sexual desire made a brief return.

Trisha Posner

Rebel with the Pause

Scenes from a Marriage

Aging forces us to decide what is important in life.

Thomas Moore

We are standing in the kitchen glaring at one another. I remind my Valentine that he's officially taken over dishwasher duty, which means loading and unloading the old workhorse; that it's now 11:00 A.M.; and that, still, the clean dishes remain lodged inside while the dirty ones languish on the counter.

I avoid mentioning that in my dishwasher-loading/unloading era, the deed was always done early and that the platters were always standing like sentries on the bottom shelf, not leaning precariously on one another. These are fighting words on a Sunday morning. We both know it. But somehow, seconds later, we burst into laughter at our own foolishness. It's Sunday—and Valentine's Day—and what difference does it really make in the long run that the dishwasher isn't unloaded or that the platters aren't in perfect order?

At this stage of our union, we finally understand the

futility of dumb arguments and while we still have them, of course, we end them sooner than we used to.

Score one for very married Valentines. Forget the plump red satin heart-shaped boxes of rich chocolate. Forget the love poems penned in passion, the wild embraces, the waltzes under crystal chandeliers. For some of us, Valentine's Day, even in all its commercial, hucksterish glory, remains a reminder that, in ordinary life, it's the little stuff that counts.

The notes left on the kitchen table in haste, signed with nicknames only we recognize. The way he remembers to pick up the exotic cheese I love, even though it means going miles out of his way. The fact that when it's raining and we're going out, he pulls the car right to the kitchen door for a presumably liberated lady.

Yes, those trifles, friends, count dearly in this season when we're reminded that love changes everything, conquers all, and makes the world go 'round.

I agree with all of the above. But I also know better.

In the autumn of a long and committed marriage, we celebrate love in quirky, not just cosmic, ways. I make chocolate pudding the old-fashioned way, the cooking, stirring, scorch-the-pot method, when I detect a certain sag to my beloved's shoulders, a certain weariness in his walk. And the fuss feels both right and rewarding.

On mornings when we both awaken not like songbirds but like terminal grouches, we deftly avoid conversation. And yes, it's a loving, not hostile, gesture. And in the sleepless dark, when the demons come, I know that I can reach over to a man who is soundly sleeping, gently wake him, and find myself in the homeland of his arms.

We haven't waltzed under a chandelier of any description in years, but every now and then, when the mood is right, my Valentine and I will dance around the kitchen to the strains of the radio, preferably to an old Frank Sinatra ballad. It's so corny that it's embarrassing, but we don't care. And some of our best moments—moments that bind and bond us and make our hearts leap—have come when we've stood in a silent, dark room and watched a grandchild sleeping. It may not be classic romance. It may not meet the rapturous hype of magazines that speak of love as primal and wild, sensual and captivating. But for two late-middle-aged Valentines, those bedside vigils are an affirmation of loving long and well—loving right into the next generation.

So when the dishwasher eruptions come—and they always do—we rely on the best gifts of Valentinehood to get us though:

Humor.

Forgiveness.

Emotional generosity.

And a love that's old enough to have a burnished glow, but not too old to sparkle and to make two midlife Valentines enormously grateful for the gift of one another.

Sally Friedman

"I just found our old love letters.
Would you like your lock of hair back?"

Orchids and Corned-Beef Hash

The love we give away is the only love we keep . . .

Elbert Hubbard

Rose was George's first true love. He met her at a luncheonette, where she worked as a waitress. He'd always order the corned-beef hash with a sunny-side-up egg atop it and a cup of black coffee. One day he snapped a picture of her behind the counter serving him his plate of hash. After he had the film developed, he showed her the picture.

"Here's a picture of the girl I'm going to marry," he said, smiling.

Rose and George dated. He put the picture of her in his wallet. When he'd go out with his friends or even when he was among strangers, he'd pull out his wallet and show them the picture.

"Here's a picture of the girl I'm going to marry," he'd say to them. "Isn't she beautiful? Her name is Rose."

Rose fell for George just as he fell for her. They soon married. A year later, they had a son—me. It was the three of us for several years until my mother died suddenly, unexpectedly, from a stroke. I remember the wake and the funeral and my father crying. I cried, too.

Several more years passed and soon I was in high school. I was getting ready to go to the senior prom with Jennie, my girlfriend at the time. My father had said he'd pick up her orchid corsage at the florist for me. Dad arrived at the florist late in the afternoon. He walked in and told the owner he was there to pick up the orchid corsage for Flynn. The man went to the case and returned with the beautiful purple and white corsage.

"That'll be fifteen dollars," the man said.

My father took out his wallet, and as he was removing the bills from their compartment, he showed the owner the picture of my mother serving him hash.

"This is my wife—isn't she beautiful?"

The old man adjusted his glasses and looked at the picture.

"Sure is," he said. "Is the orchid corsage for her?"

"No, no," my father said. "She only liked roses and daffodils. I don't think I ever gave her an orchid."

"Well, it's never too late," the man said.

My father smiled sadly and said nothing more.

Dad left the florist, and at the back parking lot, two men wearing ski masks approached him from behind. One was carrying a revolver.

"Give me your wallet," the man with the gun ordered, thrusting the revolver's muzzle into my father's ribs. My father handed it to him.

"And your watch, too," the other man said.

My father took off his gold watch and handed it to him.

"I know who you are. If you try to alert the authorities, we'll be back some night to take care of you. Understand?"

The two men fled on foot.

My father, shaken but unhurt, drove home and gave me the orchid corsage.

"Are you okay, Dad? You look pale as a ghost," I remember saying. "Is anything wrong?"

"No. Nothing's wrong. Have a good time at the prom, Son."

The next week or so my father was quiet and subdued. I knew something was wrong. After pressing him a few times, he finally told me the story.

"Did you call the police?" I asked.

"No. The robbers know who I am and where I live. If I tell the police, they'll be back for me."

Although I tried hard to persuade him to call the police, he wouldn't hear of it. What he did do was make certain all the doors and windows were locked securely each night before we went to bed. He seemed more sad, however, than afraid.

Two weeks passed. One evening, the front doorbell chimed. My father jumped—then cautiously peered out the window to see who was ringing the bell. He recognized the man as the florist who had sold him the orchid corsage. He went to the door, unlocked it, and admitted the man. The man introduced himself and then reached into his coat pocket and pulled out my father's black wallet.

"I found this in the shrubbery behind my store. I recognized the picture of your wife. It's the only thing left in it."

He opened it and showed him the picture of my mother. Gone was the name and address card, his driver's license, his union card, his social security card, the money (about forty-five dollars, my father recollected), and all other pictures and papers.

"Today is my lucky day," my father cried loudly, startling the florist. Dad tried to give him ten dollars as a reward for finding the wallet, but the florist wouldn't take it. He left and my father locked the door behind him.

"How can this be your lucky day, Dad? All your important papers and money are gone. Your watch, too."

"They can all be replaced," he said, smiling. "But there's only one picture of your mother serving me corned-beef hash. Only one picture!"

George M. Flynn

The Moment

My mother and father have been divorced for thirty-five years, and now they are together again. They reside in the same nursing home, but most of the time they are not aware of each other's presence.

They were married for twenty-eight tumultuous years. They each looked at life through a different lens. My mother was focused on financial security, and my dad spent money impulsively. This conflict caused great stress. During my teenage years, I could never have friends over because our house pulsated with anger and resentment.

My parents looked at each other with such contempt. In the end, I was glad when it was over. They were better people apart than they had been together. My mother mourned the end of the relationship and struggled with the stress of keeping the family business going: meeting deadlines, pleasing customers, and raising three adolescent daughters. She turned the business around, winning acclaim as a businesswoman and being named Michigan Photographer of the Year. But even with all that success, she always carried a torch for my father.

Dad had always dreamed of becoming an engineer, and

although he had worked as a draftsman for many years, he had only attended one year of college. Dad set his sights on passing the professional engineer's registry exam. He studied independently for years, and after four attempts, he passed the two-day exam at the age of fifty-eight, an accomplishment that few graduate engineers achieve. He was promoted and spent the remainder of his working years supervising important projects.

My mother fell victim to dementia first, at the age of eighty-one, and three years later, my father began a serious decline in mental functioning. After my father's second wife died, we brought him back to Michigan, and now he lives under the same roof that shelters my mother.

And, although they're often not responsive in the present, I have found that it is possible to help both of them reach back and connect with memories of the distant past. On a December Saturday, I packed up a box of Christmas cards and my address book and headed over to help Mom and Dad prepare Christmas cards.

When I arrived, I found Mother sitting alone, half dozing, at one of the dining tables. We worked together for an hour. I told her whom each card was for and shared a special memory before I helped her with her signature. Her face became animated and she laughed or smiled with each remembrance.

She is confined to a wheelchair now, and rarely moves about the room. I know that her days are empty; she does not talk to the other residents and she speaks to the caregivers only to complain. Sometimes, I think that the pain of a failed marriage and years of living alone have caused her to retreat inside and develop a hard, crusty exterior. As we finished the last of the cards, I could see that she was tired. I hugged and kissed her and gathered my things.

As I walked away, mother called out to me.

"Thank you, Beverly, for helping me get my cards ready. That's so nice of you." she said.

The words were precious to me because they are so rare, giving a quick glimpse of the person she used to be.

"They'll be so glad to hear from you, Mom. You rest now." She set her head against the back of the chair and closed her eyes.

I walked down the east hallway to Dad's room. He was sitting in a wingback chair, napping. Most of their days are filled with sleep. I touched his hand and said, "Dad, it's Beverly. How are you?"

"Oh, Beverly," he said, his eyes opening and welling with tears, "I'm fine, especially now that you are here."

"I came to help you get your Christmas cards out, Dad."

"Oh, wonderful, dear. That will be wonderful."

Dad's vision has deteriorated, but he was determined to sign each card. We worked for a long time, finishing all the cards, and then I suggested that we listen to some music. Dad's hearing is still good and music is a pleasure he can still savor.

"What do you want? Beethoven? Bach? Or how about Tommy Dorsey? You and Mom used to dance to this music."

"Yes, Dorsey would be good," he said, smiling.

I put the CD in and we both sat back to listen. The first piece was a swing number with a trombone solo, "Song of India."

"Notice how this piece starts real slow," he said, "but it'll pick up very soon now." Then he pursed his lips and played the notes, as if he were playing along with the trumpet.

I looked up and saw Mom at the doorway. I was surprised because she had never ventured down this hallway.

"Beverly, what are you doing here?"

"Listening to music with Dad. Do you want to come in?"

She didn't resist as I wheeled her in and situated her right in front of Dad's chair. Then I turned up the music so that Mother could hear, and I sat down on the bed.

"Mom, do you remember when you and Dad used to go to the big band dances? Aunt Fannie said that you two were quite an item on the dance floor."

She nodded her head slightly and stared at Dad, a faint smile spreading across her face.

The next song was a slow number. I had never heard it before, and I thought of pressing the button to skip ahead to the next song. I wanted something livelier, to keep their attention. But then the vocal part began—a trio of voices, in perfect harmony.

I was struck by the words, how appropriate they were, and for that brief moment I saw my parents focused, alert and remembering together. Dad reached out his hand to Mother. I got up, wheeled her closer, and she put her hand in his. How long had it been since they had touched each other like this? I sat on the bed, tears streaming down my cheeks. I had never seen them look at each other like this.

It felt so good seeing with my own eyes that my parents had loved each other. The next song began, a swing number, and the spell was broken. Dad was concentrating on the sound of the trombone and he let go of Mother's hand to conduct the band. Mother began to fidget and announced, with urgency, that she had to use the restroom. I wheeled her around and pushed her out into the hall.

"Wasn't that great, listening to the music with Dad?"

"With who?" she asked.

"With Dad. Remember?"

"Oh," she said. "Is he here?"

It had been such an intense moment; I was amazed that it had already vanished from her mind. *Well,* I thought, *they did have that moment, and it will live in my memory.*

In January, my sister, brother and I gathered with Mom and Dad around a table at the nursing home to celebrate my mother's eighty-sixth birthday. While we were enjoying cake and ice cream, I brought out the CD player and placed it on a shelf directly behind my mother. I put the Tommy Dorsey CD in while Dad and my brother talked about the music. I noticed that the other residents sat up straighter as they listened to this wonderful music of their youth. What magic this music has.

Soon, my brother began telling Dad about how his business was doing. Mom and I talked about her birthday and her presents. Then that wonderful song began, and Mom stopped listening to me. *She remembers,* I thought. *The music has brought that moment back.* She listened to the words: "Once in a while, will you try to give one little thought to me?" Then she looked across the table at Dad, and a warm smile spread across her face.

"Mmmm," she said contentedly.

Yes, I thought, *she does remember.*

The music had captured the moment.

Beverly Matulis

5

ON PARENTING

*Because I feel that, in the heavens above,
    The angels, whispering to one another,
    Can find, among their burning terms of love,
    None so devotional as that of "Mother."*

Edgar Allen Poe

More Precious Than Gold

On a warm spring day, I waited in the yard for my two girls to get off the school bus. Time had run amok, and it seemed to be the first time in days that I had simply sat. The sun began to soak into my bones and unwind all the places that stress and busyness had wound too tightly. Soon enough, there came the bus. Turned loose in the sun after a day in school, they quickly informed me it was not a day to be inside.

I happened to be drinking iced coffee—a summertime treat my six-year-old longs to share. It must have triggered a nostalgic gene, because after begging a drink, she began to reminisce. "Remember when you made iced coffee and you gave me a drink? Remember when we made clean-out-the-kitchen cookies? Remember when we made bread, and I made raisin bread and ate a lot of it? Remember when we made lunch and it was only you and me and we ate tomato sandwiches?" (Either she was hungry, or we spent entirely too much time making food memories.)

Her older sister tried, to no avail, to entice her to play. "Let's ride bikes. Let's play on the swing set. Hey, Elizabeth, want to dig in the garden?"

Elizabeth replied, "No, I'm remembering with Mommy." She walked around my chair in circles, tucking her hair behind her ears and touching me with each pass by.

"Remember when we went to the library and you drove past it and had to turn around? Remember when we went to McDonald's for lunch? Remember when we played dollhouse dolls? Remember when we read books and then took a nap?"

Then, her eyes lit up.

"Remember when you and I made a picnic lunch and ate at the little table under the trees? We made peanut butter sandwiches and lemonade and had a tea party, and it was the funnest because it was just you and me. We didn't tell Joanna. We did tell Dad, but I bet he forgets."

"But we don't forget, do we?" I asked.

She looked at me with earnest joy, and said, "Cause that's so happy, I can't forget."

Elizabeth curled into my lap, a little bit harder to accomplish as her gangly legs don't fit quite as well as they used to. Joanna sat next to me on the sidewalk, asking for increasingly complex spelling words. She had heard that third-graders only did easy words, and she had to keep in practice with hard ones. I found myself interspersing "rememberings" with words like "pollination" and "echo-location" and "daffodil," which Joanna delighted in sounding out and spelling. "It doesn't matter if they're spelled right, Mommy, because this is just for fun," she informed me.

Just the day before, April 15, I had evaluated my net worth for the previous tax year. The end balance did not add up to very much, and I found myself wondering what I had done with the rather small amount of money I had managed to add to the family coffers, which were still distressingly empty. It seemed I had traded my salary for a lot of headaches and stress. I wondered if it was worth it.

As I tucked my girls in bed that night with Elizabeth's questions ringing in my weary mind, I viewed it all differently.

I hugged Elizabeth close and reveled in the remnants of her baby scent while asking Joanna if she could spell "faucet." I knew that no matter what the checkbook balance showed, I had deposited untold riches into the memory banks of my family. They remembered the cookies, the gardens, the walk on the neighbor's farm, the times we lay on the grass and counted airplanes.

They remembered time—given much more lavishly than gifts could be.

They remembered me. Somehow, with their childlike grace and love, they reminded me that my worth was above rubies and beyond anything that could be deposited into our local bank or added to a stock portfolio.

Amy Ridgeway

What Mothers Teach

Our power is just the force of our love for our children and grandchildren.

Barbara Weidner

Many years ago, when my daughter Sara was in the fifth grade, she came to me with a life-gripping problem. As tears welled up in her big brown eyes, she began explaining her dilemma.

"Marcy hates me!" she cried. "She hates me because Kathy is my friend, too. She wants me to be her friend and nobody else's." Sara choked back her tears and said, "She won't play with me if I hang out with Kathy. But, they are both my friends!"

I tried my mommy-best to console her and let her know that we cannot control how others feel and react. Even though we should understand feelings, there are some things that are out of our control, and some decisions we can only make for ourselves.

As I was trying to decide what motherly advice I could give her, she stumped me with, "*You* talk to Marcy. *You* tell her that I like her and want to be her friend, but I can have other friends, too!"

Oh boy. I sat there staring at her for a few moments trying to figure out how I got into this mess, when suddenly the idea came to me. I excused myself and left the room, telling her I would be right back. My mind raced. It was obvious that she needed to learn that there are just some things you need to do for yourself. Only, how could I teach her this without her feeling like I had failed her?

Picking up two wicker baskets from the living room, I quickly tossed their contents onto the floor and walked back into Sara's room. She stared at me like I was nuts.

"What are those for?" she asked with big, surprised eyes.

"It's a life lesson for you," I explained. "Just sit down and let me explain."

She sat on the edge of the bed with a wary eye. Placing the littler basket inside the big one, I placed the handle of the big basket over my arm and began to slowly walk around the room as I explained.

"When everyone is born, God gives them a little basket. This little one here is yours. The big one is mine. As you grow, so does the basket. But if you notice, your little basket is inside of mine. Why do you think that is?"

She just glared at me. Nope. Not getting through yet. Not even close.

I continued. "Your little basket is in mine because when you were born, there were too many things you couldn't do for yourself. I had the responsibility of feeding you, changing you, bathing you, and doing everything else you couldn't do on your own. So I put your basket in mine and carried them both for a while."

She nodded, but so far still thought I was crazy.

"Well, as you grew older and began to do some things on your own, I began placing a few more things in your basket. When you learned to tie your shoes, that went in your basket. You wouldn't want me tying your shoes now, would you?"

She bowed her head a second and said softly, "No, that would be stupid. I can tie my own shoes."

"Right," I said. "And when you learned how to put on your own clothes, I put that in your basket. You don't even like me telling you what to wear now, never mind dressing you."

She agreed with a small nod.

"As you grow older, there will be more and more things you must do on your own." As I spoke, I gradually took her basket out of mine and handed it to her. "You will eventually carry your own basket with things only you can do, like deciding who you want to be friends with, who you will date, what college you will go to, who you will marry."

She looked up at me and said, "I understand. There are some things that I have to do for myself because they are in my basket."

Hallelujah! The light came on! "Yes," I squealed, "but it's even better than that because you decide the things that belong in your basket or someone else's. Like now, you decide who you want to be friends with. If Marcy doesn't like your decision and gets angry, whose basket needs to carry her anger?"

She smiled. "Marcy's. Right?"

I hugged her and continued with the story. "You're absolutely right. Marcy's responses aren't in your basket. They are in hers. Now, one last thing you need to understand before the basket story is over." She was smiling big now and really getting into my little skit.

I stood there for a moment, thinking of my own mother and grandmother who were living with us, reminiscing about the things they used to do for me that now I do for

them. Even though it tugged at my heart strings, I held up
the big basket and said, "One day when I'm much older,
there will be things I can no longer carry in my basket.
When that time comes, eventually you will begin taking
things out of my basket and placing them into your own.
Just like I do now for Grandma and Momma. Eventually,
the things that are in my basket will be taken out, for I
won't always be strong enough to carry everything I'm
carrying right now."

I reached over and gently took the small basket from
her hands and traded with her. As she felt the large handle
of the big basket and watched me take the little one, she
understood.

Softly, I said, "Life is a circle."

As she smiled and gave me a big hug, she said, "Mom, I
think I can put much more in my basket. Don't worry
about Marcy. I can do this."

As I put the magazines and the potpourri back into the
baskets in the living room, my own mother entered and
asked me what I was doing. Smiling, I gave her a quick
overview of my impromptu skit, feeling quite smug and
proud of myself. Mom just smiled.

A few days later, I was surprised to see one of the tini-
est baskets I've ever seen, sitting on the top of my computer desk. It was small enough to hide in the palm of my
hand. Underneath it was a note, in my mother's hand-
writing that said simply, "Just remember, your basket isn't
nearly as big as you think it is. Love, Mom."

Ferna Lary Mills

Messy Rooms: A Neat Memory

I do not love him because he is good. I love him because he is my child.

Rabindranath Tagore

I could swear it was just yesterday when she skipped beside me down the sidewalk, a happy, brown-eyed little girl singing nursery rhymes.

Already she had her own unique rituals. She'd come to a halt and carefully cross her right leg in front of her left before launching into each new song. She'd suck her left thumb while twirling her hair around her right index finger. She'd pick flowers with no stems, snapping just the heads off the marigolds, bringing the blossoms to me in her chubby little hands.

I could swear it was just yesterday. How is it, then, that I stand here in her empty room, wondering what to do with the dried blossoms from the prom corsages she left pinned to her wall?

I did surprisingly well when we said good-bye at her dorm last weekend. It was her dad who cried all the way to the airport. But what can you expect from a guy who sobbed through *Father of the Bride,* even though the mortified daughter beside him was only twelve? Everyone else in the theater saw the Steve Martin film as a comedy. Not my husband. He saw tragedy, already anticipating the day she would leave home.

I anticipated it, too, though I didn't start quite so early.

It was only about a month ago that I began waking up about 4:00 every morning with a sweat-soaked nightgown and knot of dread in my stomach.

I tried to intellectualize away my grief. I reminded myself that we were lucky she was heading off to college, that this was what we'd hoped and planned for, that we still have another child at home, that I have no business anguishing over this when some people never get to see their kids off to college because of accidents or cancer or school shootings.

You can give the brain all the arguments in the world why something isn't a loss, but the body knows. It tells the truth at 4:00 A.M. Your stomach knows what's coming. It's a lot like trying to prepare for labor and delivery. You try to minimize what's coming as only "discomfort" or "transition." But it turns out to be plain old pain. Hurts like hell. Especially now, back home in her cleaned-out room. I came down here hoping to remind myself of some things I will *not* miss. This room was easily the sorest subject between us over the years. The floor was constantly covered with piles of clothes, stacks of books, papers, music and magazines, even candy and gum wrappers. Her bed was rarely made.

When she was young, we tried positive reinforcement, metallic stars on a chore chart. Later, we went punitive, withholding allowance or television and phone privileges. Nothing worked. Eventually we resigned ourselves to simply closing her door. If this was the worst trouble she gave us, we decided, we were lucky. Still, it was our one, constant irritant. So, it's funny that our best times in her last days at home were spent in this room, cleaning out the rubble that had been the biggest rub between us.

Even she had to laugh at some of what we unearthed in her drawers, closet and under her bed: a pair of size 4–6X tights; an uncashed $5.96 income tax refund check from 1995; a Recordings for the Blind version of a May 6, 1996, *Newsweek* magazine (neither of us had any idea how she came to possess this); a one-pound chocolate heart her grandparents had given her Valentine's Day of her freshman year; a notepad from a State Farm agent in North Carolina (a state no member of our family has ever visited).

Now I sit in that empty room, scrubbing eighteen years of stickers—touting everything from Care Bears to snowboarding—off the mirror of her French Provincial dresser. And I even miss the rubble.

A child is such a presence in your life.

She leaves such an absence.

In the first of my 4:00 A.M. ruminations, I thought my dread reflected only the fact that she was going to a college so far away. That's only part of it.

Three people live here now, not four. When she sleeps under our roof again, it will be as a visitor on vacation from her real life elsewhere.

Her leaving marks the end of a life phase I've loved with all my heart. I wouldn't change a thing. But I'd sure love to do it all again.

Suddenly, I envy men my age who are remarrying, starting new families with younger women. They're having another baby. I'm having hot flashes.

At first, I chalked these up to the warm weather and my emotional turmoil. Then one hit as I stood in the frozen food aisle at my grocery store. The body knows.

I've been apart from my daughter only three days now. We once went almost two months without seeing each other, and I didn't miss her nearly this much. The body knows.

Karen McCowan

Sunshine

Mother love is the fuel that enables a normal human being to do the impossible.

Marion C. Garretty

"How long has she been skating?" the woman asked, as she took a seat next to me on the bleachers surrounding the ice rink. "She's very good."

In spite of the lump in my throat and the tears welling up in my eyes, I answered,

"She just started."

I didn't tell her she was seeing a miracle in the making. My autistic daughter had found a place she could shine—and my heart sang out, "Thank you, God . . . thank you."

I sat there with my eyes fixed on her as she skated around the icy rink, gaining confidence and speed with each revolution. She didn't seem to notice the obvious danger of falling, or even the overwhelming chill that numbed the fingers and noses of the few who joined me watching from our bench seats. My thoughts turned back to the early years as I remembered how we'd come—my child and I—to this moment.

I was almost thirty-five and my teenage daughters were testing their wings of independence. The last thing I'd expected to be holding soon was a newborn. And certainly not my own. Yet, a thirty-second phone call to my doctor's office had confirmed the fact, and I found myself exactly that—expecting. And on a crisp, but sunny morning in February 1981, my fourth daughter, Farema, was born. Her father, my husband, Cody, chose her name from his ancestral homeland of ancient Persia. I gave little thought to its rarity until one of the nurses asked, "So— you named her Farina? Like the cereal?"

"No," I answered, "it's pronounced Fa-ree-mah." I would hear that same question, many times over. I'd even resigned myself to it—if in her life she were mistaken for a breakfast food, so be it.

Before my surprise pregnancy, I'd anxiously contemplated what freedoms awaited me when my children were finally grown. Leisure lunches with a friend, no more rushing home to beat the school bus—maybe even trips to far-off places. Cody and I deserved time to ourselves after raising three daughters.

Now, a new baby meant that the smell of ocean beaches in faraway lands must succumb to the pungent odor of ammonia-laden diapers. Soothing sounds of music drifting overhead from eateries dotting the sandy strip where I lounge, watching the orange sun set over the calm blue sea—a fading fantasy. I'd be well into middle age before this child was out on her own.

"My albatross," I'd thought to myself, only to be filled with shame for thinking such a thing when I realized something was seriously wrong with my youngest daughter.

I'd seen other families burdened with a child who never left home. Now it was my own life that would be forever rearranged. But what worried me far more was what the future held for Farema.

I began to search for something that would offer my daughter a life with some amount of joy. I didn't want her to be lonely and left behind, though she never seemed to care one way or the other. By keeping her around normal, healthy children, I hoped she might imitate and become like them. That was my new dream. And though she lived in a secret world that we could not enter, her love for the outdoors and her ceaseless energy convinced me to look in the direction of sports.

I jumped at the idea of signing her up for soccer when a friend offered to coach the grade-school girls' soccer team.

"She doesn't talk much," I warned him. "But she understands everything you tell her."

Before her third practice, I knew soccer was not for her. Basketball, softball and track were just as hopeless. She was the kid no one chose for their side, leaving the coach the ultimate decision as the little girls whispered their dismay.

By the time Farema was twelve, I had run out of ideas. I had come to the end of my imagination. And by now, she'd been diagnosed with autism, a biological brain disorder with no known cure. My mind told me to accept what cannot be changed; yet my heart continued to hope for more. One evening, I noticed a short preview of the coming Olympic figure-skating competition on television, and it sparked a memory for me.

As a very young child, Farema seemed to have some mysterious pact with the elements of nature, especially when it was cold. When other children were driven indoors by the chilly weather, or bundled up against the winter wind, no amount of pleading would persuade her to keep a jacket on. And at night, she'd shed her warm covers to sleep under her bed on the hardwood floor—and never would a shiver betray her.

Now I sat on the cold bench at the skating rink with the other moms, watching that familiar smile envelop her small face and shine from her eyes to the very air around her—and I knew God had heard me. He hadn't made her normal, as I begged in prayers offered up to heaven on a sea of salty tears, but I knew from the moment she stepped out onto the ice that this day was a beginning for her. This was the beginning of her life, a life that would fit her perfectly.

Farema and I returned to the skating rink again and again. As her skills progressed, her ability to speak improved as well.

"I like ice!" She said to me in the car on our way home from the rink. I was dumbfounded to hear a complete sentence from her. Months later, she was talking incessantly.

The local ice-skating rink is truly her place. The icy mist in the air is her shadow, the breeze that caresses her body as she skates in her solitary world, her companion. With Farema's newfound happiness came friends who joined with her in a special camaraderie, as they, too, fulfilled personal goals and reached for their Olympic dreams.

My uncommon daughter, Farema, is now indistinguishable from any other young girl as she glides over the ice with a smile that illuminates her face—and my heart.

Cody and I are now approaching the retirement years of our lives. I would never have asked for the heartache and disappointment that raising a disabled child could bring, but I would not have traded the lessons I've learned, including perseverance, faith and enduring patience for all the freedoms I've sacrificed. And those faraway shores and sunsets are getting nearer every day.

Lauri Khodabandehloo

A Scarf, Earrings, Necklace, Bottle of Perfume

All that I am, or ever hope to be, I owe to my mother.

Abraham Lincoln

Growing up in the Bronx during the 1950s, I was a mama's boy—and an extreme case at that. When I started Public School 105 as a five-year-old, I couldn't last a full day because I missed my mother. I found that the quickest way to be with her was to complain that I had a stomachache. The school nurse would then call my mom, and she'd come and pick me up and take me home. But before we even reached our apartment, my stomach problem was miraculously cured.

My mother soon realized that my formal education would never be completed at the rate I was going. She decided to give me one of her pearl earrings to keep in my pocket. She said that the next time I had stomach cramps, I could reach into my pocket, touch her earring, which had magical healing powers, and I would feel better.

The next day at school, right on schedule, my stomach started acting up. I reached into my pocket, touched my mother's earring, and to my astonishment, I felt better.

I continued this healing process every day for a few weeks. Then one day, my stomachache didn't go away as quickly as it had on the other days. That afternoon I asked my mother if it was possible that the magical powers were wearing off the earring. "Sometimes that happens," she said. But she had a solution. She explained that any personal possession of hers would work. She went to her dresser and pulled out one of those white gloves that women wore back in the 1950s. The glove worked just fine for me for a couple of weeks. Then it, too, lost its power, so I selected one of my mom's scarves and used that to cure my problem. This process went on for months, eight months, in fact.

One spring morning in April, the principal announced on the public-address system that all classes needed to report to the gym. We filed in pairs down the stairs to the gym, where we were told that all the classes should form large circles by holding our neighbor's hand and then dropping it.

Mrs. Hallorhan explained that we had a serious problem at P.S. 105. One of the students had taken another student's property. She explained that she was going to point to each of us and we would then turn our pockets inside out.

Now my stomach started to really hurt. I wasn't stealing anyone else's property; I was only five years old. Yet, I knew how it would look when I emptied my pockets and all of my mother's items came tumbling out. You see, I hadn't exchanged the glove for the earring, or the scarf for the glove, and so on. I'd kept all of them in my pocket.

Slowly Mrs. Hallorhan went around the circle, my

anguish increasing as she got closer and closer. When she did reach me, I started to cry. I reluctantly turned my pockets inside out. The teachers must have thought that they had caught the Bronx cat burglar, because out came the first earring, a couple of other earrings, the white glove, the scarf, a pearl necklace, a couple of stick pins, a small bottle of perfume, various charms, and four rings.

Embarrassed and ashamed, I ran to the boys' bathroom and locked myself in a stall. I wouldn't come out until my mother came and got me.

Almost forty years later, my mother passed away. That night, the rabbi who would conduct the memorial service called my sister and asked her to tell him about our mother. Roberta spent over an hour telling him about the wonderful, humorous, loving and thoughtful person our mother was. She said that most of all, our mother loved to make people smile. Among my sister's stories was the one about the day her brother holed up in the school bathroom.

The service was respectfully sedate. Near the conclusion, the rabbi asked everyone to stand for a final prayer. He then said he wanted to tell just one more story about my mother and her son. The rabbi was a fine storyteller, and his timing was perfect. As he described the earrings, the white glove, the scarf . . . dropping out of my pocket, the laughter grew louder and louder.

I was laughing; I was crying. It was all true. I was a mama's boy. Even in her absence, my mother worked her special powers and was able to bring a smile to all of those at her funeral one more time.

Andy Strasberg

Middle-Aged Mommy

Parents learn a lot from their children about coping with life.

Muriel Spark

Being middle-aged is like being the middle child. You're not the oldest so the expectations aren't as high. You're not the baby, so you don't get spoiled. The middle child is the independent one. The one left to find her own way, to decide for herself what she wants to do, how she wants to do it and where she wants to do it. So it is with the middle ages.

That's my theory.

For me, it can only be a theory because no matter how many times I chant my mantra, "I'm an independent woman," there's always a four-year-old child who will interrupt me to say, "Mommy, will you draw me a picture of Captain Hook?" Yes, I said four-year-old. There's a six-year-old, too. It wasn't a conscious decision on my part, but I defied middle age by having children just moments before menopausal symptoms set in. Giving birth and the onset of menopause were spaced so closely together that I was practically having hot flashes during labor.

The challenge for me isn't to nurture my spirit by taking yoga classes and redecorating my living room. The challenge is to make this midforties, overweight, dimpled body run after little boys. You try climbing inside one of those tunneled mazes at a fast-food restaurant to retrieve a stubborn child; experience the challenge of finding all thirty-six pieces of a jigsaw puzzle that are now scattered between the garage and the laundry room; and learn to listen to your body when you step on a Lego in the middle of the night and suppress a howl because you don't want to wake anyone.

I chose the road less traveled by midlifers. I met the man I love when I was thirty-seven. We married when I was thirty-eight and knowing that my biological clock's alarm was sounding the final charge, we immediately set about making a baby. We did, I might add, send the wedding guests home first. Five months later, I was "with child" and six weeks shy of my fortieth birthday, our son was born. We tempted fate by trying for another right away, and boy number two was born nineteen months after the first.

When my middle-aged friends ranted on about the terrible teenage years with their own broods, I would simply have to say, "I was in the middle of the supermarket when Casey's diaper exploded," to bring dead silence to the conversation. My peers would stare at me, their mouths agape, and their eyes would roll upward as their minds took them back to their "baby" days. Their own recollections were all it took for waves of sympathy to come my way. "How do you do it?" "I could never go back to those days." "I wouldn't have the stamina!"

I never admitted that I didn't think I had the stamina, either, but miraculously when I need some, it's there.

Many of my middle-aged colleagues are rediscovering themselves or weighing their priorities in life. I don't have time for that. I'm too busy discovering how to answer the question, "Why don't you stand up when you use the potty?" While pals read self-help books, I'm relishing getting reacquainted with Dr. Seuss. How did he come up with *Green Eggs and Ham?* Why did the kids let the cat back in the house in *The Cat in the Hat Returns?* Didn't they learn their lesson the first time? These are the burning questions that keep me awake nights. Okay, not really, but surely I'm not the only one who can spend an afternoon looking for Waldo.

It isn't very often that I really take (or have) the time to assess myself in the mirror these days so I'm often surprised by the visage that appears before me in the glass. I used to look five to eight years younger than I actually was. Now I look forty-six years old. That seems so old. Then I remember. I *am* forty-six years old. And if parenting little ones right now isn't a middle-aged miracle, I don't know what is.

Karen Brown

"We thought my biological clock had run out.
Who knew it had a snooze button."

Reprinted with permission of Steve Smeltzer.

Who Called the Sheriff?

The capacity to care is the thing that gives life its deepest meaning and significance.

Pablo Casals

When my twin sons, Chad and Brad, were born, I was concerned about everything. Was the formula too hot or too cold? Was I doing everything right? Could I actually be the mother that two little boys needed? I wanted the world to be perfect for them.

Five years later, our little girl, Becky, completed our family. Would she get enough of my undivided attention? Would the boys feel neglected by the amount of time a new baby required? I wanted everybody to be healthy and happy. I worked hard to see that they were.

As the kids grew older, I worried about tonsils, earaches, throat infections and many other common childhood illnesses. I worried about their future heartaches. I didn't want anybody to make them sad. I wanted to protect them with all the strength I had.

I didn't like it when the boys spent time "warming the

bench" during Little League and midget-football games. I wondered if they felt inferior because of their smaller size. I worried about Becky when she missed the ball when she played softball. I was afraid she wouldn't make it during flag tryouts.

Many times the kids told me not worry. "Everything will be fine," they constantly reminded me. But like most moms, I worried anyway.

Before long, the teen years were upon us. I sat up late at night waiting for the boys to return home. I worried about drunk drivers on the road. I worried about how the boys would react if one of their friends did something wrong. If they were five minutes late, I panicked. Many times the thought crossed my mind that I would call the sheriff if they weren't home on time. Luckily, they always arrived home safe and sound before I had to resort to such measures.

"Please don't ever call the sheriff," one of the boys said when I threatened him after a late arrival.

The day the boys moved away to attend college was a sad day indeed. I worried about the kinds of professors they would have. Would they make good grades in school? Would they ever graduate? I worried about them being able to take care of themselves and actually cook their own meals. Would they starve?

A few months after the boys left for college, our doorbell rang in the middle of the night. It startled us when we looked at the clock and saw that it was three o'clock in the morning. "Something must be wrong," I shouted to my husband, Roy, as we both jumped up. We ran to the door, opened it and there stood a deputy sheriff.

"You need to call your sons," he sternly announced. I picked up the telephone, but unfortunately, it was dead. A line outside had been accidentally cut. Roy and I jumped into the car and took off to the nearest telephone. My stomach ached with middle-aged worry. My husband was shaking so badly that he could barely dial the number.

On the first ring, Chad answered the telephone. "What's wrong?" Roy shouted into the receiver.

"We were worried about you," Chad told him. "We've been trying to call you all night, and you didn't answer. We called the sheriff's office and asked them to go check on you."

Chad then asked to speak to me. "I was so worried, Mama," he confessed.

"Don't worry, son," I said. "Everything will be fine." For the first time in their lives, the table was turned and the boys were worried about us. And to top it off, they were the ones who actually resorted to calling the sheriff.

Nancy B. Gibbs

"Before you look at my report card,
let me remind you that I'm the only one
in this house who can get you on the Internet."

A Walk to Manhood

The walks and talks we have with our two-year-olds in red boots have a great deal to do with the values they will cherish as adults.

Edith F. Hunter

As a senior, my son Luc would be playing his last high-school football game. He would also be participating in Senior Night pregame activities where all seniors in the band, drill team, pep squad, and football team would be recognized for their four-year contribution to their school. Parents were allowed to participate alongside their son or daughter.

However, the football coach had other ideas. He wanted his players to be focused only on the game, not pregame activities. But after discussing the importance of this evening with both parents and students, the coach relented and agreed to let the parents run onto the field with their sons, probably figuring we'd pooh-pooh the running suggestion. Yet the plan was met with great excitement by the leaping gazelles of the football booster club. I, on the other hand, was filled with angst because I had not run since the eighties, and I did not want to embarrass my son as he ran onto the field dragging me behind him. And I didn't want anyone to see me run, especially from behind! I dreaded the moment when I would have to tell Luc I wouldn't be able to participate.

A few days before the big night, I seized the moment. "Luc, I won't be able to run onto the field with you Friday night. I won't be able to keep up, and I really don't want to embarrass you."

Luc thought about this for a moment then suggested, "I'll walk with you, Mom."

I looked at my boy who was on the verge of becoming a man. "Really? You'd do that for me?" I blubbered like a fool. Luc must have really wanted me with him as he took the field for the last time, I suddenly realized. Senior Night couldn't come fast enough for me after that.

Chattering like excited monkeys, we parents waited for our sons to leave the locker room and join us for our "run." The band members, cheerleaders, drill and flag teams formed a human tunnel on the field for us to run through. When they called Luc's name, we took off. The cheerleaders saluted Luc as he passed. I could feel his excitement as the crowds cheered for him, and I knew I was holding him back. I had to let him go.

"Go, Luc. Run on ahead. I'll catch up," I encouraged.

"No, Mom," he said. "I want to stay with you."

Bless his heart, he really wanted to run—I could feel it in him—so I said, "I'll be fine. Go! They're cheering for you! It's okay!"

"I love you, Mom," he said. "Are you sure?"

"Yes, now go!" Our hands held as long as they could . . . fingertips . . . and then . . . I let him go! The band played and the crowd cheered as I proudly watched my Luc run toward his life.

His rapid footsteps made the only sound in that surreal moment of suspended time. Its symbolism did not escape me, however. "This is how it should be," I thought. "He didn't leave me behind, I let him go! Good for me, and good for him!"

It's been years since that night. But I recall it clearly. For that night was the stepping-off point for me of no longer parenting a child, but of parenting a young adult. And although my place in Luc's life is continually changing, I still am, and always will be, his cheerleader.

Jeri Chrysong

Seven Days to Live

Motherhood is being available to your children whenever they need you, no matter what their age or their need.

Major Doris Pengilly

I once thought of a midlife crisis as questioning whether to pluck out the gray hairs or to let them grow in haphazardly, to get a divorce or stay in a nowhere marriage, to deal with the hormones or lack thereof. Maybe, better yet, it consisted of changing careers in midstream. At no time did I think it would consist of a phone call stating that my son has taken a turn for the worse, and if I want to see him, I'd better get there now.

That was the way my midlife crisis became defined. He went from having a stomach infection to a total non-functioning liver in a matter of hours. I scrambled to make connections from Idaho Falls to Phoenix to arrive at the Mayo Clinic to find my normally muscular son looking like "marshmallow man." His hands were swollen beyond belief as was the rest of his body. The life support was pumping away, and the tubes seemed to be coming from all parts of his body. The ICU nurse was monitoring him constantly. His only response was the single tear that rolled down his cheek when I grabbed his monstrous hand and told him that I was there and that I loved him so very much.

It seemed as if I went through everything on autopilot or, maybe I should say, with God as the pilot. The prognosis was not good. They were giving him seven days to live, and without a new liver, he would surely die. How does one grasp the fact that someone has to die in order for your son to live? How do you pray that way? The doctor said not to think of it as someone needing to die, but rather that someone is going to die and that those organs could be used rather than having the death serve no purpose whatsoever. Prayers were said all around the world. The love and support was overwhelming.

Jeremiah was put on a transplant list and the waiting seemed like an eternity but in seven days, a young man whose life was cut short by an auto accident breathed new life into my nineteen-year-old son. A new liver, so graciously and selflessly given in grief, gave the miracle he so desperately needed.

A new chapter was added to the crisis when Jeremiah began to have a toxic reaction to the antirejection medication. Once again I watched him slide into a near-death mode, first losing his speech and then having seizures and then being placed back on life support. The vigil began all over again. The bedside watch for any indication that he was going to come out of it whole was long and agonizing. Hours turned into days, but finally the life support was removed, and he once again was on the arduous path of a long, uphill climb.

He slowly started to come out of his toxic state, but the doctors had no idea how long it would take to flush the poisons from his brain or if he would ever regain total function. A month had gone by, and I had to return to my job and to register my younger son in school. I had to leave Jeremiah in the hands of the wonderful staff at the Mayo Clinic and his father. The hardest thing I ever had to do in my entire life was to walk out of that hospital room and get on an airplane. I could not say good-bye to him. All I could say were the words that I had repeated over and over to him: "I love you, Jeremiah!"

He was just starting to support himself with a walker and could barely walk without the help of a therapist. He was unable to speak. He could give thumbs up but it was more of thumbs sideways. I went back to work and some-how went through the motions to get through each day. The nurse with the transplant team gave me a daily report on his slow but steady progress.

Then I received a phone call that seemed to take an eternity. I heard from a very slow and very forced voice, "Hi, Mom," a very long pause and then a forced and slurred, "I love you, Mom!" Tears were streaming down my cheeks because they were the very words I had repeated over and over to him, "I love you!" "I love you, Jeremiah!" "I love you!" They were words that every mother longs to hear and wants to hear but probably doesn't get to hear often enough. They were words that only a mother could recognize and decipher. On October 8, 2001, Jeremiah celebrated his twenty-first birthday. My son survived because someone was able to see beyond their own grief and loss to grant my son the gift of life.

As for gray hair and hormones, let's just say I'm keeping everything in perspective because I've learned what a crisis really is. The important part of midlife is *life*—life and love are all that matters.

Mary Anne Fox

Let's Celebrate!

I celebrate the uniquely human ability to celebrate—to ritualize affirmations of our most significant events and deeply held values. Since I am a sentimental seeker of reasons and ways to celebrate, I am usually the one who engineers family events.

Our oldest daughter, Christina, however, showed the potential to be a celebrator par excellence on a certain Mother's Day, about ten years ago, when she was sixteen.

I was feeling shell-shocked that year, suffering from post-traumatic stress syndrome before the trauma of mothering three teenagers was even close to being over. I felt shaken, off-balance, unanchored in a very big, unknown sea, which I had come to feel completely unqualified to navigate. I no longer knew how to be a mother. It had been a very rough year.

I awoke that Mother's Day morning with a feeling of dread. I had never felt more like burrowing under the bedding and never coming out. But when I finally opened my door, there was Christina, grinning in triumph, her eyes glistening faintly with tears.

My firstborn had artistically laid down a "carpet" of white sheets, winding down the hallway, through the family room and kitchen to the dining room. On it she had scattered hundreds of fresh pink rose petals from our own bushes, which had perfumed the air with their deep scent. She took my arm and escorted me to the breakfast table, where my husband had waffles and strawberry butter waiting. It was a conspiracy of love.

I had never felt more grateful to be the mother of such a child, and never more successful in the job, than I did at that moment. I will never forget the blessing of that Mother's Day and its essential message of hope.

Yes, I love celebrations, and I continue to create them. But I never expect to top the celebration of the mother-daughter bond that Christina engineered with such sensitivity and flair one Mother's Day, an era ago, when she let me know, without words, that I was a mother worth celebrating.

Now every Mother's Day, in my mind, I am crowned once again Queen of Mothers amid a swirl of white bed-sheets and pink rose petals. And through my incredulous tears, I see Christina, one of three amazing God-breathed miracles—my babies all grown taller and stronger and more beautiful than I can say.

Lynell Gray

6

ACROSS THE GENERATIONS

I am a part of all that I have touched and all that has touched me.

Thomas Wolfe

Mama's New Dress

*When I stopped seeing my mother with the eyes
of a child, I saw the woman who helped me give
birth to myself.*

Nancy Friday

It was Sunday afternoon, and Mama was feeling pretty
well. So well, in fact, that she wanted a new dress for
Mother's Day. It was just one week away. Whatever
Mama wanted these days, Mama got. Only two short
months ago, she was diagnosed with pancreatic cancer—
with a big T for terminal. That day as the doctor spoke,
from somewhere deep in my spirit I heard: "She has two
months and when she goes, she'll go quickly." The doctors
did not argue when we chose to employ no heroic measures. They agreed to do whatever was necessary to keep
her comfortable for the time she had left and I brought her
to my home.

Her medicine was Tylenol and a family who loved her
so much that she had neither time, nor inclination, for self-
pity. She wanted very little. She was satisfied to have
grandchildren and great-grandchildren crawl up in bed

beside her just to feel her warmth and love. I was unable to pray for Mama to get well, only that she would not suffer. Somehow, I knew that it was her time, although she was only seventy-seven. She had long since buried her other two children, her husband, parents and most of her brothers and sisters. I was her anchor to what was left in her world.

Together we went to the mall to pick out a pretty dress for Mother's Day. We both knew exactly what that dress was for, but neither of us said the word. We knew we would recognize the perfect one when we saw it. I saw it first. By the time we got into the store, Mama had to stop to rest. I knew this would be the last outing we would ever have. She loved the dress, and we bought it on the spot. In defiance of the inevitable, we also purchased two new pantsuits. We dragged ourselves home, happy and deliciously tired.

Monday, Tuesday and Wednesday passed as I watched my mother struggling for more air. The nurse ordered oxygen, which helped little. On Thursday, I knew I would never leave my mother's side again. She said, "I think I've been hearing God calling me." Choking back tears, I hugged her and tried to say the words that would express a lifetime of unsaid "I love yous." I couldn't, but she knew, and we cried a little. I called my daughter, who was a nurse, and she calmed me and admonished me to save my strength, for we were just beginning what would be a long and difficult time.

On Friday, Mama asked, "Where is that music? Don't you hear it, 'Nearer my God to thee, nearer my God to thee . . . ?'" as she pointed to the ceiling. I did not want to hear it, but I knew. My daughter came to help me on Saturday. Together we got Mama up for her bath. She collapsed in our arms, and my daughter knew then as I did. She quickly ordered the comfort medicines the doctors had promised and called the hospice nurse to assist. We called the family together, and Mama was able to hug each precious one. As the day wore on, she rested in a peaceful, painless state as friends and family came and went.

Late in the afternoon, a pastor friend came. We circled her bed, and in prayer, he released her to the Father. Almost immediately she started to leave us for that heavenly home that awaited her. With the family gathered around, I sang hymns to her and wept silently. At 8:00 P.M., my children said they saw her last breath—to me it hung in the air as she took on the radiance of the hereafter. All I saw was one tear in the corner of her eye. I did not know if it was hers or mine.

On Sunday, we dressed Mama in her new dress and she went home to spend Mother's Day with her other children. She was beautiful. I felt no grief. She had lived two months and ten days after her diagnosis, and she had died pain-free. God had spared my mother months of suffering; I felt only gratitude. The new dress has been replaced with a white robe and a crown, but the sweet memory of that shopping day will be with me forever.

Billie Sue Moser

What Do You Have to Say for Yourself?

Memory is more indelible than ink.

Anita Loos

My dad died recently. I expected it; after all, he was eighty-six years old. He had emphysema and his heart was failing. His hands, ravaged by arthritis, could no longer grasp his coffee cup. I had not lived near him for over twenty-five years—I had my own life, four grown children, a busy career, a happy marriage, a house full of dogs.

I often heard friends talk about losing their parents. They talked about the pain of it, the loneliness, feelings of being lost without them. I thought, *But that won't be me.* I knew I would miss him, and I would surely be sorry he was gone. But lost without him? After all, what did he really provide me these days in the way of guidance or support? I had been self-sufficient for a long time. Oh, I talked to him every week, but those calls were for his reassurance, to let him know we were fine. He hardly understood the world my brother and I live in. He couldn't understand our jobs, why we flew all over the world. It wasn't that he didn't know anything about the world. Even at his age, his eyes were good and his mind was sound. He read three papers a day. He knew the political landscape better than most anyone I knew. But his children's lives always seemed beyond his comprehension.

He would begin every Saturday's call with, "Well, what do you have to say for yourself?" And every Saturday, I would have to recount what I had done, what the kids had done, where I had traveled. I also had to be up on the latest in Washington politics, know whether the Green Bay Packers had won, and preferably, who they had recently traded. It would be helpful if I was up on all recent news events, and it would really be best if I had a strong opinion about something.

I'll admit it now, sometimes I found these calls exasperating. But I realize now that this question has been a part of my life since I could speak. I remember walking home from school, knowing my dad would be there, the question on his lips. And I would sometimes dawdle a little on the way, trying to think of an answer. Had I done something clever? Had I read something interesting?

Maybe the question was just a way to open a conversation. Maybe he just wanted to know how my day had gone. But now I realize it took on much greater meaning to me.

I felt that, every day, my dad was asking me to account for myself. What was I doing? And why was I doing it? Knowing this question was coming made me think more about what I did, what I wanted, what I cared about. Even his questions about our jobs now seem not a lack of understanding on his part, but rather an implicit question about whether this was really how we wanted to spend our time.

As I got older, there were times when my dad asked,

"Well, what do you have to say for yourself?" and I would respond, "Nothing."

His eyebrows would shoot up and he would look at me over his reading glasses. Then he would say, "Nothing?"

And I would swallow hard, nod my head, and repeat, "Nothing."

He would look me up and down then respond with an exaggerated, "Mmmm . . ." Then he would shrug his shoulder in that big John Wayne-way of his and change the subject. But as he moved on to ask me about Jim's latest fishing trip or Jen's job or Brooke's college or Dan's girlfriend or Zach's latest book, I knew I had disappointed him. And that was hard to take.

Now there are no more phone calls. I am feeling a little lost. And I am finding myself wanting to answer the question "What do you have to say for yourself?"

Today no one asks me to account for myself. Certainly not my husband, not my children. At the age of fifty, I can do what I want. There's no one there on Saturday to check on what I am up to, no one to wait for the answer on whether my latest book is done or why I haven't done that Habitat for Humanity work I said I would do. Not that Dad ever asked those things outright, either. But wrapped inside the "Big Question" were many implicit little ones.

Now, without my father acting as my compass in the world, I am faced with a greater test. I must go on, remembering that, though no one is asking, I must still account for myself and my actions. Will I become a slug without his weekly question? I hardly think so. But will an occasional Saturday go by when I feel I have been let off the hook, just a little? Probably.

So today, in honor of my dad, I would like to take another opportunity to account for myself.

What do I have to say for myself?

I say that I love deeply and am loved.

I know how to think clearly and act on what I believe.

I know how to set my priorities.

And when I see my children, I now always ask them, "Well, what do you have to say for yourself?"

Thanks, Dad.

Kate Rowinski

Mother and Child

*Just as you inherit your mother's brown eyes,
you inherit a part of yourself.*

Alice Walker

She sits in an easy chair in her sunny apartment and smiles when I enter the room. Her blue eyes sparkle beneath a shock of gray hair going white. Anticipation lights her lined face as I hand her the box of chocolates. I know I have the order right: dark chocolate only, no peanut butter, no coconut, truffles, truffles, truffles, thank you.

I smile as she lifts the cover of the box and hesitates, trying to decide which morsel she will pop into her mouth. It pleases me to give her a moment's happiness in what must be another unending, worrisome day in which she naturally focuses on herself and how her body is reacting to the heart that is failing.

"Hi, Mom! How are you doing?" I ask, and sit in the matching easy chair, waiting for her to savor the last taste of chocolate. Dying isn't easy. I know from experience with my father.

My father's death was anything but easy. Haunting memories of that time color my thinking and fill me with worry. I wish I weren't so impatient for details on how the process is going for my mother. We are a family of planners, but how can we plan for death when the body that failed her so miserably in the past is suddenly determined to hold its own against the inevitable tide of heart failure?

"How am I? Oh, I don't know," she answers. "It's one of those days when I just wish the whole thing was over." She takes another bite of candy and holds the box out to me. "Want one?" She grins as if catching herself. "You can have two, if you want."

"Maybe later," I say, suddenly without appetite at the thought of my mother no longer living, calling to see how my day is going, reminiscing about my childhood, giving perspective to my life.

After some time, I leave, sad inside because we both know what the end result will be; we just don't know when. And we both know something else—she's scared.

I drive home from the assisted-living facility wondering what I can do to help her. She has always been a source of strength for the family. There must be something I can do to make the process easier, something not even the nurses' aides or people from the local hospice can do.

My thoughts flash back to the time when she was diagnosed with multiple sclerosis. That was difficult. I remember watching her in the Hubbard Tank, gaining movement in her legs after a severe attack. I cheered her on at each new milestone. Looking back, I see that she was the child and I the mother during that time.

I pull into the driveway and walk out to the back of the house, wanting, needing, to breathe deeply of the fresh air, to rejoice in the multicolored flowers scattered in beds and on the banks behind retaining walls. *Oh, how I would hate to leave this sweet Earth,* I think to myself.

I remember my mother as a younger woman, twirling around in a circle in the backyard, her arms spread as if to embrace the sky. She was like a child. It is then that I know what I will do. Just as I did many years ago, I will switch roles with my mother. She will be the child, and I will comfort her.

I lower myself into a chair on the patio, deep in thought. *Maybe,* I think, *this is what midlife is about.* It is being mother to your own children and learning to switch roles with your elders so you can give back to them what you have been given or, perhaps, what you've missed in your own life. Child and mother. Mother and child. Endless circles.

Images of other "role-switchers" come to mind. I shake my head. No, I will not speak overly loud to her as if she cannot understand a word I say, nor will I order her about like a dimwitted, stubborn infant, uttering words only a baby would enjoy. I will give her what she has given me: love, security, comfort and self-respect.

As the process continues, I see how frail my mother is becoming. The day comes when the aide greets me with the news that my mother can no longer rise from her bed. It doesn't seem fair. Movement has been difficult for her for so many years—legs numb with disease and weakened by time, constant reminders of her longtime condition. The person who could walk for miles in her youth is now unable to do much more than move slightly. Her body has become a heavy, useless shell sheltering a sweet soul that is preparing to leave me. I choke back tears so she will not see my anguish.

I enter the bedroom, struggling with this latest progression, and take her hand. She gazes up at me and asks the question I dread to answer.

"I'm not leaving this bed, am I? This is close to the end, isn't it?"

I look her squarely in the eyes and nod yes. There are no

lies between us. I owe her that.

She seems to relax. She knows my husband and I will do our part. She is content to switch roles now.

And my husband and I do what we must—laughing, touching, listening, encouraging. And then she is gone. Finally at rest. Dancing above us, we hope, like she always said she would.

Through our sorrow, we tell our children about the wonder of it all. Perhaps they, too, will switch roles when the time comes. And the endless circle will continue.

Judy Keim

Fifty, But Who's Counting?

All right, so I turned fifty this week. My mom taught me that each day is a victory, and I accept that credo. However, I've had a few setbacks of late that are shaking me to my foundation. While shopping for end-of-season bargains, I realized the lovely sweater I'd selected had a tag describing it as part of the Sag Harbor Collection. This caused me to wonder if they intended me to anchor my drooping body parts at their port.

Unfortunately, it was worse in the lingerie section, where I found, to my alarm, that someone had redesigned my favorite bra. You can move my cheese, redefine my paradigm or make me think outside my box—but don't mess with my bra.

The young sales clerk, schooled in proper fit and company jargon began her tutorial. "Ma'am, with your shape and, well, at your stage of life, you should never wear that bra. If you like, I could show you what you need."

She was tugging at the tape measure draped around her neck as I made my retreat. I'd probably been wearing the "wrong" bra since before she was born. I've felt the fires of the burn-the-bra movement and if gravity hadn't prevailed, I'd have rekindled those embers right there.

I felt a little diversion was in order and decided to indulge myself in a mindless movie. With my accumulation of years, that would include most everything released nowadays. I queued up behind Britney Spears look-alikes and the bleached blonde dudes and waited my turn. The nice young man with the tongue stud looked at me and asked, "One senior?"

I said, "Sure, why not?" I bought some popcorn with my ill-gotten gains and figured I'd enjoy it while I still had my teeth.

The next evening, my daughter and her husband, a twenty-something couple, treated me to a birthday dinner. As our waitress took our drink orders for Zinfandel, she pointed to a sign over the bar, "We Card Anyone Under 27."

"I'll need to see some ID please," she said, brushing the gray-tinged bangs from her eyes. The kids flashed their licenses, and then she turned to me. "I'll need to see yours, too, please." I readily complied as we traded winks.

"What was that all about?" My daughter asked, when the waitress left. "Is she working on a bigger tip?"

"Compassion," I said, as I kicked her under the table. "Something you'll understand in a few more decades."

Carolyn Hall

Alone Together: A Grandmother's Tale

I am a reflection of my past generations and the essence of those following after me.

Martha Kinney

We are alone. Blissfully alone. She is lying in my arms sleeping so soundly that I need constant reassurance that she is breathing.

Her mother has been sent out of the apartment, her father is at his office, and there is not a single distraction.

No TV blares.

No phones ring.

And for a blink of very precious, very remarkable time, it's just Hannah and her grandmother. What takes some getting used to is that I am that grandmother!

My oldest daughter, Jill, and her husband bestowed that title on me and, in the process, transformed me into a humbled, overwhelmed, slightly mad woman.

In the blur of those first days, Hannah and I were often in the same place at the same time, but never alone together. And I had such a longing for that experience that, I admit, I engineered my own opportunity by offering Jill an afternoon out at the precise moment when cabin fever was threatening to overcome her.

Jill succumbed. But not to the entire notion.

She would leave for an hour. Just an hour.

So, it came to pass that on a recent afternoon, I rushed my own daughter out the door to have the pleasure of *her* daughter's company.

Hannah is a perfect companion. She fits perfectly into the hollow where my shoulder meets my neck and nestles there, soft, pink and warm, without stirring. It has been too long since I've felt this blissful weight—and the perfect peace and contentment it brings.

For a full hour, Hannah asks nothing of me.

No searching questions about life or philosophy or morality or fairness.

No pouts about why I was too critical, not interested enough, too prying, too controlling.

Just an occasional, tiny little lurch or turn and, once, a small wail, just to remind me that, yes, she's really there.

The afternoon sunlight dances on the rug as Hannah and I dream our separate dreams. I marvel at her miniature perfection, kiss her tiny fingers, stroke her silky, sparse hair. I stare at a face that I am still trying to memorize, looking for clues to who this lovely little infant will turn out to be.

Will she have her mother's iron will? Her father's gentleness?

Will she be a sober, serious child or a laughing one, an eruption of joy?

Will she do to her mother what her mother did to me during that enchanting period twixt twelve and twenty, that era of slow torture called "coming of age"?

Hannah—tiny Hannah—already has a disposition, a natural bent, a network of traits that will someday define her. The notion that in my arms is a creature with all of us in her bone marrow still leaves me breathless, grateful, awed.

Suddenly, I feel tears streaming down my cheeks. Silly, sentimental, new-grandmother tears.

I realize, sitting with Hannah on a sunny afternoon in the middle of my life and the beginning of hers that she represents the last phase of this complicated, endless, precious process called parenting.

She is renewal and hope, and the person who makes waves of love swirl through rooms as she holds us, already, in her tiny grip.

And for all those reasons, my tears keep coming. I've barely composed myself when Jill rushes breathlessly into the apartment to ask, "So, how did it go?"

And I can't begin to tell her.

Sally Friedman

"Motherhood is an acquired taste. Most mothers don't acquire it until they're grandmothers."

An Unexpected Gift of Peace

Nothing ever succeeds which exuberant spirits have not helped to produce.

Freidrich Nietzsche

September 11 will be remembered by all Americans as the date of a terrible national tragedy. Thousands of us who were airborne at the time will also have personal memories of becoming grounded and stranded. The most memorable event in my own life occurred the following day, September 12.

"Your dad just called," my husband, Dick, said solemnly, as I walked back into our house from visiting our neighbor. "Your mother suffered a stroke and has slipped into a coma." It was Sunday afternoon, September 9. I immediately called my father back and heard him repeat that my mother's condition was critical.

The following morning, my father called again. "I think you should come as soon as possible," he said. "It does not look like your mother will live much longer." I told him that I would be on an airplane by that evening.

As with a lot of families today, many miles separate us from one another. But thanks to the world of aviation, getting on an airplane to go anywhere in the world has not only become a convenience but also an expected part of our lives. I was attempting to get to Oak Ridge, Tennessee, from where I lived in Carlsbad, New Mexico.

Whether it was fate or Murphy's Law, something definitely seemed to be putting my trip to Tennessee in slow motion. The commuter plane that I was taking to reach a major airport was late leaving. I could not make a connection by the time I finally reached the Albuquerque airport. Consequently, I spent the night at a hotel there. Early the next morning, I was on a flight to Phoenix, where I would connect with another flight to Nashville. It was while I was on the Phoenix-bound flight that the horrific plane crashes occurred. The plane I was on landed, but those passengers who had connecting flights became stranded. An announcement in the terminal simply told us to go to baggage claim for our luggage.

Being informed by others in the terminal of what had occurred within the past hour, their faces aghast as they focused on a television showing scenes of the plane crashes in New York, Washington, D.C., and Pennsylvania, I went to get my luggage. Passengers were lined up in the baggage-claim area to make calls on the hotel shuttle phones, in hope of finding a hotel that still had vacancies.

Upon checking into a hotel and settling in, I called my husband to let him know where I was. As the whole country seemed glued to the television that day, I, too, watched in horror and wondered how long I would be stranded in Phoenix. During the night, I was awakened by a phone call. My mother had died.

Early Wednesday morning, September 12, I was informed that no planes were yet allowed in the air. Needing to purchase some items, I walked a quarter of a mile from the hotel to a shopping center. Walking slowly back to the hotel, I started to feel very distraught. All I could think about was how our country had been attacked by an evil force, my mother had died a few hours earlier, I couldn't get there before she passed away and didn't know how long I might be stranded. Grief began to overwhelm me. Out of the blue, a beautiful white dove flew down and began walking with me. The dove continued to turn its head and look at me as we walked. I smiled through my tears and became increasingly aware that something very unusual was happening. "Are you from Heaven?" I asked the dove, as we walked, and instantly thought, *Gosh, I'm talking to a bird!* The dove just continued to walk with me and look at me. I unexpectedly began feeling that my mother's spirit was with me. When I reached the hotel, the dove and I looked at each other once more. A peace and warmth came over my entire being, and I felt God had just given me a special gift. Tranquility had replaced my feelings of fear, loneliness and desperation. I knew that God was still in control of this world.

I went back into my hotel room and called my husband. He had driven that morning to El Paso, Texas, attempting to get on a flight to Nashville. Being told that there would be no flights that day, he was booked on a flight for the next morning out of Midland, Texas. As a result, he drove the three-hour trip back home to Carlsbad. Later in the evening, he started driving to Midland to stay at a motel near the airport in order to be on an early flight the next morning. Hearing the news that flights were cancelled for the next day also, Dick turned around and drove all night to reach Phoenix the next morning. He later told me how very aware he was of God being with him in the car as he drove the 1,000 miles to reach me.

We both felt God's presence as we drove all day, all

night, all the next day (another 1,900 miles in thirty-one hours), arriving one hour before the family was to receive friends at the funeral home. The funeral service immediately followed, and we were able to share with others my unexpected gift of peace.

Linda Lipinski

My Mother's Eyebrows

In search of my mother's garden I found my own.

Alice Walker

"Can you show me how to pluck my eyebrows?" she asked. I looked askance at my mother. It's not every day that a mother asks her high-school freshman how to pluck eyebrows. She wasn't joking.

This request came from a mother whose adult life consisted of giving birth, raising eight children and keeping house as a dutiful wife trailing an Army officer from one installation to another. Surely, they had modeled Mrs. Cleaver after my mother with her ever-present apron and no-nonsense approach to everything from child-rearing matters to baking homemade bread. On rare special occasions, Mom wore perfume and orange-red cream lipstick to accessorize sleeveless dresses and other Jackie O–inspired fashions when she and Dad stepped out for the evening.

In the ignorance of my youth, I believed that my mother

was—year after year—forty-five years old. For some reason, I affixed that age to her persona. It just seemed right.
She never got older than forty-five. To my young eyes, the
age of forty-five bordered on geriatric.

It was with great pleasure that I showed my mother
how to pluck eyebrows.

The changes were gradual. Not long after, Mom began
contributing her bass voice to the Sweet Adelines; her
Singer sewing machine—at one time reserved for spitting
out summer outfits for me and my sister—began generat-
ing glittery gowns and other lush costumes. Fake eyelashes, tubs of facial cream, bottles of makeup and various
shades of lipstick began to clutter the medicine cabinet
and around the sink in her bathroom.

I remember the first time I saw Mom on-stage; I almost
didn't recognize her. The years had fallen away—she was
no longer forty-five—and all assumptions about my
mother were escorted quickly to the exit doors. Mom daz-
zled me with the way she swished around in costumes,
smiling broadly to timed steps, carefully shaped eyebrows
arching over false eyelashes and rouged cheeks.

This was not my mother.

Mom was . . . well, she was a woman!

My mother was a woman having the time of her life,
and looking every bit as young as she was feeling.

We traipsed to countless Sweet Adelines shows in support of our mother. After all, she had spent nearly thirty
years cheering each of her kids in school plays, church
choirs, jazz bands, half-time marches. Now it was her turn.
She disappeared into a world of bus trips and workshops
and competitions with the large chorus that sang barber-
shop-style, tirelessly honing scales and choreography.
Loud, boisterous ladies with husbands to match came
over to our house, filling our normally quiet lives with rau-
cous laughter, songs and jokes. We grew to love these

friends, revel in their good humor, idiosyncrasies and out-look on life.

When shows were held under the stars in the amphitheatre, we'd bring a cooler filled with sodas, cheese and crackers and kick back. After the biggest show of the year, my parents would attend the Sweet Adelines after-glow party and come home late with confetti in their hair. Year after year, confetti in their hair and flushed cheeks. Finally, when Mom made it to first row on the risers—reserved for the cream of the crop—it was a cham-pagne moment.

Several years after Mom retired from the Adelines, she and my dad were paid a surprise visit on Valentine's Day by a quartet of familiar faces who crooned a medley of romantic songs to them—a surprise gift from the family. And then on my parents' fiftieth anniversary, we reserved a table for the ladies from the "good ol' days."

"C'mon, gang!" someone shouted. "Let's sing a song!"

And there she was again. Up there with her buddies, harmonizing with arms linked around each other's waists. Nostalgia welled up as I remembered the day she asked me how to tweeze eyebrows. I snuck a look at Dad. His beaming face mirrored the pride I felt, because Mom was proving it to us all over again—that age, after all, was just an attitude.

Jennifer Oliver

Hands of Time

Mothers are really the true spiritual teachers.

I saw it before I felt it. The metamorphosis. The evolution of my own hands into the hands of my mother. There was no warning.

Graceful and elegant fingers that braided my hair, made my lunches, and brushed away my tears belonged to my mother so many years ago. Frightened animals stopped quivering when she laid her hands upon them. Those hands prepared our dinner, set the table and then scoured away the remnants left behind. They rolled pie crust so delicate it would melt upon the tongue and scrubbed stains from our clothes with a vengeance. The iron pump handle yielded to her will, spilling cool water into the bucket that hung from the spout.

Her nails were carefully tended by a monthly soaking in warm, soapy water followed by a firm scrubbing with a small brush. An orange stick pushed the cuticles back and a file shaped their ovals to perfection. Occasionally, a coat of clear polish completed the ritual.

Fancy scented creams were not an option—only the sensible healing ointments delivered by the Watkins man.

Throughout the years, I observed those beautiful hands as they ministered to the needs of our family. As time passed, her fingers picked up needle and thread, refusing to be idle. Under her touch, perfectly formed stitches matured into a plethora of colorful flowers, birds and full-skirted ladies adorning pillowcases that cradled our heads at night. Her hand-stitched quilts grace the bedrooms of children, grandchildren and great-grandchildren. Their beauty warms the soul as their weight warms the body.

Friends have told friends. From far and near the requests come for her hand-stitched wonders, every stitch done by hand, whether creating a small pillow or a bountiful covering for a king-size bed. Each creation is unique, a one-of-a-kind treasure.

Arthritis has tried to stake a claim, but her fingers defy it, refusing to give way to defeat. The freckles on the backs of her hands slowly turned into "age" spots, protesting that it was time to slow down. The once-smooth skin has become thinner, the veins playing peek-a-boo. But still her hands move, continuing to weave beauty with each new day.

My hands learned to braid hair, make lunches and brush away tears. I held my hand out to feel the down of a bird, the sleek fur of a cat, the deep coat of a dog. With patience, I would hold out my hand until they would approach. Their quivering would stop when I placed my hands upon them.

My hands can set an elegant table for company and scour the burned pans from my culinary attempts. I learned to roll pie crust. I even scrubbed our laundry, before the modern convenience of an automatic washer became available. Though once I fought to draw water from a pump, today I turn a faucet and it appears, already warm or cold, depending on my choice.

My hands pinned cloth diapers on babies and today peel off the tape to secure disposable diapers on my grandchildren. My fingers grace the keyboard of a computer, weaving words, as my mother weaves her needle and thread.

Gathering my thoughts, I look upon my hands tonight and behold the spectacle. My mother's hands have transposed themselves to my own body. The fingers are still graceful, feeling from time to time the twinge of arthritis, but refusing to slow down. A plastic pump bottle of hand lotion sits at my fingertips to be used at my leisure. Still, the "age" spots have appeared, and I see the veins peeking through. I'm not sure when it happened, but the metamorphosis is complete.

My only prayer is that my own hands have left behind memories that will be recalled with pleasure some day, when my daughters notice their hands have evolved into mine.

Carol Ann Erhardt

I Am My Mother and Proud of It

I looked in the big bay window,
And, surprise, what did I see.
I swear I saw my mom,
looking back at me.

Although she's been in heaven,
for over fourteen years,
I know I saw her smiling at me,
while I was wiping off my tears.

I had just come back from taking
my oldest sons to school.
I was having second thoughts about
the whole darn college rule.

Where moms are not allowed to stay,
in the dorms with them safe and sound.
Oh, no, they send us home to wonder,
what the heck kind of home they've found.

I was standing in my living room,
with tears running down my face,
And I thought of how my mom had felt,
when I joined that college race.

I don't remember tears that were cried,
or sad little messages sent.
I remember the freedom and life was so good,
But for Mom, I never knew what it meant.

But for now, as I look in the window,
at the face that I see as my own,
I see Mom and the smile she had given,
and I know that somehow I have grown.

Into a mom I know she is proud of,
A mom who is almost like her,
And I know that she cried, but she hid it from me,
on that day that I left on my own.

Teresa Tyma Helie

Mrs. Frieda Moves

*The teachers are everywhere. What is wanted is
   a learner . . .
The teachers are waiting as they always have,
   beyond the edge of the light.*

Wendell Berry

On my calendar in Thursday's space is written, "Mrs.
Frieda moves." Avoiding this melancholy matter had
almost convinced me everything would continue as
always. But the day I've been dreading for so long has
arrived. The phone rings. Frieda wonders if I could come
over for a few minutes; she wants to say good-bye.

When my husband and I moved into the neighborhood
ten years ago, Thomas was almost a year old and Barrett
was four. Frieda, a sweet elderly widow who lives next
door, grew fond of our children and tolerated their typi-
cally boyish behavior with an astonishing amount of
good-natured grace.

When Barrett was six or seven, he decided on a whim to
see if a rock, when hurled over our fence, could land on

Frieda's roof. It did not. With a mighty crash, it collided with her living-room window. Frieda was in a bedroom in the back of the house and almost suffered heart failure on the spot. But when I marched Barrett over to apologize, the corners of her mouth trembled with an ill-concealed smile, and she said, "I wasn't worried; it didn't break, but if it did, I knew you'd look after it."

The boys decided that Mrs. Frieda, as we christened her, has a better driveway than ours for hockey. It is shared with the people living next to her and, as a result, is wonderfully wide. The boisterous game at some point spilled over into her yard and before Mrs. Frieda knew it, her property became a giant rink filled with shouting boys, hockey sticks, pucks and nets. I wasn't aware of this development until she phoned me to say that hockey is a healthy exercise, and the boys are very good at it, but she was a little concerned for her shrubs.

On hot summer nights, Barrett would sleep out in a tent with his friends, and in the morning, I would see it set up over at Mrs. Frieda's. Thomas went through a bow-and-arrow phase and homemade arrows regularly littered her lawn and impaled her shrubbery. At Halloween she would shower my kids with goodies. Those minitreats wouldn't do for Mrs. Frieda; she filled their bags with full-size chocolate bars, bags of chips and cans of pop.

Her affection was returned enthusiastically. Without being asked, the boys would often shovel her driveway, their little arms straining to push the heavy snow. They took her garbage out to the curb faithfully every Thursday morning on their way to school. One day I searched everywhere for Thomas only to find him in Mrs. Frieda's backyard, helping her rake leaves and stuff them into bags. I made them deliver countless dinners. "What do you have for me today?" she always asked and the boys would dutifully recite the menu. She sent them back with packets of instant oatmeal, eucalyptus throat lozenges and cans of fruit cocktail, lingering at her door to watch them peering into the bag as they hurried home.

One sleet-filled night, Thomas went over to Mrs. Frieda's with a huge piece of cherry cheesecake and fell. He came back covered in cheesecake, crying and carrying an empty plate. In the morning, we saw cherries, chunks of cake and pieces of graham cracker crust all over the sidewalk; for days, this unappetizing conglomeration remained congealed and frozen in the ice. Years later, all Thomas has to say is, "Remember the cheesecake?" and we burst out laughing.

Sitting in Mrs. Frieda's kitchen for the last time, chatting about the nursing home she'll be moving into at two o'clock, my eyes fill with tears. Her hair, freshly cut, curled and colored an unusual shade of taupe, is held firmly in place by a shiny brown net. Her green cardigan is buttoned up to the neck and a mustard yellow blouse peeks out over the top. Her wedding rings are too loose on her thin fingers and her breathing is shallow and rapid, but she smiles that precious smile I love so much and asks me if I'd like a cookie. She has packed a tin of salmon, a box of pudding mix and a piece of leftover Christmas cake for me.

Her things are waiting by the door. Such a meager, lonely assortment, an inadequate sum of a richly significant life. A small blue suitcase stands upright, tarnished locks clipped shut. A worn plaid mohair coat lies over the back of a chair. An ancient alarm clock and some toiletries are set out beside her oxygen equipment.

Life is filled with these heart-wrenching chapters, yet turning their pages never seems to become any easier. Mrs. Frieda's sight is failing; she doesn't notice me wiping my eyes as she puts together her talking-book tapes and asks me to mail them back to the Canadian National

Institute for the Blind if it's not too inconvenient.

I should be glad; she is moving down the street into a new facility where she'll be well cared for, and I will visit her often, but something dear is slipping from my grasp. Mrs. Frieda is the reason my children have learned to appreciate and enjoy the elderly. She is why they think of others. She is why they believe neighbors should be kind to each other. Such priceless lessons they have learned trudging up the sidewalk with plates of food and dragging bags of garbage out to the curb. Mrs. Frieda has thanked me often for my generosity, but she has given me something far greater than I could ever give her—the opportunity to teach my children how to be beautiful human beings.

Rachel Wallace-Oberle

A Mother Sings

Life can only be understood backward but it must be lived forward.

Soren Kierkegaard

Jill paused halfway down our front steps. She turned and said, "Mom, will you sing to me? Will you hold me and sing like you used to when I was a little girl?" Her husband and her two little stepdaughters stopped and looked back.

I always sang to my kids when they were young. Jill and her older brother shared a bedroom, and I knelt between them, holding one's hand and stroking the blond head of the other. I sang and crooned through "Dona, Dona" and "Kumbaya." I swayed in rhythm to "Swing Low, Sweet Chariot." I never missed a verse of "Hush, Little Baby." I made up songs, too, a habit that drove my husband crazy. On nights when I was out, the kids begged, "Sing 'The Horse Broke the Fence,' Daddy," or "No, we want 'The Big Wheel' song." And they didn't mean "Proud Mary," which he might have managed, although he really couldn't carry a tune even when he knew the words.

But the kids and I always finished with "All Things Bright and Beautiful," as I watched their active bodies quiet and their eyes grow dreamy as they imagined the purple-headed mountains and ripe fruit in the garden of the old hymn. By the time I warbled my way through the refrain for the last time, one of them had usually twitched and fallen asleep.

As Jill grew from child to adult, it became apparent that she had inherited her father's trouble carrying a melody. She cuddles with her girls every night and she reads to them, but she just can't sing to them.

Recently, I baby-sat for our granddaughters. After I tucked them into our king-size bed, I sang "Dona, Dona," "Kumbaya," and all the others. Hannah, the six-year-old, lay still as a stone, gazing at the ceiling. Four-year-old Brianna came forward onto her hands and knees, staring into my eyes from so close that her features blurred. In the dim light coming through the open door, I saw her lips parted, glistening. Trance-like, she held perfectly still, listening as if she wanted to inhale the songs directly from my mouth.

It was a few days later Jill asked me to once again sing to her. She said, "The girls talked about your singing, Mom, and it brought back all the wonderful memories. I remember my cool pillow and your hand on my hair. I remember my nightgown with the sunbonnet dolls on it and the pink ice-cream cone quilt you made. Sometimes I would wake up when you kissed me one last time."

That's when she turned and asked, "Mom, will you sing to me, again?"

Her husband stood beneath the street lamp with a child balanced on each hip. Her father and brothers stood behind me, illuminated by the porch light. She's very tall, this girl of mine. Standing on the step below me, she still had to stoop to put her head against my chest. I wrapped my fingers in her long hair, and she wound her arms around my waist.

"What shall I sing, Jill?" I asked.

"You know, Mom," she said, looking up and smiling.

"'All Things Bright and Beautiful'?"

"Of course." She snuggled closer. "All the verses."

I kissed the top of her head and began to sing.

Swallowing a lump in my throat and stroking her back, I continued through the verses. Off-key, she joined in.

She began to cry, and so did I, but the words still flowed from my mouth as my mind drifted back over the years. I remembered her birth, how ecstatic I was to have a daughter—what an easy child she was. I remembered how she loved to please others—and still does. This girl who married young and took on the daunting task of raising another woman's children is no longer under my wing. She's a young woman now, and I can't tuck the ice-cream cone quilt around her shoulders each night. I can't protect her from pain, from hurt and from mature responsibility. I can't make growing up any easier for her.

Jill's tears soaked through my T-shirt that night and mine dropped onto her bowed head. She clung tightly and then looked up into my face.

"The purple-headed mountains. Don't forget the purple-headed mountains," she whispered, staring at me through the dim light, just as Brianna had a few nights earlier, drinking in the words, the memories, the song. Drinking in my love.

My voice cracked, and I could sing no more. We stood locked together on the stairs. I know the enormity of the task she's taken on is sometimes almost more than she can handle. I know how hard she's working to create a home.

Cradling her in maternal love, allowing her to remember falling asleep to a mother's singing, was the best I could offer my daughter this night. Jill squeezed me tightly and then turned toward her husband and her step-daughters. Her dad hugged me as we watched her settle the girls into the back seat of their car—and then I heard the hymn again. I strained my ears, listening. Jill was still humming the refrain. Then Brianna's thin, little child's voice burbled from the open car window as they pulled away from the curb: "All things wise and wonderful, the Lord God made them all."

Peggy Vincent

The Gift of Memory

How we remember, and what we remember, and why we remember form the most personal map of our individuality.

Christina Baldwin

It was Amy's idea from the start. Our middle daughter, now a thirty-something TV producer, kept raising the notion of videotaping her grandmother, chronicling her life and memories in order to preserve them.

And I kept resisting.

"Mom . . . Mom won't want to," I argued. "She'll be uncomfortable," I told Amy, projecting, perhaps, my own feelings about video cameras.

Amy would have none of it. And because she and her grandmother have always had a connection that is as mighty as it is indefinable, Amy ultimately prevailed.

So on a recent weekend, Amy arrived at my mother's city apartment carrying a sophisticated video camera and a grand plan for recording the life and times of her beloved grandmother. The gift of my mother's life on tape, I came to realize, would be invaluable to us. As a middle-aged daughter, I began to realize how finite our time together is—and how precious.

The "star" of the show was initially most concerned about feeding Amy and those few of us who were to be observers of this milestone: my sister, my husband and me.

After we had been stuffed with bagels and fruit and cookies, a small, beautiful lady with shining green eyes faced the camera and began. Nobody had told Mom what to do or say because, in some ways, the format had to be hers.

And after Amy asked the first broad questions, my ninety-one-year-old mother was off and running.

There we sat listening to the story of a woman born to immigrant parents—a woman who had lived the first years of her life behind the family grocery store on a gritty city street—who would go on to see granddaughters graduate from Ivy League schools.

We heard what it was like for her to witness her own mother giving birth to the flamboyant younger sister who would then take center stage in the family's life. We listened as my mother described the father she loved so much, a frail man for whom my own oldest daughter is named. Joseph Goldberg was gone before I had a chance to know him well, and has remained a somewhat shadowy figure in my memory bank. But sitting in my mother's apartment that Saturday afternoon, listening to her talk about him, my grandfather suddenly came alive for me. It was moving—and marvelous.

As the camera rolled, what it tracked was a deeply personal chronicle of what life was like when the twentieth century itself was young, and when just being born in this country was considered a gift. But not an unqualified one.

The story of how my mother faced rampant anti-Semitism on her first job search, when the name "Goldberg" was clearly not an asset, was profoundly disturbing. I'd never known that to get her first job, my mother had assumed a name she invented because it seemed safe. "Gould," she reasoned at eighteen, was surely less telling than Goldberg. And as Lillian Gould, she was on her way.

How my parents met, their first official date, the richly textured tale of my mother buying her wedding dress and feeling, in her words, "like a princess" because a dashing lawyer had asked her to be his wife: priceless.

As Amy let the camera do its work, the stories kept coming. It was as if my mother had been given this astounding gift she couldn't let go of as she reflected and processed a long, full, richly-textured life.

I know there were moments when she forgot the camera was there, and they, of course, were the best moments of all. That camera rolled for hours, pausing only when we "young ones" worried about Mom's stamina and insisted on periodic breaks. But Mom—Mom could have gone on and on, remembering the magnificent and mundane moments of her life: her first job, the birth of her daughters, the war years, the sweetness of walking into her first home as a mother.

She could talk of my late father with humor, with candor and only occasionally with what my sister and I recognized as "revisionist history." He was a wonderful, brilliant, complicated, difficult, impractical man—and the video camera now holds that rich and complex marital history for all time.

Her becoming a grandmother, and then, miracle of all miracles, a great-grandmother—all recorded on that marvelous piece of modern technology.

Only when darkness began to fall, and other obligations beckoned, did Amy shut off the video camera. Only then did we pause to realize what a treasure it held, and how right Amy had been all along.

A life—a history—a part of us—has been preserved for

all time. We have a true treasure in that deceptively
simple-looking cassette. And as we summoned up the
energy to return to the tensions of the present, we realized
that there was no way to thank my mother for this
astounding gift of memory.

There are only feeble ways to try.

Sally Friedman

The Gray Slipper

"It's only a matter of time now," the doctors told me. Mom's eighty-three-year-old body was saying, "Enough." I consoled myself, knowing death would provide relief from pain and usher in a whole new, wonderful experience.

Still, all I could think about was the gray slipper.

As the oldest daughter of five, and the only one who lived in the same town as Mom, care-taking responsibilities had rested on my shoulders for the past ten years. Throughout the course of this slow debilitating process, my mother and I have grown very close. Visiting doctors, finding support care, moving her into various eldercare homes as her condition worsened made for quality time, and sometimes, humorous episodes.

I still remember her first night at the convalescent home. After tucking Mom in for the night, I left for home, assuring her I'd be back to check on her in the morning. I got a phone call that night from a nurse, complaining that my mother wasn't sharing the TV.

"What do you mean?" I asked.

"She says she wants to watch *Wheel of Fortune,* and that's

all there is to it. Her two other roommates want to watch something else."

Knowing that my mother is nearly incapable of getting in and out of bed by herself, I asked the obvious, "Why don't you just turn the channel?"

"She doesn't want us to!" the nurse exclaimed.

I laughed inside. Mom always had a way of controlling a situation. I knew the same obstinacy had allowed her to live so long in spite of bad health. Maybe that's why seeing her in the hospital now, so docile and weak, was taxing to my soul.

Only two weeks ago, my mother had been admitted to the hospital for what they believed was a cracked hip. The X rays proved negative, so she was released and sent back to the convalescent home. That night, the hospital called me to report she had left behind one gray slipper. Knowing I had just purchased a new pair for her, and realizing she was probably through traipsing the halls anyway, I instructed them to throw it out. While visiting my mom at the convalescent home that night, I told her about the stray slipper. "I love those slippers. They are so cozy," she whined.

"I already told them to throw it out. Besides, you have this nice new pair," I assured her.

"Go get the other one. Please!" Mom begged.

"I can't. It's late. I'm tired, and it's probably already at the bottom of the trash bin."

When I left that night I felt a tinge of guilt, but at the same time, remained firm in my resolve.

Now two weeks later, standing beside her hospital bed again, guilt gave way to remorse. I know people often live with regrets, good-byes left unsaid, deeds left undone, but I was determined such a fate would not befall me. I wished for another chance to tell my mother I care: I care enough to give you hope for a slipper you'll never be able to walk in; to give you comfort in familiar things; to give you a feeling of worth, dignity and control when all around you seems helpless, and your personhood stripped.

I knew, if given the chance again, I would not betray a trust.

The hours ticked away and Mom drifted in and out of sleep. My stomach growled.

I kissed her cheek and slipped away for a quick bite. My sister arrived, agreeing to keep vigil. As I sat alone in the cafeteria with my contrite conscience, I couldn't help but wonder about the people dining around me.

Do they know how precious life is? That each day is a gift from God? Do they realize the opportunity they have to tenderly touch another life, leaving what might be their last impression on them?

I knew my mother would forgive me for the lost slipper; we had too good a history to hold grudges. Still, I felt a shadow of regret that I acted so hastily. I finished the last of my coffee and headed back up to the room. When I walked back in, Mom was awake. She looked happy to see me.

"Oh look," my sister said, "a policeman came in and made me sign for this; said it belongs to Mom." I blinked in utter disbelief. It was the gray slipper.

"I don't care who you think brought that in," I told my sister. "An angel sent this to me."

"A slipper?" my sister asked. "Mom can't even walk. She doesn't need it."

"It's not for her," I said holding it to my chest. "It's for me."

Pearl Nelson
As told to Lynne M. Thompson

[EDITORS' NOTE: *Alberta Anderson passed away on July 2, 2000. The gray slippers remain in Pearl's closet.*]

The Folks Next Door

Occasionally, I say something that's guaranteed to evoke a strong response. I tell people, "I live next door to my parents." Their reaction tells me a lot about the relationship they have with their own parents. I've heard everything from abject horror, to wistful sighs accompanied by, "That must be so nice."

In case you're wondering, I'm not some psychologically dependent cling-on. My parents and I haven't always been neighbors. For most of my adult life, I lived in a completely different (though, come to think of it, neighboring) community.

It was my last move, six years ago, that led us to share lot lines, garbage pick-up days and the same view of the night sky. My husband, three kids and I were looking for a larger home. At the same time, my parents wanted to downsize to a smaller, low-maintenance house. My husband, Greg, and I chose a subdivision and watched as our new house progressed from a hole in the ground to completion.

After looking at existing homes, my parents visited our builder to look at floor plans. They liked the area, but the visit was really a lark, or at least that's the story I was told.

As it turned out, the house they loved was offered only on the lot next to ours. After they studied the room layout and toured a model, my mom asked, "Would you mind if we lived so close?" She assured me that they wouldn't be offended if we didn't like the idea. Greg and I thought it would work out fine, and luckily, it has.

I can't complain—the benefits have been enormous. Vacations are worry-free because we know that each of us will watch the other's house, pick up the mail and collect the newspapers. We're available for each other in the event that furniture needs moving (them) or kids need watching (us). My oldest son's first paying job was mowing their lawn. And when we say it's no trouble to bring back more takeout from the Chinese restaurant or pick up additional stamps at the post office, it really isn't.

I've found that my parents are the only neighbors I can be brutally honest with. When my dad bragged about his cost-effective, makeshift central air-conditioning cover, I took him over to my kitchen window. I showed him how aesthetically pleasing his plastic garbage bag secured with duct tape was from our viewpoint. Shortly thereafter, the bag was replaced with a less creative, traditional cover.

Our kitchen windows are the only direct view of each other's homes. Sometimes the timing of our kitchen duty will coincide, and I'll wave from my side. If they notice me, they'll wave back. Only once has this view posed a problem. On that occasion, I got up in the middle of the night to get a drink of water and noticed my mom awake in her kitchen. On a whim, I dialed her phone number. The frantic way she catapulted out of her chair made me realize there are times it's best not to call.

I've learned that respecting each other's time and space is the key to successfully living close to family members. Other relatives don't believe me when I tell them days go by when I don't even talk to my parents. My three sisters (they of the "better you than me" philosophy) will call asking, "Where are Mom and Dad? I've been trying to reach them all day."

I usually don't have an answer. Who can keep track of busy retired people? "You could do what I do when I can't get hold of them," I suggest.

"What?" they ask, waiting for the next-door neighbor secret.

"Leave a message on their machine. When they get home they'll call you back."

For some, life is a boardgame of cross-country moves to better job opportunities and bigger houses. Families keep in touch by phone, letter and e-mail and somehow they make it work. But I believe there's no substitute for being nearby. My children know my parents in a way I never knew my own grandparents. On a warm summer day, my kids will interrupt valuable playing time to dash over to my parents' yard for a hug from Grandma or to help Grandpa water his plants. It's good for a kid to have a haven close to home.

This parent–next-door thing has been working out so well that I'm already thinking ahead to my own retirement. I try to imagine one of my three children as a future next-door neighbor. When asked about that possibility, thirteen-year-old Charlie said, "I probably will want to live as far away from you as possible."

The younger two are far more agreeable, in fact six-year-old Jack has said he wants to live with me forever. That may be a little too close—but if he wants to move in with Grandma and Grandpa, it's a deal.

Karen McQuestion

Missing

I am born connected. I am born remembering the rivers flowing from my mother's body into my body.

Meinrad Craighead

The chocolate cake presented to me for my birthday startled me. On top of the dark fudge frosting were words emblazoned in neon orange frosting to celebrate the Halloween season and my birthday, which revealed the truth, "Happy Fiftieth Birthday."

Family and friends had joined in my celebration. Joviality ensued, with toasts galore to roast the hostess. I was either over-the-hill or on the verge of a midlife crisis. But one dear friend's toast was the most endearing of them all, "Here's to middle age. Remember, it's nifty to be fifty. In case you don't know what nifty means, I looked it up. It means marvelous, particularly excellent. May you have fifty more marvelous years."

As the merriment continued, I scanned the room and remembered a very important person was missing. The person who once said to me, "One day you're going to be celebrating a birthday, and you'll be older than I will ever admit to." It was hilarious at the time. The beginning of the middle years, my fiftieth had arrived, the year that very important person, my mom, had referred to. She never acknowledged publicly that she was fifty, she was forty-nine and holding. Even as the years passed, she was still forty-nine and holding.

Yes, Mom was missing—lost in time and private memories. Originally, her diagnosis was senile dementia but was later determined to be the beginning of Alzheimer's disease. As a patient, she is referred to as "pleasantly confused." My dear mom, a widow, an independent woman, suddenly incapable of caring for herself or her affairs and no longer able to live on her own after almost burning down her house, is a resident in a convalescent facility. And I live 2,500 miles away in California.

Each time I visit her, I hold her hand. She smiles and asks, "What is your name?" or "Who are you?" Caretakers say she is the same with all family and friends. But it doesn't make me feel any better.

No matter how many times I say my name, she doesn't remember I am her daughter. I fight back the tears and pretend it doesn't matter. A conversation between us is impossible. I've shared my accomplishments, my dreams, my thoughts and my goals with her anyway, longing for a glimmer of recognition.

I am reminded of the last visit. She was waiting in the lobby, wearing her favorite outfit: a navy-blue-and-white dotted dress, white shoes and matching white purse. As I approached her, she announced, "I'm all dressed up. My daughter is coming to visit me from California."

I gave her a big hug and announced my arrival from California. She seemed bewildered and didn't recognize me. Of course, I stayed anyway. Mom motioned for me to sit down. "You can visit with me until my daughter arrives. I don't have many visitors. Tell me all about yourself."

Hiding my sorrow and disappointment, I took her hand and smiled at her, making a feeble effort at bits and pieces of conversation. Remembering her love of flowers and gardening, I mentioned the flowers I could view from the window. She yawned; her interest in flowers had vanished. It was time for me to leave. But first, I told her, "I'm going to be celebrating my fiftieth birthday."

Mom asked, "Really? Are you having a party?" Not waiting for an answer, she added, "I think my daughter in California is having a birthday real soon."

Hoping this was the glimmer of recognition I'd been waiting for, I answered, "Yes, I am having a party. How old will your daughter be?"

"She is forty-nine and holding, just like me." Mom giggled.

Astonished by her reply, I made no comment. She stammered, "My daughter is very late. I want to go back to my room now."

"I'll help you," I said. I held Mom's arm as we walked down the hall to her room. She pulled away, so I only squeezed her hand. Carefully, I chose my words of farewell, since time—today, tomorrow and yesterday—are insignificant to her. "I'll visit you real soon." She nodded and waved as I left her room.

Suddenly, I realized I'd been lost in my own thoughts in the middle of my fiftieth birthday party. Tears streamed down my face. Several friends standing nearby stared at me. Concerned, they asked, "Are you all right?"

Feeling flushed, I wiped away my tears, proclaiming loudly, "I want to make a toast."

"I wish to thank everyone for helping me celebrate my fiftieth birthday. I hope you'll all join me for fifty more. Having such wonderful family and friends is what makes my life worthwhile. Together, we'll cope with middle age. But remember, from this day forth, no matter how many candles are on my cake, I'll remain forty-nine and holding."

I think Mom would toast to that.

Georgia A. Hubley

Marathon Women

*The great thing about getting older is that you
don't lose all the other ages you've been.*

Madeleine L'Engle

On an ordinary afternoon in March, Eliza, my sixteen-
year-old daughter, plopped her backpack at my feet,
waved a brochure so close it grazed my nose and made a
declaration. "I'm signing up for the Marine Corps
Marathon. I'll be running with a group that raises money
for AIDS and trains Sunday mornings at seven."

"Seven A.M.—are you crazy?" Then, pausing for less
time than it takes to say "PowerBar," I added, "Tell you
what, I'll sign up with you." It was as though, for just this
microsecond, I had morphed into Jane Fonda.

Now alone, I began to confront different questions. Was
I doing this for myself or for Eliza? Or to bolster my athletic image with friends and acquaintances? Was I willing
to risk injury and, in turn, all the skiing and swing dancing that filled the void left by my divorce? Wasn't there a
simpler bonding opportunity with Eliza? And an easier

way to meet guys? Would I ever find a sports bra that worked? And why would I give up six months of Sunday mornings to arrive at my weekly training sessions earlier than the newspaper arrived on my doorstep? Surely not because running 26.2 miles with thousands of other Type A's had always been my dream. More likely, my interest could have been called curiosity.

Nonetheless, I attended an orientation meeting with Eliza where we signed up and exchanged motives with other hopefuls. A trim secretary, seated beside me, told the group, "My best friend is dying from AIDS. He can't run, so I'm going to do it for him." Ashamed of my ego-centric motivation, I sheepishly introduced myself and expressed my desire to regain a sense of focus in my life. When Eliza announced that she looked forward to training with her mom and raising money for AIDS, I felt exonerated.

At our first weekly training session, we were assigned partners and placed in pace groups. These were the people with whom we would work out as well as run the actual marathon. Eliza's tight-abs pack lined up near the front; despite our neon CoolMax costumes, my partner, Rayford, and I found ourselves in the rear among the less hurried. In the weeks that followed, the pain of placing one foot in front of the other was eased, ironically, by Rayford's sagas of his partner's death from AIDS and living with his own HIV. After we got through a twelve-mile Sunday run by exchanging the ordeals of Rayford's coming out and the final year of my marriage, we agreed on "single in the seventies" as our topic for the upcoming three-hour, fourteen-mile run.

If I were still married, I would have bristled at the idea of striding the equivalent of halfway from Washington to Baltimore (or if you compute all the training miles, round trip to Scarsdale). Isn't it striking how a major life change, like divorce, can transform you into the opposite of who you thought you were? Yet, dim recollections suggested that the marathoner was who I originally was. It seemed that marriage had molded me, temporarily, into someone far more sedentary.

Sometimes I imagined Eliza and myself as two inter-secting rings. I worried that I was treading on her exclu-sive territory when I asked her, "Would you mind if I try to keep up with your group on next week's six-mile mainte-nance run? It might be my only chance to jog with you before the distance increases."

Even before she answered, her response was evident in her bright eyes, lit up the way they did on the trail when her group, in their homestretch, passed me as I was still huffing my way to the halfway mark, and her fellow speed-mates cheered, "Go, Liza's mom."

As Eliza and I planned a party for the fundraising com-ponent of our marathon, she asked, "Mom, how can I take credit for half the donations? They'll be mostly from your friends." I told her that so many of my friends were the parents of her friends and that we were in this together—a partnership. We not only jointly crafted invitations and baked brownies, but we also explained to our guests what raising money for drug therapies that offered hope to people with HIV/AIDS meant to us. I reminded Eliza that, without her, this expansion of my world would never have occurred.

As the training distances mounted, I began to believe that I could actually make it to the finish line. New queries surfaced. Would Eliza wait at the finish line on marathon day until I completed the course? Wasn't it backward—shouldn't the mother be the one to soak up her little girl's I-did-it grin as she crossed the finish line? Or was this one of those role reversals dealt to us by the passing years? On my birthday, Eliza hauled out a cake she had baked and shouted, "Yay!" when I extinguished the candles in one blow.

And on marathon day, there I was sailing by on my merry-go-round as I cried, "Look at me!" Eliza jumped and waved and cheered my victory—hers, mine, ours.

Susan Fishman Orlins

A Gift Through the Generations

My grandmother was of average height, with hazel eyes and salt-and-pepper hair that framed a round face. She had lots of laugh lines and a smile that said she had plenty of love to give. When you hugged her, there was plenty to hang on to. I know because I hugged her a lot.

She wasn't beautiful by today's definition. She didn't turn heads when she walked into a room. If you saw her on the street, you would probably have walked by her without a second glance. There are millions of overweight grandmothers in the world—mine would have blended right in.

But if you did walk by her, if you didn't notice her, you would have been missing someone special.

When I was growing up, going over to my grandmother's was always a special occasion. Although there was little money for new furniture or fancy knickknacks, the house was filled with food and love, in equal amounts. Even now when I think of her, more than thirty years after her death, I find it hard to separate my memories of her from the food she made.

Mostly, I remember her baking. The kitchen table would be covered with flour and she would be up to her arms in dough, her short, nimble fingers able to turn the most mundane ingredients into light, flaky treats from the old country. While my contribution to the baking was often no more than carrying ingredients from the fridge to the table, I took my role as her assistant very seriously.

I don't think I ever felt as close to her as I did then, when it was just the two of us in the kitchen. The older grandchildren would be out shopping or at the movies, too old or too sophisticated to want to spend time with a grandmother who wasn't up on the latest fashion or music group.

Not me. I was exactly where I wanted to be—in a cramped kitchen helping my grandmother. While she measured and kneaded, whipped and stirred, she talked to me. Not about the big world out there, but about the little world in which we lived. The day-to-day stuff: school, food and family.

Mostly what she did was to make me feel loved and wanted. In that kitchen, while I was with her, I was the most important person in her life.

I didn't inherit my grandmother's culinary talents, but I did inherit her eyes, her sense of humor and, unfortunately, her build. For the longest time, I saw that as a curse. Instead of being tall and slender, I was short and dumpy. More peasant stock than royalty.

I blamed my excess padding on both my grandmother and my mother. They were the ones who gave me one hip that's a good inch lower than the other one.

Hips that in the old country would be considered good childbearing hips, but which in this country are too wide.

During my teens and into my twenties, every time I looked in the mirror, I saw only my defects. I was too short, too round-faced, too wide in the hips, too this and too that. There was nothing about my body that I liked.

It was all their fault.

Now, when I look back, I can see how much time and energy I wasted blaming them for passing on their less-than-perfect physical traits. Because I was so focused on what I saw as their negative traits, I forgot the thing that mattered most—their real beauty.

I would look at the last picture ever taken of my grandmother and would feel how much I missed her. But I was missing more than her. I was missing my heritage. Luckily, as I got older, and maybe a little bit wiser, I began to understand and to reach out for it.

My mother is now older than my grandmother was when she died. Over the years, my mother has begun to look more and more like my grandmother. Her hair is starting to go salt-and-pepper and she has begun to put on a little more weight around the middle. There are also more lines on her face than there used to be.

The family resemblance is becoming stronger and stronger with each passing year.

In watching my mother grow more like my grandmother, I am rediscovering just how beautiful my grandmother was and how beautiful my mother is. And in rediscovering their beauty, I am also discovering mine. No, not the textbook definition of beauty, but my own definition. One that is right for me.

I no longer complain quite as much when my mother visits and brings me boxes of food. I now understand that, like her mother before her, my mother sees food as love. While she doesn't bake quite as well as my grandmother did—no one ever will—my mother bakes love into everything she makes.

As I get older, the family resemblance is coming out more and more in me, too. The hazel eyes, the laugh lines, the hair with the first gray ones appearing and, yes, the figure with the full hips and expanding middle. Only now I don't see them as a curse, but as a blessing.

All of these things form a bond between me, my mother, my grandmother and all their mothers who came before them. I only have to look in the mirror to see that I belong to a long line of very special women.

Of course, I expect to get more and more beautiful as I get older, with each laugh line and each gray hair tying me more closely to those who have come before me.

After all, in my family, beauty is a family tradition.

Harriet Cooper

$\overline{7}$

INSIGHTS

In youth we learn; in age we understand.

Marie Ebner-Eschenbach

Sunken Treasure

He who trembles is not bored.

Stendhal

My son's suggestion that we take a scuba diving class together was met with little apprehension. I've always been fascinated with the ocean and readily accepted the idea. I pictured myself exploring ancient shipwrecks in the Caribbean, fighting off man-eating sharks with my trusty dive knife and guiding my son on amazing underwater adventures through colorful coral reefs.

But, from the first day of class, it was apparent that I was no Cousteau. Concentrating on breathing condensed air through a mouth regulator was more difficult than I had imagined. Instead of reveling in the wonder of my new world, I found myself constantly struggling with my equipment and worrying about being thrown into a life-threatening situation.

During our first trip to perform an open-water dive, I discovered an element about diving that isn't in any of the textbooks. It is difficult to cry underwater. It not only floods your mask, but no one can hear your distress.

On my fourth attempt at going under, I gave the sign that I needed to ascend and began inflating my vest without waiting for any acknowledgment from my instructor, Mark. I was twice the age of most of my class, and I knew they were waiting at the bottom shaking their heads, wondering how I ever passed the physical to take a scuba-diving course, anyway. As I broke the surface, I threw back my mask, let the regulator fall from my mouth and took a deep breath of real air.

"Are you okay?" Mark had followed me up, patiently continuing what had become our main line of dialogue.

"My mask keeps flooding, and I can't clear it. I need a different mask." This was a new excuse for me, but it sounded much better than the truth.

He nodded and pointed toward the shore, "Let's go see what we can do."

I kicked rocks and threw equipment, frustrated that I couldn't do this when the other students were adapting with such ease. I have never been one to quit, but I felt there was no way I could finish this class. I ripped off my wetsuit and sat on the shore and screamed.

Mark sat with me, quiet at first, allowing me time to finish my tantrum. "It's okay. You just need to go slower."

"Slower? I'm already the slowest in the class. I just can't do this. I thought I could, but I was wrong." I lowered my head and tried to concentrate on the sound of the waves coming in.

"Everyone has their own pace," he offered.

I let out a deep sigh. "Well, some of us have no pace at all."

"Why don't we meet out here next Saturday, without the rest of the class? We'll take it nice and easy. I know you can do this. There's nothing to be afraid of," he said in an understanding tone.

"Afraid? I'm not afraid of anything," I said with little conviction, looking around to make sure no one else had heard. But he had said the word, and from the hint of a smile I noticed on his face, he was familiar with my reply.

I finally nodded, thankful that he wasn't giving up on me as easily as I was giving up on myself, but not sure if I was going to show up next Saturday or not.

Twenty years ago, scuba diving would have been easy for me. But somewhere between high school and pre-menopause, the daredevil in me had become a worrywart. I spent the week dwelling on the upcoming dive. Although my list of excuses for not making it continued to grow, I knew I really only had two choices. I could either resolve myself to the safe life of a spectator, or I could fight for the adventurer that my mind told me still resided within. As Saturday approached, I knew I at least had to try one more time.

The weather was beautiful, the water calm. My son had joined us to provide me with moral support. Mark held my hand, and together we walked into the water until the bottom disappeared beneath us. As we began our descent, I started to panic, but instead of heading to shore, I shut my eyes and tried to relax. I can do this, I told myself over and over. When I opened my eyes, Mark signaled, "Are you okay?" I hesitated momentarily, and then nodded. We eased along the bottom, my son in front to guide the way.

After a brief exchange with my son via hand signals, Mark nodded his head and pointed toward a deeper area of the dive park. I shook my head, not knowing the agreed-upon destination, but sure they intended to drag me along. I saw my son's eyes through his mask and knew that he was smiling, as he swam to my right side and grabbed my free hand.

Deeper and deeper we went. According to my depth gauge, we were at forty feet, but it seemed like a thousand to me. I focused on breathing and kept my eyes trained on the bottom.

My son tapped my shoulder and pointed ahead. I looked up and could make out a vague outline of a large object in the distance. I stayed between the two and let them guide me.

She lay almost perfectly erect, her topside covered with growth, areas of her side still gleaming white in the water. I released my grip on my two guides and brushed my hand across the small sailboat, wondering what had happened to sentence her to a watery grave. I didn't really want to know the truth, my imagination providing a story of its own.

I caught a glint of something in the silt off her stern and swam toward it. I reached for it and began digging with my hands, eventually revealing a shiny aluminum can that had been part of the sailboat's small cargo at one time. I held it up for my son to see, and he nodded approvingly. Mark clapped his hands and asked if I was okay. This time, I remembered my hand signals and told him I was fine.

As we swam back toward shore, my can safely tucked inside my vest, I allowed the tranquility of the underwater world to envelop me and realized I had been breathing without having to think about it. My mask began to flood, and I cleared it without incident, confidence slowly starting to replace my fear.

I was a long way from the romantic wrecks of the Caribbean, but I had officially made my first wreck dive and retrieved a sunken treasure. I knew the recently awakened adventurer in me would one day take me to that sea, but I was satisfied to go slowly—one aluminum can at a time. Although crying underwater is difficult to do, smiling isn't.

Kelly Gamble

In One Split Second

In the depth of winter, I finally learned that there was in me an invincible summer.

Albert Camus

I had settled into my life. My oldest daughter had just moved away from home to attend college, my son was a junior in high school and my youngest daughter was in seventh grade. My husband of twenty-three years and I had just done some soul-searching and decided we were ready for a change in our careers and wanted to work together, so we opened a closet-designing business in the spring of 2000. It was coming home from work on a rainy night in December that my life suddenly changed. I was looking forward to going home, getting into some warm, comfortable clothes, turning on some holiday music, lighting the Christmas tree and having a hot cup of tea before starting dinner.

I was rounding the bend in front of my daughter's middle school when I was hit head-on by a young girl who had been driving only a few months. She was coming down a hill and around a curve when she lost control of her car. I never saw it coming. The only part of the accident that I do remember is looking out the window into the rain and giving a woman my husband's cell-phone number. It would be a week before I was aware of anything else.

My first moments of awareness are still foggy. I didn't realize it, but I had been in a coma for a week. It was comforting to have my family at my side when I awoke. It was then that I learned about the accident. But I also had some information to share with my family. Although I had been unconscious, I had had a conversation with God during that first week in the hospital.

I was being wheeled into a room for some procedure when I spotted the light. It was only an overhead fluorescent light, but looking into the light I heard THE VOICE. The skeptics in my life have offered their opinions of whom I was talking to (probably the doctor or a nurse), but I know it was God. He told me that I would be okay. I asked if I was going to die, and he assured me in these exact words, "YOU WILL LIVE AND BE IN HEAVEN." When I questioned him—I thought you had to die to go to heaven—he replied, "I'M SENDING YOU BACK TO YOUR FAMILY, AND THAT IN ITSELF IS HEAVEN." Oh, how right he is.

Once I was finally awake, my family was trying to be strong for me and doing what they could to comfort me. And there I was trying to comfort my family, telling them that I knew I would be okay because God had spoken to me. What I didn't know was the extent of my injuries.

I had broken my left foot, my left leg and both wrists. I had lacerated my right knee and left elbow. My lungs had collapsed, my spleen and intestines had ruptured and my right foot had done a 360-degree turn, crushing all the bones in my ankle. According to my doctor, I was lucky to be alive.

I was released from the hospital on Christmas Eve and arrived home to find my home aglow with lights. My family had set up a bedroom for me in our family room so that I could be close to all the activity. I would be bedridden for the next four months, but with the help of my wonderfully devoted husband and three children, I slowly recovered. This whole experience pulled our family together in a way that was pure testimony to our love for one another. I was also blessed to have a fulltime, dedicated nurse and a compassionate but no-nonsense physical therapist. I had to learn to use my hands again and first stand then walk again. The pain was overwhelming, but God answered my prayers for help every time without fail.

For the four months that I was bedridden, every Monday, Wednesday and Friday night my wonderful friends and neighbors provided a full meal from soup to nuts to my family.

I am now in my eleventh month of recovery, and through ongoing physical therapy, I am learning how to walk again. I can't bend my ankle, so some of the activities I loved to do will probably no longer be part of my life— gardening, tennis, camping and driving a car will be severely limited. Even the ability to do my job has been seriously restricted. But I am okay with that. It has given me a chance to reflect on my priorities, to reevaluate what is important and what I want to do with the rest of my life. What difference can I make? I have always enjoyed life; I feel blessed. But now it is even more important that nothing is ever taken for granted again. I have not felt even a moment of anger or resentment or questioned, Why me? God allowed me the peace of mind right from the beginning—that everything would be okay. And it is.

At this stage of my life, I am ready for a new challenge. What I have been through will not change. So I have only to go forward and make the best of it. Life for any of us can change in just one split second. It's how we deal with it that makes the outcome either a disaster or an opportunity. Personally, I am looking forward to the next chapter of my life—certainly less physical but probably more rewarding.

Cecelia Albanese

Everyday Sacred

During my senior year of high school, I worked as an intern at a nonprofit, biweekly newspaper. The newspaper had a board of directors that met monthly. It was during one of those board meetings that I met Janet. She was a wiry, white-haired woman who seemed to burst with energy, vitality and intelligence. She was a writer and social activist who volunteered her time to a number of organizations, one of which was our little paper.

About halfway through my internship, our editor was called away to Belgium for a conference, and Janet was asked to fill in. Almost as soon as she took over, she seemed to transmit her passion for life to the staff. We became more enthusiastic about our work and the stories that we were researching and writing. She definitely gave us a much-needed lift and we found ourselves hoping (with great guilt) that our regular editor wouldn't return. As an intern, there really wasn't a whole lot for me to do, so during the two weeks that Janet was my boss, she tried to make my experience of working at the paper as much fun as possible. Even though a courier service would have been quicker and more efficient, she often sent me out to deliver a package of one type or another with the instruction, "Please deliver this package, but spend the afternoon exploring the city. Enjoy this beautiful spring weather. And don't worry about rushing back. Take your time." For a teenager from the suburbs, this was a wonderful gift of freedom.

One day, Larry, the reporter whom I was assisting, told me that he had met someone at a party who knew Janet and who confided an amazing story. Back in the sixties, Janet had been a CBC radio producer, and one of her assignments had been to produce the 1967 Massey Lectures by Dr. Martin Luther King. Dr. King appreciated her so much that after the talks were broadcast he phoned and offered Janet a job as his personal speechwriter. "Come down and help me heal a sick nation," he had said to her on the phone. Needless to say, it was the opportunity of a lifetime. But Janet declined Dr. King's offer. It seems that the job would have required that she move to Atlanta, and unfortunately, her mother was very sick and needed Janet to care for her. Larry told me that when he first heard the story, he hadn't completely believed it. After all, he had been friends with Janet for over a decade, and she had never even mentioned that she had ever met Dr. King. But, when Larry repeated the story to Janet, she admitted that it was true. Larry told me how amazed he was—first, that a radio producer from Toronto could have been offered such a powerful position; second, that she so unselfishly turned down the position in order to meet her familial obligations; and third, that she never once boasted or bragged about the opportunity she had turned down. As I rode the train home that evening, I thought a lot about what Larry had told me. At the age of eighteen, contemplating a career in journalism, I was very ambitious, and I had trouble understanding how Janet could have given up the writing assignment of a lifetime to play nursemaid. After all, didn't she know what was important?

The next day at work, the editorial assistant was giving

me some instructions on the archiving of some files when Janet called from across the room, "Joanne, can you come over here for a second?"

"Sure, Janet, just give me five minutes," I called over my shoulder.

"No, no, now. Hurry, come quick."

I practically dropped the armful of files I was carrying as I rushed over to where she was standing. "What is it?" I asked, expecting to be filled in on some sort of crisis.

Instead, Janet smiled, put her arm around my shoulders and turned me in the direction of the window. "Look out there. Isn't that the most beautiful thing you have ever seen?"

It took me a few seconds to realize what she was referring to. Among the dilapidated buildings of Toronto's east waterfront was a small vacant lot. The grass was incredibly long and a forceful spring breeze blew the blades gently in unison. At that moment, the vacant lot almost looked like blue-green brushed suede.

We looked at the view together for a few moments, then she said, "I just wanted to share that with you. You can go back to what you were doing." I think I probably looked at her as though she had just lost her mind. At the time, I didn't understand or appreciate the lesson she was trying to teach me. But the memory stayed with me. And it wasn't until years later that I understood that Janet wasn't showing me blades of grass blowing in the breeze, but she was showing me how to see the extraordinary in the ordinary.

Now I realize that, for Janet, spending the last precious years with her mother was more important than providing a voice to one of the great leaders of our time. Janet was wise enough to know that everyday events can carry more profound beauty and meaning than the "big" opportunities. And that the ability to find beauty in the mundane is an incredible gift because it means that beauty is always abundant. Even in a vacant lot.

Joanne Morrison

A Perfect Moment

The cream of enjoyment in this life is always impromptu. The chance walk; the unexpected visit; the unpremeditated journey; the unsought conversation or acquaintance.

Fanny Fern

It was the weekend of my parents' sixtieth wedding anniversary party, and there was a lot to do. I had traveled from my home in Chicago, where I live, to my parents' home in northern New Jersey on Friday, and my two brothers, my sister-in-law and I had been working almost nonstop to put all of the final details in place. My brother Jerry had to call the caterer; his wife, Mary, had to buy the paper goods; I had to call the guests who hadn't responded to find out if they were coming; and my brother Rick had to pick up the cake. Along with these tasks, we had my parents' health needs to contend with. My parents were both in their eighties. My mother had suffered a stroke, and now needed help with many routine activities, and my father had been receiving chemotherapy for the leukemia that had recently been diagnosed.

It was stressful, to say the least. In addition to contend-
ing with the immediate tasks associated with the party, my
brothers and I had stayed up late Saturday night discussing
our parents' precarious health, and the challenges we
would certainly face in the near future. We talked about it
often, on the phone and whenever we got together, but
there was never enough time. My parents' health needs
changed in often sudden and unpredictable ways, so it was
impossible to really plan for the future. We all worried
about what the next few years, months, or even days might
bring.

The party was scheduled for Sunday afternoon. It was
to be an open house at my parents' home; more than fifty
people were expected to show up and squeeze into the
modest, three-bedroom ranch house. I woke up early on
Sunday, already thinking of everything I had to do: set up
chairs, move the dining-room table, take my mother to get
her hair and her nails done. I was feeling stressed before I
even got out of bed.

My parents were still sleeping, and my brothers
wouldn't be coming over for another couple of hours, so I
decided to go for a run. Maybe that would help relieve my
stress. I quickly pulled on my sweat pants and sweatshirt
and a windbreaker, and stepped outside, quietly pulling
the door closed behind me.

I jogged down the quiet street and up the next block, a
long, winding street with many large, beautifully land-
scaped homes. The last time I was here it was late summer,
and the yards were an explosion of color, flowers and
bushes of every kind spilling over the lawns and porches,
and children's bicycles strewn in the driveways.

But now in the last weekend of March, it was chilly,
gray and drizzling slightly. The ground was muddy, the
grass sparse. I shivered and I pulled the hood of my windbreaker over my head and ran a little faster as I crossed

into the country club on the other side of the highway. My footsteps were the only sound, slapping on the damp pavement as I jogged down the road.

Usually, I enjoyed this route and the routine of running. But today, I was distracted. It was cold and the flowerbeds were still bare, and I had so much on my mind. I was completely engrossed in my thoughts, worrying about my parents' long-term needs and also about the things I still needed to do today to prepare for the party. I barely noticed my surroundings.

I was jogging along, head down, when I slipped. Suddenly, I was sprawled in the wet grass on the side of the road. I knew immediately that I wasn't hurt, but I was out of breath and my shoe was untied. As I tied my shoe, I looked up for the first time and noticed exactly where I was. I had jogged a little more than halfway around the lake that sits in the middle of the country club. When I was here last, in the summer, there were children splashing in the water, ducks quacking, bright flowers lining the road.

But today the lake was completely still. The trees, still leafless in early spring, stood out sharply against the gray sky, their trunks darkened by the mist. The ground along the edge of the lake was barren, with no hint of the riot of color that would burst from the soil in less than a month's time. And there was not another person to be seen, not a single car on the road, not even the cry of a bird or a duck to break the silence.

It was utterly pristine and perfect, and I thought it was the most beautiful thing I had ever seen. I sat there for several more minutes, just watching the stillness, listening to the silence.

Now that I wasn't running, I started to feel cold, so I reluctantly got up and started back towards my parents' house. But now I was acutely aware of what I was seeing, of where I was at that moment. I realized that I couldn't even remember the first half of my run. I had been so focused on the things that would come after, on everything I had to do, that I hadn't noticed whether there were buds on the forsythia bush at the entrance to the country club, or whether the house on the corner that had been half-built in the summer was finished yet, or whether Maynard, the elderly dog belonging to my parents' equally elderly neighbor, was lying in his usual spot on the front porch.

When I got back to the house, my parents were both up. My mother was sitting at the kitchen table in her bathrobe, reading the morning paper. My father was at the stove, making coffee. They looked up and greeted me as I came in.

"Hi, honey," my mother said, as she took my hand and squeezed it; her hands were soft and warm.

"How was your walk? Do you want some coffee?" my father asked, smiling.

It was late; I had been gone longer than I'd planned, and there was so much to do. *I really should go take my shower, get dressed and get to work right away,* I thought.

But it was warm in the kitchen, and the coffee smelled wonderful, and my parents were both there—it was an utterly perfect moment.

"I'd love some coffee," I said.

In the end, everything I needed to do for the party got done in time. And the party itself was wonderful. Celebrating sixty years of marriage is, of course, an amazing achievement. And for my parents, being able to share that celebration with their family and their oldest and closest friends was especially rewarding.

But for me, the best part of the whole day was that hour I spent sitting in the kitchen with my parents that morning, drinking coffee—just enjoying the moment, unburdened by the past or the future.

I know, of course, that I can't always have that luxury. As my parents grow older, the problems and the worries I have about them aren't likely to go away, and I'm going to have to continue to deal with them. But I think it's going to be a little easier now, because my focus has changed. Even though it's important to plan for the future, I'm going to make sure I'm not looking so far ahead all the time that I overlook the special and perfect moments that still happen, every day. I'm going to make sure I look for those moments, and savor them.

Phyllis L. Nutkis

The Reason

The spur of delight comes in small ways.

Robert L. Stevenson

It was Easter Sunday, 1990. The trees were now more than halfway green. I remember being slightly nervous, but it had helped that we had done lots of singing in the Easter Service earlier in the morning. Even though I was nervous, I was ready. I enjoyed being a part of The Son-Shine Singers. I enjoyed ministering to the sick, the old, the abandoned and the hopeless through singing, worshiping, talking and praying with these precious people.

As I pulled into the parking lot of the rickety old nursing home, I saw the familiar faces I had grown to love gathered together in a circle of prayer. This had been our custom since the group was formed nearly a year ago. I parked the car and hurried to join them.

After the prayer had ended and everyone had received greetings and hugs, Tim, the lead guitarist, asked to speak to me. Getting right to the point, he said, "We weren't supposed to come here till next Sunday. The charge nurse is pretty upset because we're here. She wasn't ready for us, but she said to go ahead, as long as we were here. Did you have the right date?"

"I'm pretty sure I did," I replied. "Let me check my book." I went back to the car and found the book in which I meticulously noted all of our upcoming engagements. Sure enough, I had penciled in the next Sunday for Brookside. I felt stupid and embarrassed. I had never made this kind of mistake before. I walked back to Tim.

"I blew it, Tim," I said sheepishly. "I'm sorry. I don't know how I managed to mess the dates up. Gettin' old, I guess."

Tim just smiled and shrugged. "C'mon. It's time to do it. Don't worry about it." Still, a feeling of apprehension began to creep over me.

The residents were just being escorted into the Activities Room when we walked through the door. Ken and Frank were tuning their guitars. Dawn was arranging the music stands. Kenny and Sheila were helping to seat patients and roll in wheelchairs. The charge nurse was glowering at us.

Looking out at the faces as I prepared to open the program, I saw the cruel results of age and disease: Alzheimer's, crippling arthritis, diabetes, strokes—the list seemed endless. But I knew that what we were doing was worthwhile. We cared for these people, and we were there to share ourselves with them, if only for a few hours.

I started in the usual way by introducing our group and encouraging everyone to sing along if they knew the words. I don't remember all the songs we sang, nor do I remember most of the things I said. However, I do remember that when we started to sing "Amazing Grace," one dear old soul sitting in the front shouted, "I hate that song! Please don't you sing that song!"

Of course, the music and the singing stopped. I turned around to look at the group. We had never encountered this before. Hearing no suggestions, I turned back toward the elderly lady, and gently said, "We're sorry if we offended you in any way. If you'd rather we didn't sing that song, we won't."

"Can't you see I'm blind?" she asked. "He never gave me back my sight. How come? The song says, '. . . was blind but now I see.' Well, I don't see! So, please don't sing that song!"

I glanced at the charge nurse. She was smiling at me. But it was a smile of disdain. The whole day was starting to disintegrate. Recovering my wits, I whispered to Tim, "Let's do 'I'll Fly Away.'" It took me until the third stanza to fully regain my voice.

At the end of our performance, it came to me to close in a different way than usual. "How many of you know the song, 'Jesus Loves Me'?" I asked. "Would you sing it with me?" The group quickly joined in.

I thanked everyone for the opportunity to be there. I began to walk around and to talk to people. After about five minutes, I saw the charge nurse headed toward me. "Are you just about finished?" she demanded. "We have other things we have to do." I nodded my head and walked back toward the makeshift stage. I was feeling defeated, foolish and unwanted. I couldn't wait to leave.

"Excuse me, sir?"

I stopped. Fearing more trouble, I turned to face the little woman who was smiling at me. "Yes?" I smiled back. "Can I help you?" I could see that she had tears in her eyes.

"I just wanted to tell you something. You see that man over there?" she asked, pointing to the corner. "That's my husband. He's a retired minister. He had a bad stroke five years ago, and I had no choice but to bring him here. I couldn't take care of him. And I came here to live with him a year ago. He hasn't spoken for almost two years. About three weeks ago, I began praying that God would send someone here today, Easter, so we could worship together, like we did for almost forty-five years. But, oh, how I prayed for a miracle! I just wanted you to know that when you started to sing 'Jesus Loves Me,' my Harold started to sing. Can you imagine? He started to sing! I just wanted to thank you. God bless you. You came. Just like I asked for."

She took a step and wrapped her frail arms around me in a hug. I looked up and saw the charge nurse crying. She had overheard our conversation. Her face was somehow different now. And then I knew why the schedule book had been "wrong." We had been on God's schedule, not ours.

Donald S. Verkow

The Gift of the Middle

As a nurse for the past twenty-five years, I've spent the majority of my life helping others get back to "health," ignoring my own as it steadily declined—until last year, when I hit the wall, so to speak. Seems like one day I woke up and found myself grossly obese, falling on my knees— not in prayer (that came later) but because they wouldn't hold me up any longer. I was also graced (yes, graced) with arthritis, degenerative disc disease, spinal stenosis, fibromyalgia and sleep apnea—all at the same time. In general, I was a mess, unable to work and fearing the loss of my independence and financial ruin.

I started to pray, "God, please make me healthy again. I've got so much more to do." That's how it started.

And as time went by, with knee surgery, therapy, gas-troplasty and the loss of 160 pounds, I was able to go back to work, am doing great and am looking forward to fifty at full-speed. I call this past year the "Gift of the Middle," for it really has been a gift—every ache and pain a ribbon, and all the misery and despair the wrapping.

The real gift was that I learned to pray, not just to ask for something, but actually to have a one-on-one conversation with God. Lying on the stretcher, waiting to be taken in for my gastroplasty, I was scared but too tired and fed up with everything to want to even deal with it, much less handle it. That's when I had that first talk with God. It was the first time I have ever just given my life over to him and said, "Okay, God, you handle it." It was so easy, just letting him have it. I can't say I knew everything would be okay—I didn't—but I knew that whatever happened, it would be his doing. And that was okay. I felt immediate release, like someone had finally lifted a load off my soul. I felt at peace with whatever the outcome.

And so, as I start out on this journey of life, on the other side of the middle, I begin each day with, "Okay God, you're in charge. Take the rest of me—and make the best of me." I look forward to each day, including every ache and pain—the ribbons and bows on my Gift of the Middle.

Sandra B. Smith

Crayons, Notebooks and Pencil Bags

Walking into my local supermarket this week, I was surprised to discover parents and kids stuffing carts with Technicolor folders, dazzling bright nylon backpacks and crisp cellophane packets of yellow #2 pencils and blue-black pens. It's August in Texas, back-to-school time. I felt wistful and more than a little sad watching them buying school supplies, for this annual ritual is no longer mine, my sons' school days long behind them and our grandchild only six months old.

When the boys were school-age, I viewed the ritual as a challenge, trying to see how many items I, too, could buy before the first day of school. From experience, I knew there would be no risk in stocking a dozen plastic zippered pencil bags, reams of notebook paper, dozens of folders and portfolios, boxes of pencils and crayons, a few pairs of scissors and some bottles of glue. I'd purchase sheets of poster board, ready for the night a child would suddenly cry at bedtime, "Mom, I have to have a poster for Safety Day tomorrow." No hurried trip to the store for us. In fact, I could offer not just plain vanilla poster board, but black, yellow, green and blue.

But I may have overdone this buying-in-advance-of-need. Rearranging my study closet last month, I found several unopened packets of notebook paper, a few pristine spirals, some pocket folders, and that staple of the elementary school list, the plastic pencil bag. Finding the pencil bag surprised me because my youngest child, the one who went through pencil bags as though they were made of tissue paper, is now thirty-one. Why did I keep buying school supplies so long after there was no longer a need?

And why did I feel sad this week in the store when I realized this was no longer my ritual? I remembered that much of the joy I derived from participating in this ritual when the boys were school-age was the knowledge that it marked the end of the summer. In a few blessed days, my time would become my own again. No matter how nice it had been having the children around for the summer months, it was going to be even nicer having them back in school and someone else's responsibility for a few hours a day. So I shopped liberally—no child of mine was going to be sent home from school for not having all the essentials. But now all my time is my own, to squander or spend wisely as I choose.

Maybe I'm yearning for the simplicity of family life when a closet full of school supplies was assurance I could satisfy my sons' future needs—a new box of crayons enough to get a day off to a good start, a colorful sheet of poster board enough to stir the imagination, a crisp portfolio incentive enough to write a book report. But life is more complex now. Buying supplies no longer serves to protect my children from unhappiness, and the supplies themselves no longer provide effective armor for life's journeys. No spiral organizer will be sufficient equipment to help one son through the decision of changing careers, and no glossy lunch box will console another for the pain of a divorce.

Seeing these parents buying supplies stirs up a restlessness inside me, perhaps a need for a goal as clear-cut as the objectives for each grade, whether memorizing the multiplication tables or mastering phonics. Perhaps I, too, want to equip myself for some task that I cannot yet describe. Or, perhaps what I miss the most is living, through the children and the start of school, the limitless possibility of new beginnings. Sharpened pencils with tender pink erasers and three-ring binders full of blank ruled paper openly proclaim that it's always possible to begin again.

A new school year brings the possibility of friendships, activities and abilities not yet manifest, all as fresh as the school supplies spilling from supermarket shelves. Maybe I simply want to feel like a kid starting school again, sharing the spirit of adventure and hopeful newness. If this is it, the cure is simple. The next time I go shopping, I'll just buy myself some crayons and a notebook. I already have a pencil bag.

SuzAnne C. Cole

The Circle of Life

I have a tradition of displaying the cards my family receives for life's many events. My husband's birthday was our most recent milestone so the windowsill in the kitchen holds the few greetings that arrived to mark his thirty-fifth. Lately, however, the window has crowded: colorful cards are lined up, all cozy along the sill, while others hang from grown wooden mullions above. To my husband's disappointment, these latest arrivals are not in his honor, as his birthday has arrived on the heels of a more substantially acknowledged event: the birth of our second son, Aidan. Aidan's welcoming cards, adorned with lambs and moons and jumping cows, continue to trickle in day after day, and admittedly look a little out of place next to the cards poking fun of my husband's "advanced" age. Still, I keep them together for tradition's sake.

It's the cards I've added of late that make me question the whole arrangement: the ones with hazy pictures of flower gardens, deserted beach scenes and mountain-top views; whose greetings read, "You're in Our Thoughts" and "With Sympathy." These are the sentiments that don't seem to fit with the party hats and teddy bears and balloons.

They have trouble fitting in my heart as well.

I am as full and as conflicted as that window, flooded with an uneasy coupling of joy and sorrow, celebration and mourning—torn by the juxtaposition of events in my life, and blessed with the grace bestowed from the experience of both birth and death occurring within weeks of each other.

This year, I have received the gift of motherhood again, only to have my own mother stolen away by disease; she was given two months to live while I had two months left in my pregnancy. The two of us, hundreds of miles apart, agonizingly separated by the birth of a child who would be such a blessing at this time of loss. To me, it seemed as if my mother and I were engaged in some kind of parallel dance; one spinning toward death, the other toward life. Each facing an ending and a beginning; both crossing a threshold of no return. Sometimes, rather than moving together, it felt like we were on some terrible collision course, and inwardly I feared that the birth of my child would bring on her death. As I began the work of labor with its all-consuming pain, I was acutely aware of my mother's suffering, and of how, in many ways, we were sharing in the same process—one of struggle and surrender, both surrounded by loved ones who helped "midwife" our passage.

A week earlier than expected, I gave birth to our son, Aidan, in our home in Vermont. Three hundred miles away, my mother lay in a hospital bed in her own home by the sea, unable to walk or even sit, but there to answer the phone when I called with the news. I don't think I'll ever forget that moment. I was so painfully aware that she'd probably never meet her new grandson, and yet I was so grateful that she was there in this moment to share in my joy and accomplishment.

Bonnie Kelly Bradley, age fifty-seven, outlived her

sentence of two months by several weeks. She died on the morning of my husband's thirty-fifth birthday, weaving our lives even closer together in her death. My mother passed from this world surrounded by her eight children, including my nursing babe who cried out just as she took her last breaths. I don't know that I'll ever fully comprehend the connection between their two emerging souls, but it certainly was a powerful one.

It's funny how life gets dished out sometimes . . . with heaps of sorrow or heaps of joy, or in my case, heaps of both at once. Holding both the season of death and the season of birth is a mind-altering experience, I can tell you. As these seasons pass, I've looked at the strange collection of cards in my window and realized why I've kept them together. . . . I am trying to become whole. If I can integrate these experiences on my windowsill, perhaps I can integrate them in my heart and life as well.

I've learned so much being present to both life and loss, and it has helped me to be open to the gifts that each brings. There was an abundance of blessings in the pain of losing my mother. It was the depth of our sorrow that made the expression of our love so powerful, so very palpable—as if the two emotions needed each other, as if they were meant to be held together.

One of my greatest lessons came in the quiet hours sitting at my mother's side with baby Aidan on her lap napping. Ever watch a baby sleep? It's a profoundly spiritual experience, deeply soothing and meditative. What struck me most is how at one moment Aidan's face would light up with a smile, and in the next, his lips would quiver, his brow wrinkle, and he'd let out a whimper that could pierce your heart. I love those sleepy smiles, but I've always worked to chase away the cries. And then it occurred to me: Maybe they belong together. Maybe Aidan, in these early days, was being prepared to be present to both the joy and loss his life would hold.

Children seem to know this without reflection, as does Mother Earth. For on the morning of my mother's death, the sun shone brightly, and a beautiful ocean breeze blew through the windows of her newly vacant home. Her grandsons jumped on the trampoline outside the window where she lay in final sleep, while her young granddaughters sat beside her, lovingly touching her face without any hesitation, and talking casually about their own deaths one day.

There was so much healing in the fullness of my experience, and I'll hold it close as I walk the days of my life. When I'm faced with a new challenge, I draw upon my labor and birth, and upon the death of my mother as a well of strength. On those days when I feel I can't handle a fussy baby, another diaper change, or the cold and darkness that sometimes grow inside me, I remember Aidan's delivery, I remember my mother's passing, and I know that beauty lies within this moment, too, if I choose to see it; my life a reflection of how I hold each and every experience.

My son Aidan is two months old now, and his face has begun to reflect back that which he has received: countless hours of love and wonder and devotion. It was the same with my mother. In the end, all that she had given in life was reflected upon her.

Kelly Salasin

I Worked Hard for That Furrowed Brow

Just because the FDA has approved of Botox doesn't mean that I have to. In fact, since 835,000 people have already had their foreheads injected with the paralyzing fluid that keeps them from being able to frown, I figure that somebody has to frown for them.

When I first read about Botox as a cosmetic, I thought there was something vaguely charming about the idea. After all, the microbe created by the U.S. Army to inflict botulism poisoning on our enemies was now being used for domestic and aesthetic purposes. Talk about beating your swords into tweezers.

But even before the FDA gave the green light, we heard that Botox gatherings of women had become the Tupperware parties of the twenty-first century. Only what's being preserved are the women, not the leftovers.

This is not, I promise you, a screed about the political incorrectness of plastic surgery or vanity. Nor is it about how beauty is only skin deep.

Over the years, my attitudes—like my jaw line—have softened toward women who choose to change their faces rather than live with them. I know there's a line between those who "need" to be "fixed" and those who don't,

between those who need surgery—think burn victim—
and those who need therapy—think Michael Jackson. But
I'm less inclined to draw it for anyone else.

When forty-seven-year-old Greta Van Susteren became
the poster anchor for plastic surgery, I thought the criti-
cism was way over the top. As she said, "Having plastic
surgery isn't shoplifting." If it were, nearly every female-
and-fifty face on TV would be behind bars. After all, most
of us choose, earn, some self-improvement. Where is the
unacceptable point on the aesthetic slope between braces
and face-lifts? Aging gracefully does not mean that you
have to age gray-ly. So, you tell me the cut-off between
hair color and collagen.

Nevertheless.

As a woman of a certain age—the age targeted by the
hefty $53 million ad campaign being launched by
Allergan, the maker of Botox—every time someone I
know, or watch, has some "work" done, I have a vague
feeling of being deserted. It's as if they'd left a threatened
neighborhood, the endangered, natural species free range,
and sided with the image-makers.

Remember back when Gloria Steinem turned forty? (If
you do, it's probably too late for Botox, anyway.) She said:
"This is what forty looks like." At that time, it was a state-
ment that said proudly: We are not your grandmother's
forty-year-old.

Of course, forty never did necessarily look like Gloria.
But what happens when fifty is supposed to look like
forty? Does that mean the whole standard of aging has
changed? Do we think sixty should look like fifty? Does,
say, a seventy-year-old Barbara Walters actually change
the future for older women on TV? Or is an older woman
only accepted if she doesn't look her age?

Chemical peels. Endoscopic lifts. Microfat injections.
Eyelid lifts. Face-lifts. Botox marketed to women the way

Viagra is to men (never mind). How long before looking "your age" is regarded as a slatternly failure of effort? How long before any woman who doesn't try one of the above is dismissed as someone who is "letting herself go"?

I have always loved the expression, "letting yourself go." Where do you go, when you let yourself? To the recycle bin or to freedom? On Oscar night, in a sea of nipped and tucked, siliconed and surgeried women, the only seamed faces over fifty belonged to the likes of Judi Dench, Maggie Smith and Helen Mirren. They are all character actors. Is that where they let themselves go? Into character?

In the past few years, I have found myself looking at older women as harbingers of the future. I'm looking for energy and confidence, and yes, attractiveness. Who do I want to be when I grow up? I am sure there are young women searching for the same clues. But there's no way to find them on the Botox party masks. This is the real symbolism of Botox. It eliminates lines temporarily by paralyzing muscles. It offers an actual trade-off. You trade the ability, literally, to express your emotions—furrow that brow, crinkle that eye—for a flawless appearance. In the search for approval from others, you hide what you are feeling. Especially anger.

This seems to my cranky eye and creased eyebrow to be exactly the opposite of my goal to become an outspoken, maybe even outrageous, laugh-out-loud, nothing-left-to-lose old lady. Spare me the Botox. I plan to remain the kind of character actor who wears her emotions, not on her sleeve or on her surgeon's bill, but on her face.

Ellen Goodman

Body Work

Some think it's holding on that makes one strong, but sometimes it's letting go.

Sylvia Robinson

I remember the moment when it first happened, the first time I found myself dissatisfied with my body. I was fourteen, lying on my back. I noticed with displeasure that my stomach did not curve inward the way my friend Lisa's did.

Since then I have been on a roller-coaster ride. I have been alternately pleased by and disgusted with my body. I have received some positive comments—but also many negative ones—about my physique. One time while out jogging, I heard a man yell out to me, "Keep it up! You need to do *a lot* of running!" Even my family has gotten into the act, telling me when I am "plump" or advising me when my face has gotten "full."

I have had ambivalent feelings about my body most of my life. Pretty women—reed *thin* women—reap the rewards in our society, whether it's men, attention or jobs.

If a woman is not attractive—and slender—she is ignored. So, like most women, I have wanted to be slim. But I have never gone on a strict diet or embarked on a rigorous exercise program. Clearly, part of me desires to have the perfect body while another part wishes it weren't so important.

A couple of years ago, I started volunteering for the Meals on Wheels chapter in my community. The people I brought meals to certainly weren't obsessing over their appearance and their weight. They had more important things to think about, like long-term illnesses and perilous financial situations. I realized then that striving for the perfect body is a superficial pursuit, to say the least.

I realized something further. There is only so much I can do to alter my shape. I can exercise regularly and eat healthfully, but I will never measure up to the impossible ideal our society has set. Sure, there's starvation and plastic surgery, but I prefer not to resort to such extreme and potentially dangerous methods.

On the other hand, there is a lot I can do about my feelings of compassion for those less fortunate, my understanding of cultures different from my own and my actions on behalf of people not as healthy and fit as I am. I have decided to focus on these pursuits rather than the futile quest for a better body.

After all, I would rather be admired for the breadth of my kindness than the length of my legs, the size of my heart than the fullness of my breasts, and the shape of my thoughts rather than the proportions of my body. It's taken me twenty-seven years, but I've learned to love my body—after all, it's where I live.

Carol Ayer

The Leap

It is not the mountain we conquer, but ourselves.

Sir Edmund Hillary

I slowly became aware that I was at the bottom of a ravine watching bright drops of red blood splash onto green leaves inches from my face. I heard Marylou call down to me. My first thought crystallized abruptly: *Damn! I am old.*

I had seen the rope swing the day before, when a friend had pointed it out—a thick braid hanging from a towering cedar that stood a few yards down a steep-sloped ravine. Tied to a limb more than fifty feet above the ground, the rope hung invitingly within reach. That sight tugged at something in me, seemed to beckon—or challenge. I reluctantly walked away, but the next day I was back on the trail, this time with my friend Marylou. I didn't mention the rope swing to her, but I knew that's where we were heading.

Early spring sunlight filtered through the tall cedars

and scraggly oaks, warming us as we walked along a path that followed the irrigation canal through our hilly neighborhood. Dogwood trees were on the verge of blooming, their white buds plump with promise. White butterflies flitted around the trees, looking like blossoms that had taken flight. The only sound aside from our voices was the murmuring water flowing alongside the trail. My pulse quickened as we neared the spot. I stopped and showed the rope to Marylou.

A few months earlier, I had turned forty and had plunged into a self-critical—and self-pitying—assessment of my life. I was noticing physical changes—none of which were improvements—progressing at a startling rate. I saw my dentist frequently as my old fillings crumbled and needed replacing; I found more gray in my hair every morning; I suddenly noticed wrinkles, instead of laugh lines; my body seemed to be threatening mutiny at every turn. I was confronting the inevitable physical decline of aging—and it had left me sullen.

And what had I done with my life? My sixteen-year marriage had settled into a comfortable but dull routine, and my two preteens were requiring less and less of my attention. I seemed to have spent my life driving kids around, taking the dog to the vet, and doing countless loads of laundry. Taking care of home and family—that hadn't even been considered a *real* job in several decades. And just look at all the things I *hadn't* done. I hadn't paddled down the Amazon; I hadn't competed in the Olympics; I hadn't negotiated world peace. In other words, I was a complete failure.

I was in this dejected frame of mind when I stood before the rope.

In some less-than-logical twist of reasoning, this rope seemed to be offering me a chance to defy my age—a chance to prove that I hadn't lost the enthusiastic, vibrant, adventurous spirit of youth. I fought against my fear and better judgment as I carefully made my way down the leaf-strewn bank. The rope felt heavy and coarse in my suddenly sweaty palms. As I looked out over the ravine, above the tops of trees, a blend of fear and exhilaration engulfed me. I wavered between apprehension and desire. *Should I do this?* In my mind ensued the debate between cautious common sense and the impulse to "fly." I was thinking that common sense would prevail, until Marylou, who waited nervously on the trail above, told me that this was something she would have done when she was *younger*, but not now.

That settled it. A deep breath and in an instant I was off the ground, swinging out over the ravine, above treetops, flying into the cloudless sky, surprised by the length of my swing before I paused, suspended briefly in midair, and followed an equally long, graceful descent back toward the bank. Filled with euphoria, beaming, I sailed through the air as if in slow motion, embracing every thrilling moment.

When I arrived back at my starting point, I planted my feet triumphantly on the hillside. But the steep hillside was slippery with fallen leaves and loose dirt. When I thought I was safely on the ground—when I released the rope—I found myself suddenly plummeting down the hill. The law of gravity that defined the course of my flight, the same law responsible for my sagging body parts, was now compelling me toward the bottom of the ravine. I ran fast, trying to get my balance, trying to make my feet catch up with my head, but I could see the boulders and trees below were my inevitable destination. Here was the time I should have been thinking, *Tuck and roll*, but all I could manage was, *This is not good*, before plunging headlong down the bank.

And then, lying on the ground and watching blood drip

from my head, I was certain that this was irrefutable proof I was past my prime. I tried to push that dismal thought aside and concentrate on climbing back up the slippery bank to the trail. Still numb, I scaled the hill, my bruised hands clutching at the underbrush, not daring to look either up or down—my recent fearlessness apparently left in the dirt along with layers of skin from my hands and knees. I reached the trail, and Marylou looked anxious as she surveyed the damage. Blood was dripping in a steady stream from the side of my head, and a piece of skin was laid open on the bridge of my nose. I had unwisely stopped my fall by landing face-first against a large rock.

But I was up—walking and talking—and since I couldn't see my injuries, since the adrenaline was still keeping the pain at bay, my immediate concern was my pride. *How stupid! How really, incredibly stupid!* Marylou took off her white T-shirt and dipped it in the canal so that I could clean the dirt and blood from my face (this slight variation on tradition binds us together forever in my mind as blood-sisters), and then she led me to the nearest house for help.

I wore the evidence of the fall on my face for weeks: two black eyes, which weren't really black but dark purple, followed by red in progressively lighter shades that eventually settled into a sickly yellow-green. Black spiderlike stitches crawled across my head and nose. (My broken nose had to be "set," which involved the sadistic use of a metal rod up one nostril.) A plastic splint affixed to my nose with white medical tape completed my new look. I found myself having to explain my appearance over and over again. I considered lying—a car accident would have been less embarrassing.

But something odd happened when I told people the story, admitting to swinging out over a steep ravine on a rope. Something like awe was mixed with their concern and surprise. And instead of confirmation of my aging condition, my lost youth, I was repeatedly told, with words or raised eyebrows, that I must still be a kid. Who but a kid would do this? Marylou started calling me Sheena, Queen of the Jungle.

Not long after that leap, I went back to school full-time. I started dyeing my hair, adding just a hint of red. I joined a book group. I started writing again. And now, when I look in the mirror, I no longer see the wrinkles—not first, anyway. I see the C-shaped scar on my nose, I see blue sky and treetops, I feel the fresh spring air rushing against my face—and I remember that I can fly!

Marjorie Woodall

I Never Saw My Mother Do a Sit-Up

We turn not older in years, but every day.

Emily Dickinson

The dress was a full-length sheath the color of sweetened condensed milk, its simplicity the perfect canvas for the hemline's hand-painted flowers. Wearing it, I was a fashion success and I basked in the symphony of compliments it garnered.

But fitting into the dress year after year was difficult, for although shapeless by design, I had to stay in shape to wear it. Despite daily exercise, sometime between birthdays fifty-one and fifty-two, my metabolism slipped into a coma and my svelte figure, along with my derriere, disappeared. Although I'd noticed my pants were snug at the waist and baggy in back, it was my husband who questioned the geographic relocation of my rear. "Where'd your butt go?" was his eloquent query.

To reveal my buttocks' travel plan, I tried on the dress. With my head and arms through the appropriate openings, the barometer by which I judged weight gain followed gravity and flowed southward. But unlike in previous migrations, the dress stopped its journey mid-way. Gently tugging on one side, then the other, I eased the fabric down my hips and over my thighs. Then I looked in the closet mirror. From waist to knees, the dress clung to what appeared to be a lunar landscape made of dough. I'd found my butt.

Determined to wear the dress to an upcoming family celebration, I immediately began starving and sweating calories.

For several weeks, I worked out with a variety of video partners and a thigh gizmo (the purchase about which I was so embarrassed, I set the box and its packaging in the alley by a neighbor's trash can). I nibbled foods befitting the rodent culture and stuck my nose in the Oreo package to sniff dessert. I was miserable but determined to fit into that dress.

It was during a crunch session with Miss Abs of Steel that I suddenly recalled I'd never seen my mother do a sit-up. It wasn't as if she hadn't had side rolls and a tummy bulge. My mother had managed her flab by wearing a girdle.

I remembered sitting cross-legged on my parents' quilted bedspread and watching as Mama prepared for a special evening out with Daddy. Stepping into her All-in-One, she'd grip the sides and pull upward, while at the same time doing the most wonderful dance . . . a perfor-mance that involved much shimmying and shoving and squishing and shaking until everything loose between her knees and armpits was encased in latex. With her firmly curvy, hourglass figure, she'd looked like Sophia Loren. *Sophia Loren!*

Grabbing the dress, I headed to the mall to buy myself a girdle. I soon learned that yesterday's shapewear is today's control undergarment. With names like Thigh Trimmer, Minimizer, Smoothie, Belly Buster, Body

Reformer, Invisible Shaper and Slim-O-Matic, it wasn't difficult to envision their purpose—a quick lump-and-bump fix.

I tried on the shapewear and like my mother, I danced my looseness into the slimming casing of each. When 100-percent squished, I slipped on the dress and watched in the department store mirror as it glided over a spandex highway and journeyed to my ankles. Preening, I appraised my silhouette, now a smooth and slinky curve. For the price of $27.00, the lunar landscape was gone, and I'd reincarnated the figure of my inner babe, who in the dim dressing room, surprisingly resembled Sophia Loren.

I don't dress my inner babe every day, but when fitting her into a pretty dress means "lifting the fallen," it's spandex, not sit-ups I now turn to.

I am, after all, my mother's daughter.

EllynAnne Geisel

Life Lessons Well Learned

I attended an all-girls, private Catholic high school, and in retrospect, the four years I spent roaming the hallowed halls of that institution were undeniably the best part of my youth. The classroom education was second to none, and the everyday demand for excellence by the good sisters who staffed the institution provided me with a personal life foundation that has always served me well.

It was the atmosphere of my alma mater outside of the classroom, however, that had the greatest impact on my life. The freedom to relate to 134 girls of the class of 1969, minus any male presence or social pressure, made each one of us keenly aware of our independent, individual abilities and talents.

We ran the student government, organized fund-raising and charitable programs, and took responsibility for our day-to-day school lives. There were no young men to assume control or take center stage. It was all up to us. Definitely an empowering and bonding experience.

Oddly enough, despite my strong feelings about my old school, I had not returned there once in the three decades since my graduation. Over the years, I did manage to stay in touch with a few of my classmates and attend the occasional reunion, but overall, my alumnae experience could most accurately be summed up as "a view from afar." That is, until now.

Recently, I received an alumnae newsletter. Inside, a notice for volunteers to speak at a senior seminar on careers and employment opportunities for women caught my eye. I put the newsletter on my desk. I carefully glanced at it, in passing, for the better part of a week. Should I or shouldn't I? That was the question. It had been thirty years since I had crossed that revered threshold and a lot of water had gone under the proverbial bridge since then. Did I really have a place there anymore? Did I truly have something to offer?

Finally, I decided to call the contact number. Just an informational exercise, I told myself. The voice on the other end of the line brightly stated they would be happy to include me as a guest speaker. When I asked about speech content, I was advised that they were looking for information on education and resultant career choices, at which point I immediately blurted out that perhaps I was not the alumna of their dreams, as unfortunately, I had never earned a college degree. Additionally, time-wise, the greatest percentage of my career fell into the work-related fields of motherhood and domestic engineering. "Still of value," this seemingly imperturbable woman insisted. So, somewhat hesitantly, I signed on.

I faced my day of reckoning with a reluctant enthusiasm. I wondered if, after so many years, the school would seem diminished in any way. I also wondered if any of the nuns who appeared to be so ancient during my academic years, could still possibly be holding court in their same arcane classrooms.

As I made the turn around the circular drive, passing the modern auditorium with its silver lettering, snatches of conversations and life-altering moments flooded my memory. I was amazed at how fresh it all seemed, as if the time had passed in moments rather than years.

I opened the familiar cream-colored parking lot door to a ceremonious greeting and a location assignment of the third-floor library. I climbed the three speckled green/gray marbled flights of stairs, momentarily pausing on each landing. Everything looked just as I'd left it. Only the kelly-green tone of the newly painted lockers disturbed my thirty-year-old memories.

I reached the third floor and wound my way, turning right, then left, then right. A four-year practiced pattern that led me directly to the library. I took a deep breath before entering. My last memorable experience in this particular room involved a senior prank, innocently planned, to check out all the library books on the same day. Unbeknownst to our class, the librarian's mother had passed away the very morning of our playful endeavor. Our well-planned idea of harmless fun sent that poor woman right over the edge. The subsequent image of our principal storming down the hall after us was an image not easily forgotten!

I carefully strode into the room and took a seat. The other chairs were all occupied by younger, more professional-looking women. I nervously started to glow. Suddenly, the class bell rang and it was time to begin. A steady stream of young uniformed girls filed into the room taking seats facing the speakers' table. In a matter of seconds, I was awash in a sea of freshly scrubbed faces balancing precariously on the edge of womanhood. I wondered, was there ever a time in my life that I even resembled such youthful innocence?

Suddenly, I heard my name called as the moderator summoned me to speak. I stood and introduced myself as a graduate of the class of 1969. I revealed tidbits of information that I thought would be pertinent. I began to reminisce about my personal history at "our" school. I then looped that thread into my patchwork career of motherhood, newspaper writer and editor, aerobics instructor, cheerleading coach, gym teacher, horse trainer, restaurant manager, officer manager and freelance writer. The girls seemed interested. They even asked questions. I finally began to relax.

Perhaps this experience would be rewarding, after all. Then the unthinkable happened. As I was relating my life's successes to my alma mater's caring faculty and the sense of independence fostered among our student body, the feeling of close-knit family and security from my high-school years began to return.

Without warning or explanation, I was eighteen again and completely at home. Caught off guard by the intensity of the moment, I began choking back tears. The words of my speech swallowed within my trembling voice. And despite the best of efforts, I found that I could do nothing but stand before those sophisticated alumnae and teenage girls and emotionally lose my composure. But at the same moment, I also realized the true reason I had returned— the insight I could impart that might make a difference.

Struggling for control, I took a deep breath. Then while exhaling, I bluntly advised the collection of intent, youthful women that they should never allow anyone to try to tell them who they are or what they should do with their lives. Neither parents, teachers, relatives, nor friends. Then, with one last gulp, I told them to listen to their own voices, follow their own hearts and realize that, ultimately, they had the ability to make their individual lives whatever they could dream. Thirty years later, a lesson well-remembered . . . gratefully acknowledged and shared.

Christina M. Abt

Small Present, Huge Gift

Problems cannot be solved at the same level of awareness that created them.

Albert Einstein

She was what everyone in my family referred to as "eccentric," but to me, Aunt Madeline was a bright star in an otherwise mundane sky. Aunt Mad, as we all called her, always appeared a bit disheveled, her jet-black hair moving in directions as surprising to me as the direction of her thoughts, values and shared perceptions. I can't recall that she ever wore a bit of makeup, and her colorful attire screamed of independent creativity.

An artist as passionate about her work as she was about life itself, she taught me many important lessons, but none more enlightening than during the holidays in the tenth year of my impressionable childhood.

The whole family had gathered for the holidays in New York—grandparents, aunts, uncles and a gaggle of cousins. Each of the adults, in turn, would announce the holiday gifts with great fanfare and proudly pass them to the child whose name appeared on the package. Within minutes, there was a flurry of loud activity with all the children tearing into boxes and wrapping paper flying in all directions. The adults looked on to see who had out-done the others in this year's gift-giving competition.

The room filled with toys and stuffed animals, and kids peddling their new toy cars through a river of endless wrapping paper and ribbon.

After the initial flurry, the excitement began to calm; the kids lost interest in all the newly acquired clutter. It was then that Aunt Mad quietly stood and walked over to each child, and handed us a small, colorfully woven three-inch tube that was made of a kind of flexible construction paper. There was no wrapping, and no explanation. She smiled the way she did when she challenged us to find the incredible beauty in one of "nature's sculptures," a rock laying in the woods bathed in sunlight.

We each immediately began to examine this seemingly odd gift. It only took about three minutes for every child to have both index fingers stuck securely in each end of the tube. Each time we would try to remove our fingers, the tube would hug more tightly and leave us captive in this wonderful mystery, which Aunt Mad called a Chinese finger puzzle.

Since it was the end of a long happy day and time to go home, my brother, sister and I were piled into the back of our car as we began our three-hour journey back to Pennsylvania. Almost immediately, Mom said to Dad, "Did you see the ridiculous gift Madeline gave to the children? It couldn't have cost more than twenty-five cents a piece! And not even gift-wrapped!"

What my mother failed to notice was how the three of us were sitting quietly in the back seat, all struggling to free our fingers from the only gift that had managed to capture (literally and figuratively) our rapt attention for more than a few minutes.

When we arrived home, my brother and sister asked my parents to rescue them. This was accomplished with careful surgical removal of the Chinese finger puzzle using a pair of scissors. My request was for assistance in calling Aunt Mad, as rotary phones were hard to dial without use of the index fingers.

When I asked my aunt for the secret of how to solve this problem, she laughed and said, "It is best to solve this as you would any problem you may encounter in life. Stop trying so hard. Let go of the struggle and you will be released. Good luck and good night." With that, she hung up.

I sighed deeply, not exactly understanding what she meant. I tried hard to not try hard, but wasn't sure how to do that. I was so tired I went to bed with my clothes on and my fingers tucked safely in the magical prison and quickly fell sound asleep. In the morning, the finger puzzle was lying next to me in bed.

After school the next day I cautiously placed my fingers back in the finger puzzle. I realized that if I pulled, the tube would tighten, but if I relaxed and actually moved my fingers toward each other, the tube would loosen enough to simply remove my fingers.

That was many years ago, many holidays and gifts past . . . yet, I can honestly say that was the best gift anyone ever gave me. And while I no longer have the finger puzzle and have only memories of Aunt Mad to make me smile, I will always have the benefit of that simple gift and the wondrous "hands-on" life lesson it offered.

Now, at age forty-nine, when I find myself struggling to find a way out of some life challenge, I take a deep breath and relax into the problem. As Aunt Mad had advised, I "let go of the struggle and I am released." More often than not, just like that little finger puzzle, I find the answer in the morning.

Jenna Cassell

The Miracle

The marvelous richness of human experience would lose something of rewarding joy if there were no limitations to overcome. The hilltop hour would not be half so wonderful if there were no dark valleys to traverse.

Helen Keller

Until last year, I thought that death was something that happened to other people. Then suddenly, without warning, death showed up at my door.

It all started two summers ago as I was thumbing through one of my favorite magazines, the *Shambhala Sun*. I came across an advertisement for a spiritual pilgrimage to the roof of the world, exploring Buddhism in Tibet and Nepal, two places that I had always wanted to go. The trip was being led by master teachers of Tibetan Buddhism, which I had recently been studying and, to top it off, the trip coincided with my birthday! It seemed like it was meant for me to go, so I quickly sent in my registration.

When I got the itinerary, it read like an Indiana Jones

movie: arrive in Bangkok, fly to Kathmandu and cross the Brahmaputra River by local ferryboat in Tibet. I knew that this pilgrimage was going to be transformative for me. I started cutting out pictures of Tibet and began making entries in my travel journal on the three stages of a pilgrimage. A pilgrimage begins with letting go of what no longer serves you well, followed by opening to receive the gifts that are there for you to receive and, finally, coming back ready to take on a larger life after having been changed by the experience. I also got a copy of a book by Tulku Thondup Rinpoche, one of the teachers going on the trip, *The Healing Power of Mind,* and began reading it. As the holidays approached, all seemed well in my world.

After the first of the year, however, I began noticing pressure in my abdomen and thought that I might have a bladder infection. Because I didn't want to have any problems on the trip, I went to the doctor for what I thought would be a routine exam. Little did I know that I was about to embark on the most significant emotional experience of my life.

I had always prided myself in being healthy, so when the doctor said that he suspected ovarian cancer, I was shocked! The ultrasound report indicated that I had a pelvic mass the size of a soccer ball being contained by my left ovary. My doctor wanted to do a radical hysterectomy, including the removal of my lymph nodes, my appendix and anything else that could have been affected. He said that I had one week to get ready for surgery and that I would need at least six weeks for recovery. I couldn't believe that this was suddenly happening to me at fifty-three; it must be some mistake. After all, I couldn't take six weeks off. I had classes to teach, work to do and a trip to get ready for. He simply said, "You'll have to cancel them."

After a lot of soul searching, and several other opinions, I finally agreed. Fortunately, he said that it might be possible for me to go back to my classes in four weeks, if someone would drive me and that I could go on my trip to Tibet in eight weeks, if everything went well.

All of a sudden, I found myself faced with my own mortality. I realized that I was as vulnerable as anyone else to major illness, death and dying. I had no special immunity and very little time to prepare.

I had thought that my trip to Tibet was going to be the most transformative experience in my life, when actually it turned out that my trip to the hospital was. Clearly, the message for me had been that I needed to let go of what no longer served me well. I just had no idea that it would include body parts!

Never before had I felt so totally vulnerable, helpless and dependent on others. The whole experience was giving me the opportunity to practice letting go, surrendering, trusting and allowing things to be the way they are.

As they wheeled me into the operating room, I was able to let go of my attachment or aversion to a specific outcome, which allowed me to move freely through the experience without getting caught up in all of my hopes and fears. I was able to see everything as a gift and be grateful. I was grateful for the doctors, the nurses, the hospital, my insurance, all my friends, my spiritual practice, my Buddhist teachers, my Shambhala training, for all of life and especially for my left ovary for containing the cancer until it could be removed.

Paradoxically, coming so close to death has been life-giving. It's given me a greater appreciation for the blue sky, the warmth of the sun, the smell of fresh-cut grass, the sound of birds singing, the cool refreshing taste of water and the experience of being alive.

Midlife seems to be a time when we can reinvent ourselves with a new lease on life, if we choose to. It's an opportunity to make some needed changes and course corrections to be more in alignment with what really matters most to us.

During my recovery, I had plenty of time to reflect on my life. I discovered that what was most important to me were my relationships. All the people who were there for me were a blessing when I needed help getting home from the hospital, preparing meals or just generally taking care of myself. I couldn't have done it without them.

I also became keenly aware that there was a power greater than myself moving in my life. I realized that if I had not been going to Tibet, I probably would not have gone in so quickly for the exam in time for it to have saved my life.

The miracle is just being alive and the blessing is realizing it.

Oh, and by the way, the trip to Tibet and Nepal was fantastic—but that's another story.

Renette Meltebeke

Midlife Lessons Worth Learning

Trust in yourself. Your perceptions are often far more accurate than you are willing to believe.

Claudia Black

What is midlife, and when do you reach it? I have decided to live to be one-hundred, so I guess I will arrive there in nine years. I hear the term "midlife crisis" so often these days. At forty-one, I find nearing midlife a wonderful time. I can truly say this is the happiest and most peaceful time of my existence. I find myself "not sweating the small stuff" anymore.

When I was young, I took everything personally. There was me, and there was everyone else. Two groups in the world. I didn't like the way I walked, talked, looked or thought. But, over the last few years, I have come to the great realization that everyone felt the same way at that young age. It's wonderful now to just be part of the group. To realize that we are all different and all the same. I realize that it's okay to have my own thoughts that may be different from others, to not be concerned so much about what everyone else does or thinks, to enjoy life and just have fun being me.

I have also come to realize, upon turning forty, that I can still do anything I want to do. I can still *be* anything I want to be. I will never reach an age where I have achieved all I ever can. Each day, truly, is a new day. Each day is a gift. Each day is a new book, and I am the author.

At this time in my life, I have made new friends, started a business, found skills I never knew I possessed, overcome fears and pursued my dream of writing.

I have also lost a good friend and realized that death knows no age boundary. We must reach out and grab all of the life we can each day because we never know what tomorrow may bring.

I have developed a respect for those older than me. Although experience is the best teacher, we could save ourselves a lot of hard lessons by listening to those older and wiser.

I have learned not to be so judgmental and that listening more and speaking less can be a wonderful and beneficial thing.

I have learned that the small, inexpensive things in life always bring me the most joy. A walk on a fall day, renting an enjoyable movie, reading a good book or eating a delicious cheeseburger are hard to top. It's good to have money, but you really don't need it to be happy in life.

It's nice to be old enough to make your own decisions. It's nice to know that you really can do what you dream.

Youth is a place that was nice to visit, but I wouldn't want to live there. Being older has so many more rewards.

Sheri Harney

Golf, Like Midlife, Is Absolutely Unfair

When I turned fifty, I discovered three essential facts of middle age: periodontics, bifocals and golf.

Golf? Did she say golf?

Let me explain. I once assumed golf was a sport for elderly Country Club Republicans. The sort of men who wore green pants with whale belts and protected their clubs with fuzzy duck-head covers.

Golf was Dwight David Eisenhower. My family was Adlai Stevenson.

In my twenties, I thought golf was God's way of telling you you had too much time on your hands. In my thirties, I decided a low handicap was admissible evidence of child neglect in any custody dispute. In my forties, as a fairly decent tennis and squash player, I couldn't imagine hitting a ball while it was standing still.

Quite frankly, it seemed unfair.

But somewhere along the way, somewhere between Bill Clinton and Big Bertha and Tiger Woods, between chiropractors and knee surgery and Advil, I had an epiphany (that's something close to a muscle spasm) that said: Golf is my next sport. To wit: my last sport. I better learn it now.

This was a decision aided and abetted by a quirky

nine-hole golf course in Maine where people still stroll and stop to look at the view.

It was also aided and abetted by a quirky husband (more Bobby Kennedy than Adlai Stevenson) who enthusiastically gave me all his clubs. This was an act of generosity I didn't immediately recognize for what it was. A ploy for him to get new equipment.

Now, as I approach Columbus Day weekend with a full set of clubs and big plans, I feel fully qualified at last to offer up my views on why golf begins at fifty. Yes, I know one sign of a new and erratic duffer is the penchant for turning golf into a good walk through midlife spoiled. For reasons that remain unclear, golf has spawned more philosophical rambles than fairways.

Nobody compares tennis to life. A love game? Ken Burns and several million fans talk about baseball as the collective field of youthful dreams, but there's no senior tour on the diamonds.

Today there are, I hasten to add, some 25 million golfers and 16,010 golf courses. There are speed golfers and networking golfers and boring golfers. There is even, for reasons that escape me, a golf channel. All golf, all day long.

There is a business writer who actually correlated the handicaps of CEOs with their stock performance. And there are the very, very serious golf professionals who sit around discussing whether they should ban new, improved clubs because they are making the game too easy. Say what? But from my perspective, golf is the midlife sport of choice for very different reasons. First of all, it's easier to reach your goals. In midlife, after all, it's a snap to have a handicap below your age and a score below your weight. And getting easier all the time.

Golf is like midlife because only now do you realize the course you have set upon is governed by rules so vast, so arcane and so arbitrary that the average person—you—will never figure it all out.

Golf is like midlife because it is absolutely unfair. As a young person, you carry the illusion that if you do your homework, study and work overtime, you'll get it all right. By middle age, you know every time you've got it all together—work, family, putt, pitch—some piece is about to unravel. I promise you.

Golf, like midlife, is played against only one opponent: yourself. By the time you reach fifty, you had better figure out that doing well doesn't depend on others doing badly. You don't have to wish them ill. They're not the reason you are shanking the ball.

Golf is like middle age, because—ah, you knew this was coming—in these years, you really do have to play it as it lies. You don't get to start everything all over again. The most you get is a mulligan. If it's an unplayable lie, everybody sympathizes, but you still have to take a penalty.

On the other hand, golf, like midlife, also offers another chance.

No matter how badly you hit one ball, you can still recover on the next. Of course, no matter how well you hit one ball, you can always screw up the next.

Finally, golf is like midlife because at some time on a beautiful October day, when you are searching for a ball, or for that matter your swing, you look around and realize for the first or fiftieth time that, in this game, you're the one keeping your own score.

Ellen Goodman

Aging Gracefully

You need to claim the events of your life to make yourself you.

Anne Wilson-Schaef

My mother is a pretty woman, although I didn't think so while I was growing up. She had me, the last of seven daughters, in her late thirties, and from my childhood perspective, she always looked old.

My mom had wrinkles. Lines and creases unashamedly traced around her prim mouth and catlike eyes and across her forehead like the lines in my spiral notebooks. And she did very little with herself to try to not look old.

Except for a smattering of cold cream, a dab of red lipstick and an occasional stroke of eyebrow pencil, my mother didn't spend much time putting on cosmetics. No mascara, eyeliner, powder-blue shadow or blush (she called it rouge). Not that she was going for that au naturel look, which was never in style for women over forty anyway; she just couldn't be bothered. She didn't have the patience or the time to endure rigorous beauty regimens, steamy facials and manicures.

Mom didn't fuss with her hair, other than winding it up into pin curls every Saturday night since 1941 for church the next morning. Otherwise, her hair was twisted, out of the way, into a tiny bun on the top of her head. She never gave in to color rinses, even when her auburn waves thinned and faded to a drab brown. She didn't make appointments at the beauty shop like my friends' moms did, claiming she didn't want anyone back-combing her hair into a rat. The beehive was a great look for a lot of sixties moms but, unfortunately (I thought then), not my mother—my mom has no style.

My sisters and I never understood our mother's lack of interest in Miss Clairol and Maybelline. In our teenage years, we obsessed over our beauty flaws.

Now that we are all well over forty, we obsess even more and determine our self-esteem by ruefully scanning the magazine covers at the supermarket checkout. We agonize over our gray hairs, sagging skin and crow's feet scratching out in every direction. We forever experiment with the latest miracle creams and makeup that promise to defy time and gravity. And none of us knows our true hair color any more.

"You are what you are. Just be yourself," Mom has advised us over the years. Her words are simple and true, and yet, we do not abide by them. We have fallen prey to what our society deems attractive; for women over forty, looking good means looking youthful. So we repeatedly ignore our mother's advice and head back to the cosmetics counter for more snake oil, quelling our panic of what old age has yet in store for us.

Mom turned eighty last spring. She has more than her fair share of health problems and whiles away the long days without complaint in an easy chair in front of the TV, writing letters, solving crossword puzzles. My sisters and

I visit her every Sunday afternoon, take her to her doctors' appointments, do her grocery shopping and housework. Her hair is silvery white now, and Mom gives in to a cut and a perm every couple of months.

My perspective of my mother has changed many times during my life, especially now that I'm in the throes of motherhood. I am able to understand the woman she once was, even though I've stepped into her shoes long after she's stepped out of them.

I have discovered the aura of beauty surrounding her that has remained constant over the years. I envy her. She is both accepting and grateful for everything God has given her. Neither vain nor self-pitying, she has known all along what is important and true in life. The lines and creases are her badges of womanhood. She's earned them over her lifetime, and she's proud to wear them.

What my sisters and I always dismissed as "no style" was actually Mom's style. Her beauty transcends time with grace and shines outward, oblivious to the imperfections. Her eyes sparkle when her children and grandchildren gather around her. Her withered lips draw up into a smooth pink bow when she smiles. Her creamy skin, in spite of the wrinkles, is as fresh and translucent as her wisdom: "You are what you are. Just be yourself."

Cyndy Salamati

Be Careful What You Ask For

We are all pencils in the hand of God.

Mother Teresa

I had dreamed of being an author for as long as I can remember. Like many writers, though, I found the publishing road littered with barricades, sand traps and stonewalls. Over the twenty-some-odd years I had been writing, I had accumulated enough rejection slips to wallpaper both bathrooms as well as the living room, dining room, three bedrooms and kitchen of my house.

In my heart, though, I was sure that my mission in life was to inspire others through the written word. So one afternoon, after a particularly discouraging rejection letter, I got down on my knees and asked for divine intervention. I wanted a miracle, a miracle that would allow a publisher to see the importance of my work. *Surely,* I prayed, *if you have given me the talent to write, you will find a publisher for my work.*

A few months later, that divine intervention arrived, but it didn't come in the form of a publisher or a book contract. It came in the form of a midlife meltdown. At first I didn't recognize my miracle. In fact, it was just the opposite. I thought I was going crazy. I was experiencing night sweats, memory lapses, mood swings and an overwhelming sense of anxiety. I literally had no idea what was happening to my body. My internist thought I had panic disorder. Another physician thought I was just overly stressed. After months and months of not knowing what was causing my symptoms, I was finally diagnosed by an endocrinologist as being menopausal.

The physical diagnosis of menopause certainly eradicated the fear that I was losing my mind, but it didn't help ease the bitterness I felt toward God. I was sure that he had forsaken me. After all, I had asked for a miracle, not menopause. How could he have possibly mixed up the word miracle with menopause? Had I been that unclear? Frustrated and indignant, I turned off my computer, stopped writing and gave up on my dream altogether.

As the menopausal symptoms increased, I tried everything in my power to ease them. The hormone replacement therapy certainly helped, but deep in my heart I knew that something was desperately missing from my life. Angered by my initial misdiagnosis of panic disorder, and still feeling a lot of emotional pain over what I saw as God's betrayal, I set out on a quest to find out what menopause was really all about. I read every book that I could find on the subject. I also talked with every woman over fifty who would answer my intrusive questioning about the change. What I discovered was that menopause is more than just a physical transformation; it is a spiritual journey. It is about a woman's spirit trying to regain a sense of symmetry in a distorted, asymmetrical world. It is also about a pilgrimage in which a woman returns to the sacred land at the core of her soul, called home.

As I began to uncover the truths behind menopause, I

began to write them down. I also began to enter into discussions with other women. I witnessed their menopausal journeys, and I allowed them to witness mine. I knew in my heart that sharing my experience and hearing theirs would ultimately complete the healing circle of menopause for me. For only by sharing our painful stories do we truly learn from them. As I conversed with these women, I also found a common thread among all of our stories. It seemed that there were seven distinct stages that women go through on their passage through midlife. Pinpointing these stages helped me see that menopause was a process, and that this process was really about a woman giving birth to herself, to her dreams and to her spiritual mission in life.

And so, after nine months of midlife labor pains, and unearthing every truth I could possibly discover about the spiritual journey of menopause, I returned to my computer and began to birth my story in the form of a book. I believe my own healing circle was completed the moment I finished writing *The Seven Sacred Rites of Menopause: The Spiritual Journey to the Wise Woman Years* and started sharing it with others. This circle expanded every time I shared my manuscript and story with another woman. I have received letters from individual women whose painful menopausal experience was eased by reading my story.

In retrospect, I see that the miracle I had asked for was granted almost immediately. I just didn't recognize it. In many ways, I was waiting for validation from the outside world, instead of making that journey inward to discover my own authenticity. And, as is often the case, it took uncovering some very painful truths in my life to turn my vision into a reality.

Achieving my dream has also made me realize that miracles don't always come in the time frame that we want, and opened doors don't always arrive in the shapes and colors that we expect. Moreover, it has reminded me that once we ask the universe to open the door that will make our dream a reality, we have to be prepared to welcome the dream, no matter how it arrives.

My miracle, my dream, arrived in the form of menopause. It certainly didn't look like I expected it to, and it certainly didn't have that feel-good experience that is often associated with miracles. But once I opened the door and began to move through it, I was able to receive its blessings. And now, in looking back at its form, I relish its sharp edges and its dark, shadowy color. For in the end, not only was I able to find my dream through this door, I was able to open it wide enough for my sisters to move through it, as well.

Kristi Boylan

A Lesson in Surrender

Console thyself.
For thou would not seek Me if thou had not already found Me.

Blaise Pascal

At the end of my daughter's senior year in high school, we decided to take a trip to the island in British Columbia where she was born. Neither of us had been back since she, her father and I had left some sixteen years earlier.

Shortly after we arrived, we visited an old friend who's a jeweler. When she noticed me admiring one of her "chrysanthemum rocks," she offered to make me a piece of jewelry if I found the right stone while on the island.

From that moment on, I was on a quest. Every time I went for a walk, I would scour the beach. I must have picked up several hundred stones. After days of intensive hunting, I began to notice that I had become obsessed with finding "the perfect rock." Without having realized it, I had gotten to the point where I was no longer enjoying myself. In fact, I was making myself miserable. Here I was in this idyllic setting, and I felt as stressed out as I was in Los Angeles. I had become so driven to find a keepsake of our trip that I was missing the actual experience. I called off my search, and for the first time since arriving, I began to feel like I was on vacation.

A few days later, I ran into an old friend who invited me to go on a picnic. We rode our bikes to a deserted beach. As we lay on our stomachs at the water's edge, I suddenly noticed something tickling my palm. I looked down and there was a jet black stone with a perfectly formed circle etched on its oval surface. The stone was exactly the right size for my ring finger. I was speechless. I had let go, given up, and having expended no effort, I had found the very thing I had been looking for.

I began to think about how fear had driven much of my life. My self-assured veneer had camouflaged how truly frightened I had been—frightened that if I didn't push, nothing would happen. Perhaps, after this experience, I could begin to loosen my grip and allow myself to be carried more by life. Perhaps it was time to get my ego out of the way and allow something deeper to motivate me. Perhaps it was less about "making it happen" than it was about allowing myself to be guided by a deeper voice—a voice that has always existed, but one to which I had only intermittently listened. Perhaps it was time to allow the wisdom of my authentic self to be more present in my life—to heed the truth that I knew to be correct, but had too often ignored.

Since that experience, I began to practice trusting whenever, wherever, however I found an opportunity. Each time we choose to trust, and it's not always easy, our faith grows incrementally stronger. On those occasions when I feel fear rising in the pit of my stomach, I glance down at my ring as a concrete reminder of what's possible for each of us when we open ourselves and surrender.

Stephanie Marston

It's Never Too Late To . . .

Act on your dreams.
Be what you want to be.
Change your future.
Do things differently.
Enrich others' lives.
Face your fears.
Get out of neutral.
Have fun.
Initiate friendships.
Jumpstart possibilities.
Knock the "t" off can't.
Live enthusiastically.
Make a difference.
be Nonjudgmental.
Orchestrate your legacy.
Plan for tomorrow.
Question your priorities.
Reinvent yourself.
Stop keeping score.
Take a leap of faith.
Uncork your mind.

Value who you are.
Wake up your luck.
e**X**plore your spirituality.
Yearn for fulfillment.
Zoom in on love.

Meiji Stewart

More Chicken Soup?

Many of the stories and poems you have read in this book were submitted by readers like you who had read earlier *Chicken Soup for the Soul* books. We publish at least five or six *Chicken Soup for the Soul* books every year. We invite you to contribute a story to one of these future volumes.

Stories may be up to twelve-hundred words and must uplift or inspire. You may submit an original piece, something you have read or your favorite quotation on your refrigerator door.

To obtain a copy of our submission guidelines and a listing of upcoming *Chicken Soup* books, please write, fax or check our Web site.

Please send your submissions to:

Chicken Soup for the Soul
P.O. Box 30880, Santa Barbara, CA 93130
fax: 805-563-2945
Web site: *www.chickensoup.com*

We will be sure that both you and the author are credited for your submission.

For information about speaking engagements, other books, audiotapes, workshops and training programs, please contact any of our authors directly.

Peace Through the Magic of Story

In the spirit of giving voice to peace for American adults and children, the publisher and coauthors of *Chicken Soup to Inspire a Woman's Soul* will make a donation to Peace Tales.

Peace Tales is a nonprofit organization that produces compact disc recordings that give lessons in peacemaking to American audiences through the magic of story. The first such production, "Holding Up the Sky: Peace Tales for Kids" (©2003) features New Mexico school social worker and storyteller Sarah Malone. The fifty-six-minute CD includes multicultural stories, music and poetry that provide peaceful approaches to typical conflicts like jealousy, teasing and bullying. Author/storyteller Joe Hayes calls the recording a "weapon of mass instruction!" One hundred percent of the proceeds benefit peace causes: children affected by armed conflict overseas (through The Women's Commission for Refugee Women & Children) and Peace Talks Radio, a New Mexico radio forum for nonviolence and peacemaking.

Further information on Peace Tales is available at: *www.peacetales.org* and *www.womenscommission.org.*

Who Is Jack Canfield?

Jack Canfield is one of America's leading experts in the development of human potential and personal effectiveness. He is both a dynamic, entertaining speaker and a highly sought-after trainer. Jack has a wonderful ability to inform and inspire audiences toward increased levels of self-esteem and peak performance.

He is the author and narrator of several bestselling audio- and videocassette programs, including *Self-Esteem and Peak Performance, How to Build High Self-Esteem, Self-Esteem in the Classroom* and *Chicken Soup for the Soul—Live.* He is regularly seen on television shows such as *Good Morning America, 20/20* and *NBC Nightly News.* Jack has coauthored numerous books, including the *Chicken Soup for the Soul* series, *Dare to Win* and *The Aladdin Factor* (all with Mark Victor Hansen), *100 Ways to Build Self-Concept in the Classroom* (with Harold C. Wells), *Heart at Work* (with Jacqueline Miller), *The Power of Focus* (with Les Hewitt and Mark Victor Hansen) and *Chicken Soup for the Soul Life Lessons.*

Jack is a regularly featured speaker for professional associations, school districts, government agencies, churches, hospitals, sales organizations and corporations. His clients have included the American Dental Association, the American Management Association, AT&T, Campbell's Soup, Clairol, Domino's Pizza, GE, ITT, Hartford Insurance, Johnson & Johnson, the Million Dollar Roundtable, NCR, New England Telephone, Re/Max, Scott Paper, TRW and Virgin Records. Jack has taught on the faculty of Income Builders International, a school for entrepreneurs.

Jack conducts an annual seven-day Training of Trainers program in the areas of self-esteem and peak performance. It attracts entrepreneurs, educators, counselors, parenting trainers, corporate trainers, professional speakers, ministers and others interested in developing their speaking and seminar-leading skills.

Look for Jack's latest book, *The Success Principles,* in January 2005.

Self-Esteem Seminars
P.O. Box 30880
Santa Barbara, CA 93130
phone: 805-563-2935 • fax: 805-563-2945
Web site: *www.jackcanfield.com*

Who Is Mark Victor Hansen?

In the area of human potential, no one is more respected than Mark Victor Hansen. For more than thirty years, Mark has focused solely on helping people from all walks of life reshape their personal vision of what's possible. His powerful messages of possibility, opportunity and action have created powerful change in thousands of organizations and millions of individuals worldwide.

He is a sought-after keynote speaker, bestselling author and marketing maven. Mark's credentials include a lifetime of entrepreneurial success and an extensive academic background. He is a prolific writer with many bestselling books such as *The One Minute Millionaire, The Power of Focus, The Aladdin Factor* and *Dare to Win,* in addition to the *Chicken Soup for the Soul* series. Mark has made a profound influence through his library of audios, videos and articles in the areas of big thinking, sales achievement, wealth building, publishing success, and personal and professional development.

Mark is the founder of the MEGA Seminar Series. MEGA Book Marketing University and Building Your MEGA Speaking Empire are annual conferences where Mark coaches and teaches new and aspiring authors, speakers and experts on building lucrative publishing and speaking careers. Other MEGA events include MEGA Marketing Magic and My MEGA Life.

He has appeared on television (*Oprah,* CNN and *The Today Show*), in print (*Time, U.S. News & World Report, USA Today, New York Times* and *Entrepreneur*) and on countless radio interviews, assuring our planet's people that "You can easily create the life you deserve."

As a philanthropist and humanitarian, Mark works tirelessly for organizations such as Habitat for Humanity, American Red Cross, March of Dimes, Childhelp USA and many others. He is the recipient of numerous awards that honor his entrepreneurial spirit, philanthropic heart and business acumen. He is a lifetime member of the Horatio Alger Association of Distinguished Americans, an organization that honored Mark with the prestigious Horatio Alger Award for his extraordinary life achievements.

Mark Victor Hansen is an enthusiastic crusader of what's possible and is driven to make the world a better place.

Mark Victor Hansen & Associates, Inc.
P.O. Box 7665
Newport Beach, CA 92658
phone: 949-764-2640
fax: 949-722-6912
Visit Mark online at: *www.markvictorhansen.com*

Who Is Stephanie Marston?

Stephanie Marston is an internationally published author, acclaimed speaker and life-quality expert. She is the author of *Chicken Soup for the Soul Life Lessons*, *If Not Now, When?*, *The Magic of Encouragement* and *The Divorced Parent*. Stephanie is also the creator of Chicken Soup's Life Coaching for Parents: Six Weeks to Sanity.

Stephanie is a licensed Marriage, Family Therapist with more than twenty-five years' experience in women's issues and parenting.

Ms. Marston has appeared on numerous radio and television programs such as *The Oprah Winfrey Show*, *The Early Show*, and *Women-to-Women*.

Stephanie is one of the most sought-after experts in the country offering her sage wisdom on a host of life-quality and family issues, especially how to balance life's competing priorities and create a high-quality life. She has conducted seminars for more than 50,000 women, parents, and mental health professionals internationally.

Stephanie delivers keynote addresses, seminars and workshops to women's organizations, corporations, parent groups, professional conferences, associations and the general public. Some of her clients have included Los Angeles Department of Water and Power, Chanel, The Young Presidents Organization, Union Bank, Northrop Corporation, ARCO Corporation, Paramount Studios, Cedar-Sinai Medical Center, Jackson Lewis Attorneys at Law, Parkville Hospital, WCI Communities and The Junior Leagues of America.

Whether you're a career woman struggling to balance the demands of work and family, a midlife woman trying to navigate this challenging transition, a frustrated parent who wants to create greater harmony in your home, or a woman who is simply tired of living an overloaded existence, Stephanie Marston has the answers.

For further information about Stephanie's books, tapes and programs, or to schedule her for a presentation, please contact:

Life Quality Seminars
Box 31453
Santa Fe, NM 87594-1453
Phone: 505-989-7596 • fax: 505-989-4486
Web site: *www.stephaniemarston.com*

Contributors

Several of the stories in this book were taken from previously published sources, such as books, magazines and newspapers. These sources are acknowledged in the Permissions section. If you would like to contact any of the contributors for information about their writing or would like to invite them to speak in your community, look for their contact information included in their biographies.

The remainder of the stories were submitted by readers of our previous *Chicken Soup for the Soul* books who responded to our requests for stories. We have also included information about them.

Christina M. Abt is a newspaper columnist, magazine contributor and radio commentator. Her work has been featured in *Chicken Soup for the Soul of America* and on the Heartwarmers.com Web site as well as in the Heartwarmer's series of books and Petwarmer's CD. She is the wife of one awesome husband, the mother of two terrific kids and a great son-in-law and will always be her mother's daughter. She can be reached at *christinabt@hotmail.com*.

Dee Adams' Web site (*www.minniepauz.com*) has been noted by many major newspapers such as *USAToday, LA Times, Detroit News* and London's *The Times*. She has been interviewed on Detroit's ABC and NBC affiliates, as well as the site being shown on CNN. She has illustrated books, made personal appearances at medical conferences and is currently working on her first book.

Cecelia Albanese, the mother of three, married her high school sweetheart Sal. She moved from Philadelphia to Atlanta thirteen years ago. Being published for the first time has encouraged her to continue writing. She also enjoys reading, painting, arts and crafts and traveling with her husband in their RV. She can be reached at *cecelia13@charter.net*.

Carol Ayer holds a B.A. in English from UC Berkeley and an M.A. in educational psychology from Cal State Hayward. She works as a freelance writer and a library clerk. She has had several poems published in the e-zine *Poetic Voices* and a short story published in *Woman's World*. She lives in northern California.

Barbara Bent graduated from Jackson Memorial High School in Massillon, Ohio, in the late fifties and went on to receive a B.A. in psychology/education and an MBA in finance. She has lived and worked in New York City for thirty-six years. Currently she is compiling a collection of her published short love stories called *Love on the Light Side*. E-mail *barbbent@aol.com*.

Peggy Bird lives in Vancouver, Washington. Her writing has appeared in such publications as *The Christian Science Monitor, Collectors News, Miniature Quilts* and *Clay Times*. Most recently her work was included in the anthologies *Dear Mom* and *A Christmas Collection*. She can be reached via e-mail at: *friedbird@juno.com*.

Joyce Briggs holds a bachelor of science degree in business administration. She teaches children with special needs in Sarasota, Florida. Joyce is married and has a daughter, thirteen and a son, eight who keep her very busy. She and her partner are working on writing inspirational books for children and adults. Joyce can be reached at *vkandjb@aol.com*.

Kristi Meisenbach Boylan is the author of *The Seven Sacred Rites of Menopause: The Spiritual Journey to the Wise Woman Years, Born to Be Wild: Freeing the Spirit of the Hyperactive Child* and *The Seven Sacred Rites of Menarche: The Spiritual Journey of the Adolescent Girl*. Her Web site is *www.KristiBoylan.com*.

Karen Brown is a copywriter and radio host in Quincy, Illinois. She holds degrees in theater and, in a previous life, managed a community theater, directed plays, overacted in some of them and wrote theater reviews. She and husband Ron have two sons, Casey and Jesse. Contact Karen at *rbrown@ksni.net*.

Bill Canty's cartoons have appeared in many national magazines, including *Reader's Digest, Saturday Evening Post, Good Housekeeping, Better Homes and Gardens, Woman's World, National Review* and *Medical Economics*. His syndicated feature *All About Town* runs in thirty-five newspapers. Bill can be reached at 205 Sand Piper Dr., Poinciana, Florida. Bill can be reached at (863) 427-4135. E-mail him at: *wcanty@solivita.net*.

Dave Carpenter has been a full-time cartoonist since 1981. His cartoons have appeared in such publications as *Harvard Business Review, Barron's, The Wall Street Journal, Reader's Digest, Good Housekeeping* and *Better Homes and Gardens*. Dave can be reached at *davecarp@ncn.net* or through his Web site at *www.carptoons.com*.

Jenna Cassell is a freelance writer, independent consultant, media producer, educator, speaker and founder of an American Sign Language media company. She has received over twenty media production awards and is published in *Chicken Soup for the Volunteer's Soul* and included in multiple *Who's Who* listings. She can be reached by e-mail: *jencass@san.rr.com*.

Jeri Chrysong, a legal secretary, resides in Huntington Beach, California, with her son Sam and pugs Puddy and Mabel. Her son, Luc Alexander, featured in "A Walk to Manhood," is currently playing football for Hastings College in Nebraska. Besides writing, Jeri's hobbies include photography and traveling. Her work has been featured in several inspirational books.

Leslie J. Clark grew up in Florida. She now lives in Colorado, where she took her first sailing lesson in her mid-thirties on a local reservoir. Leslie and her husband, John, enjoy the lifestyle of Colorado, where she writes, works and pursues her new love . . . tennis. Contact her at *www.midlifeodyssey.com*.

A former community college English instructor, **SuzAnne C. Cole** now concentrates on writing. She's published more than 250 works in magazines, newspapers, journals and anthologies; plays have been produced in Houston and New York. Her next book will be the joys of being a crone. Contact her at: *SuzAnneCC@aol.com.*

David Cooney's cartoons and illustrations have appeared in numerous *Chicken Soup for the Soul* books as well as magazines including *First for Women* and *Good Housekeeping.* David is a work-from-home dad, cartoonist, illustrator and photographer. David and his wife, Marcia, live in the small Pennsylvania town of Mifflinburg with their two children, Sarah and Andrew. David's Web site is *www.DavidCooney.com* and he can be reached at *david@davidcooney.com.*

Harriet Cooper is a freelance humorist and essayist living in Toronto, Canada. Her humor, essays, articles, short stories and poetry have appeared in newspapers, magazines, Web sites, newsletters, anthologies, radio and a coffee can. She specializes in writing about family, relationships, cats, psychology and health. Contact her at: *harcoop@hotmail.com.*

Suzan Davis is author of *Babes on Blades, Drop Physical, Mental and Spiritual Flab Though Inline Skating* (Wish Publishing), a baby boomer's guide to self-empowerment. Suzan started a club called Babes on Blades that grew to 2,000 members and included women (Babes), men (He-Babes) and children (Wee Babes). Contact her at *suzandavis@rcsis.com* or *www.wishpublishing.com.*

Joan Downey writes about experiences, feelings and memories as a way of better understanding herself and others. Besides writing, she enjoys her family, reading, baseball and other simple pleasures. She graduated from Doane College in Crete, Nebraska, with a degree in human relations. E-mail: *Downey_J@msn.com.*

Carol Ann Erhardt is a marketing assistant living in central Ohio with her husband, Ron, and their cat, Sarah. They have eight children and sixteen grandchildren. She has previously published poetry and short stories, and is currently writing a romantic suspense novel. E-mail: *carolann@novellady.com.*

George M. Flynn is a husband, father of three, freelance writer and seventh-grade English teacher. He is also an avid gardener and the author of *Maggie's Heart and Other Stories,* a collection of twenty-four heartwarming gardening stories. The book is available by contacting him at 23 Kemah-Mecca Lake Road, Newton, NJ 07860.

Ginny Foster, a retired high-school teacher from Portland, Oregon, has returned to her first love, writing. She has won national and regional awards for play writing. Her e-mail address is *gingame@portland.quik.com.*

Mary Anne Fox was born and raised in Minnesota. She has a B.A. in sociology/social work/psychology from the University of Great Falls. She asks that people share her story and promote organ donations so others may live. Her address is PO Box 3553, Idaho Falls, ID 83403-3553.

Sally Friedman, an essayist from New Jersey, is a graduate of the University of Pennsylvania who writes for newspapers and magazines. The mother of three daughters, the grandmother of six and the wife of a retired judge, she is an admitted workaholic and chocaholic.

Kelly Gamble is the author of the young adult novel *The Dreamkeepers: Saving the Senoi.* She is the owner of 24-7 CPR Solutions in Henderson, Nevada. Kelly enjoys traveling, diving and spending time with her family. Contact her at *Kelly@247CPR.com.*

EllynAnne Geisel is the creator of APRON CHRONICLES, a traveling exhibit that documents people's responses to aprons. The exhibit is comprised of 200 vintage aprons, photographer Kristina Loggia's environmental portraits of the forty-five contributors and their stories. For exhibit information, visit *www.apronchronicles.com.*

Nancy B. Gibbs is a pastor's wife, mother and grandmother. The author of *Celebrate Life . . . Just for Today,* she is also a weekly religion columnist and freelance writer. Her stories have appeared in numerous books and magazines. She has contributed several stories to the *Chicken Soup for the Soul* series. Contact her at *Daiseydood@aol.com.*

Lynell Gray has taught both elementary school and university classes, and has served as a writing project consultant/presenter. She is a published author of professional teacher materials and inspirational writings. For information on her original posters, cards and gift books available for purchase, please contact her at *l.gray@eee.org.*

Carolyn Hall is a freelance writer, a consumer advocate and a registered dietitian. She is a member of the Kansas City Writer's Group and Whispering Prairie Press. Carolyn's hobbies include adventuring with her husband, John, and stonescaping with native Kansas limestone. Contact her at 913-441-4386 or *chall711@kcnet.com.*

Sheri Harney works as an administrative assistant, owns her own personalized candy business, Chocoholic Chick, and also enjoys writing. She has written articles for *Focus on Forty Magazine* and wishes to publish children's stories. Her plate is always happily full! She can be reached at *chocholicchick@fuse.net.*

Peggy Haslar is a writer who lives in La Jara, Colorado, with her husband and two sons. At the school where she serves as K–12 counselor, she sponsors a "Writer's Club" where she encourages junior-high students to nurture their dreams, some of which include being writers themselves.

Teresa Tyma Helie is Mom to her most precious gifts from God, her children, Sean, Adam and Cory. She collects angels and lighthouses, sings karaoke for relaxation, and is working on her B.A. in sociology. She credits her family for encouraging her to write, and her mom for insisting (when she was discouraged) that she write a page a day. Reach her at *mykidsmom3@charter.net.*

Patricia A. Hoyt received her master of education degree from the University of Oregon. She taught elementary school for over twenty years and is now happily retired. Patricia enjoys seeing God's handiwork all around her, and spends her extra time raising exotic chickens, gardening and working with youth in her church.

Georgia A. Hubley retired after twenty years in financial management. She enjoys writing nostalgia and fiction. Her work has appeared in *Chicken Soup for the Gardener's Soul, Good Old Days Magazine, Capper's Magazine* and numerous Knight Ridder publications. She resides with her husband in Carmel, California. Contact her at *GEOHUB@aol.com.*

Marie D. Jones is a New Thought Minister and author of *Looking Good in All the Wrong Places.* Her stories, essays, book reviews and articles have appeared in dozens of national publications. She is married and has one son, Max. She can be contacted via her Web site *www.m-powered.org.*

Lauri Khodabandehloo lives in Eugene, Oregon, where she and her husband have raised four daughters. She enjoys working with developmentally challenged young adults and leads a special young adults life-group. Lauri is currently writing a book about her daughter, the true story about an autistic girl and her miraculous transformation. The book tells about God's grace in answering her prayers that her daughter have a "real life." Please reach her at *laurie_kh@hotmail.com.*

Judy Keim has always loved books and stories. Three of her children's stories have been published in magazines; an adult story appears in *Summer in Mossy Creek,* the third book in a series published by Belle Books. Presently, she is working on women's fiction and children's stories. Contact her at *judykeim@comcast.net.*

Alice Ann (Conger) Knisely is a native Nebraskan, born and raised in Loup City. She attended Nebraska Wesleyan University and became a kindergarten teacher and elementary music instructor. She is married to Jim Knisely and is the mother of four, grandmother of three, and great-grandmother of three. After moving to Bella Vista, Arkansas, five years ago, she is a member of the Nebraska Writers' Guild and the Northwest Arkansas Writers' Guild. Several of her poems have been published and she writes a column, "Through the Looking Glass," in *The Weekly Vista.* Her published book, *Keep Smiling,* was copyrighted in 2002 and she is at work on the sequel, *And Then What Happened, Mom?*

Charlotte A. Lanham is a frequent contributor to *Chicken Soup for the Soul.* She and her husband, Ray, are cofounders of a nonprofit organization called Abbi's Room, providing beds and bedding for children of Habitat for Humanity families. Her midlife inspiration comes from her four beautiful grandchildren: Darbi, Raphaella, Abbi, Matteo. E-mail: *charlotte.lanham@sbcglobal.net.*

Linda Lipinski is the creator of the inspirational genealogy scrapbook/album entitled *A Legacy to Remember.* After listening to the elderly reflecting back on their lives, sharing wisdom learned through the years, and the terminally ill desiring to leave a special gift to their family, she created this product to help individuals put a "love letter" together as a beautiful gift. For more information, see *www.alegacytoremember.com* or e-mail *richlin@richlingroup.com*.

Mary Clare Lockman is a registered nurse in a busy Oncology/Hospice Unit. She also enjoys spending time with family and friends, reading, traveling and writing. "Paper Suits Me" is an excerpt from her book, *Warning! Family Vacations May Be Hazardous to Your Health*. She can be reached at (651) 646-7984; or *mclock man@msn.com*.

Beverly Matulis is an elementary school teacher. She is also codirector of the Saginaw Bay Writing Project where she helps teachers hone their skill as writers, empowering them to be better teachers of writing. Beverly lives with her husband Mike in Midland, Michigan. Her e-mail address is *Bmatulis@ chartermi.net*.

Joyce Maynard is the author of the memoir *At Home in the World* (St. Martin's Press) and numerous other books, most recently the novel *The Usual Rules* (St. Martin's, 2003). The mother of three grown children, she lives in Northern California. She can be reached at *www.joycemaynard.com*.

Karen McCowan is a reporter for *The Register-Guard* in Eugene, Oregon. She and her husband, Joel, have been married for thirty years. They have two adult daughters, Kelsey and Keeley.

Karen McQuestion is a writer whose work has appeared in *Newsweek, The Chicago Tribune, Denver Post* and the *Wisconsin Academy Review*, among others. In addition, she was awarded a winter/spring 2003 Ragdale Foundation residency for fiction. She resides in Hartland, Wisconsin, with her husband and three children and can be reached through her Web site *www.karen mcquestion.com*.

Renette Meltebeke is a professional career counselor in private practice in Oregon. She serves as an adjunct faculty for both Lewis & Clark College and Marylhurst University. Renette is featured in the Marquis *Who's Who of American Women* and specializes in helping people to fulfill their creative potential. Renette can be reached at *www.responsiblestewardship.com*.

Anne Merle is a freelance writer living in Evanston, Illinois. Her health and family features appear in Chicago area Pioneer Press newspapers; travel articles at *TravelingToday.com*; director's column and theatrical commentary in trade papers ITVA News and Performink. Mother of two, she's also a professional actress. Contact her at *ajacqmerle@aol.com*.

Ferna Lary Mills is the director of Rainbow Faith, a Christian grief ministry, and author of *The Rainbow: Words of Inspiration, Faith and Hope*. Many of Ferna's poems and stories have been published in various magazines and anthologies. Reach her at (903) 445-0915 or by e-mail at *ferna@rainbowfaith.com*.

Joanne Morrison lives in the Toronto area with her husband and two young sons. She works as a freelance writer and editor and is looking forward to publishing her children's book *The Half-Baked Couch Potato*. She may be reached at *joanne77@allstream.net*.

Billie Sue Moser is a homemaker and a retiree from long-term elderly care management. She and her husband, John, have four children and seven grandchildren. She writes nonfiction and poetry from a deep faith and rich life experience. A member of Inspirational Writers Alive, she writes because she breathes.

Jane Mozena lives in Portland, Oregon, where she writes short fiction and personal essays. Her work has been seen in *Holiday Tales* and *Dear Mom, Letters of Love, Loss and Longing*, and her short story "The Dissection" won an award in the 1999 Clark College Fiction Contest.

Phyllis L. Nutkis is a teacher and writer in Skokie, Illinois. She is the author of many professional articles on education, has presented workshops on early childhood education, and recently published her first children's book. In addition to writing, Phyllis enjoys spending time with her husband, children and grandchildren. You may contact her at *Norman8631@aol.com*.

Shelah Brewer Ogletree writes from her North Carolina home. She enjoys helping her husband, Mike, with the church orchestra he directs. Four children Michael, nineteen; Nathan, six; Joseph, six; and Kayla Elizabeth, five, keep her busy and provide fodder for her work. Shelah and her husband have collaborated on a book entitled *How to Build an Orchestra from Scratch*. Please reach her at: *maestroOL@earthlink.net*.

Jennifer Oliver hails from Killeen, Texas, and lives too far away from her mother. Surrounded by four awesome kids and househubby Stephen, she works full time for the government, publishes a weekly e-zine, and is writing her first romance novel. Contact her at *four_ears@msn.com*.

Susan Fishman Orlins is a writer living in Washington, D.C. Her work has appeared in *The New York Times* and *The Washington Post*. She is currently working on a collection of essays.

Mark Parisi's *off the mark* comic panel has been syndicated since 1987 and is distributed by United Media. Mark's humor also graces greeting cards, T-shirts, calendars, magazines (such as *Billboard*), newsletters and books. His cartoons can be found in the pages of many *Chicken Soup for the Soul* books. Lynn is his wife/business partner and their daughter Jenny contributes with inspiration (as does their cat).

Margie Pasero has been living her dream since January 2000. She facilitates drum circles at local events and teaches hand-drumming and world-rhythms to ages preschool through adult in the Pacific Northwest. Margie's loves are her husband, children and grandchildren; hiking; playing the clarinet and piano; reading and knitting. She is excited about her new love—

playing the fiddle. Please contact her at the following: Web site: *http://pages.prodigy.net/heartbeats1;* E-mail: *heartbeats1@prodigy.net.* Phone: (360) 829-1843.

Laurel A. Pilon-Weick is from a family of thirteen children. She has three daughters and four grandchildren and is a graduate of The Children's Institute of Literature. Since her husband, Neal, recently retired, they hope to travel. Neal was her inspiration for "His Hands." She says that, "It seems that we take so much for granted, and it wasn't until I was dying that the Lord showed me all that Neal's hands had done for me. How blessed I am!"

Trisha Posner was in fashion and music for twenty years in London and New York. She has researched seven books with her husband, Gerald. Trisha lectures on women's health and fitness. She is the author of *This is Not Your Mother's Menopause* and *No Hormones, No Fear.* Check out *www.trishaposner.com.*

Carol McAdoo Rehme has five dozen inspirational stories in anthologies, including ten books in the *Chicken Soup* series. Although her four children have emptied her nest, she feathers it now with writing, storytelling and public speaking. For her, midlife includes a new adventure: founding Vintage Voices Inc., a nonprofit agency that provides programs in eldercare facilities. Contact: *carol@rehme.com* or *www.rehme.com.*

Amy Ridgeway holds a bachelor's degree in child development and a master's degree in education. She is a full-time mom to two beautiful daughters and lives happily with her husband in West Virginia. In her spare time, she teaches school. She can be reached at *JARidgeway@aol.com.*

Kate Rowinski is a writer and consultant. Her credits include a number of children's books as well as several books of non-fiction for adults. Kate and her husband, Jim, have four grown children who have left the nest. Their numerous dogs, who have chosen not to leave the nest, live with them in Charlottesville, Virginia.

Kelly Salasin turned forty this year, and is birthing her first home! She secretly wants to be a dancer when she grows up (even though she's never been able to touch her toes). Kelly lives and writes in the Green Mountains of Vermont with three wonderful men. You might reach her along the circles of life at *kel@sover.net.*

Cyndy Salamati received her B.A. in English from the University of Wisconsin-Milwaukee. She has had essays published in *The Chicago Tribune* and *Old House Interiors.* She lives in Wisconsin with her husband and two sons.

Lois Schmidt, a graduate of Milwaukee Downer College, is a published author of children's stories, interviews, special features, and has a romance novel pending. Her husband, family and friends are foremost in her life. She's a duplicate bridge player, and loves a heated political discussion. Contact her at *arlenem2427@yahoo.com.*

Cartooning is a combination of writing and drawing, so it is the perfect vocation for **Harley Schwadron**. After working as a newspaper reporter in Connecticut and a university PR editor in Michigan, he switched to full-time cartooning in 1984 and he's still turning out his humorous drawings. His work appears in *Barron's, Reader's Digest, Harvard Business Review* and others. He can be reached at P.O. Box 1347, Ann Arbor, Michigan, 48106, phone/fax: 734-426-8433.

Peg Sherry, a "closet" writer for years, invested her energies in family and academia: four children, master's degree, teaching regular and gifted students at all levels, including college. Upon retiring, she focused on submitting her writings. Her work is in local and state magazines and in her published books of poems and essays. E-mail: *mtsherry@aol.com.*

Deborah Shouse is a writer, speaker, editor and creativity catalyst. Her work has appeared in periodicals such as *Reader's Digest, Newsweek, Woman's Day* and *Family Circle.* She is the coauthor of *Antiquing For Dummies* and *Working Woman's Communications Survival Guide.* She and her partner do keynote presentations and workshops. Visit her Web site at *www.thecreativityconnection.com.*

Sandra B. Smith lives in Alabama with her husband of twenty-nine years, and her children, two-legged and four-legged ones. She has been a nurse for twenty-seven years, and feels that nursing is a blessing that has not only fed her family, but her soul as well. She writes to validate her feelings, and to hopefully, bring a smile or an uplifting moment to others.

Sharon M. Stanford is a retired social worker. She has been the chairman of the Detroit Writers Guild and a freelance writer for the Michigan Chronicle. In 2000, she won the Grand Prize in Ebony Magazine's Short Story Contest. She is currently working on her second novel. She can be reached at *stanfords@ameritech.net.*

Meiji Stewart has written several ABC poems including *Children Are, Dare To, Don't Quit, Great Teachers, May You Always Have* and many more. These are available on a variety of posters, prints and other gift products from your local gift store or from Portal Publications. To view more ABC poems, to send an *ABCeCard,* or for more information about Meiji's projects please visit *www. puddledancer.com* or call 858-759-6963.

In his twenty-two years with the San Diego Padres, **Andy Strasberg** established himself as one of the sports world's most innovative marketers. During his tenure in San Diego, Strasberg oversaw all aspects of the Padres marketing and sales efforts. Upon leaving the Padres in 1996, Strasberg created ACME Marketing, which since that time has provided valuable service to a diverse roster of clients. Strasberg is a native New Yorker and a cum laude graduate of Long Island University. Andy resides in San Diego, California, with his wife, Patti, and their dog, Stanley.

This is **Benita Tobin**'s first story. Being published "right out the gate," has encouraged Benita to write more. Besides, she says, "Any work I can do from home while still in my 'jammies' is a great gig!" Home is Portland, Oregon, shared with her husband, David, and dog, Sydney.

Lynne M. Thompson is a freelance writer for the Christian market. She regularly publishes with Focus on the Family, teaches workshops to beginning writers, and is currently writing a young adult series. She has also contributed to Stories from a Soldier's Heart (multnomah). You may visit her Web site at *Kidfishy.com*.

Always curious, **Cappy Tosetti** enjoys life as a magazine writer and national conference speaker. When not on assignment or at the computer, Tosetti is usually in her garden on the Oregon coast, breaking dishes and tiles for mosaic art projects. Contact her at *cappy@harborside.com; www.bumpercrop marketing.com*.

Diane M. Vanover received her AGS degree, with high honors, in 2000 when she was a grandmother of five. She was inducted into the Phi Theta Kappa Society, represented in The National Dean's List, and elected to Who's Who Among Students in American Junior Colleges. Please e-mail her at: *dmvanover@aol.com*.

Donald S. Verkow is an assistant principal at Paramount Charter Academy in Kalamazoo, Michigan. Education is a second career for Don, who spent twenty-five years in various manufacturing positions before graduating with a teaching degree from Western Michigan University in 1998. He is currently working to complete a master's degree in educational leadership. Don and his wife, Katie, are the parents of a son and daughter. An avid student of history, Don also enjoys writing, reading, traveling, music and golf.

Peggy Vincent is author of a memoir, *Baby Catcher: Chronicles of a Modern Midwife* (Scribner 2002). After "catching" nearly 3,000 babies as a Berkeley, California, midwife, Peggy is now a full-time writer. She lives in Oakland with her husband and teenaged son; two older children live nearby. Contact: *PV@peggyvincent.com*.

Rachel Wallace-Oberle has an education in radio and television broadcasting as well as journalism/print. She is a freelance writer/editor and has written for numerous publications. She cohosts a weekly Christian radio program and loves walking, classical music and canaries. Rachel can be reached at *rachelw-o@rogers.com*.

Paul Weller is a full-time vagabond and a part-time versifier. He and his wife, Trudy, make their home in an RV and are currently "out there" on the highways of America, somewhere between the Land of Milk and Honey and the State of Confusion.

Bonnie West has written essays and articles for national magazines. Her first love is fiction. She teaches yoga and has stretching and relaxation audiotapes and CDs available. She has also made a "Relax into Writing" CD. She can be e-mailed at *yogabonnie@yahoo.com*.

Diane Dean White is a former newspaper reporter and currently a freelance writer and author of the book *Beach Walks* and the soon-to-be released *Carolina in the Morning*. She and her husband, Stephen, are the parents of three grown children and two grand-gals. She can be reached at *thelamb212@aol.com*.

Marian Wilson is a freelance writer and registered nurse living in North Idaho. She is a columnist for the *Spokesman-Review* newspaper and has published short stories, essays and poetry. Marian enjoys hiking with her dogs, biking and kayaking. Please reach her at: *pobdjw@nidlink.com*.

Marjorie Woodall received a bachelor's degree in English from California State University, Sacramento, in January 2000. She lives in the beautiful Sierra Nevada foothills community of Nevada City in northern California where she works as a freelance copy editor, proofreader and writer. She can be reached at: *marjoriewoodall@hotmail.com*.

Rosalie Wright was born in San Jose, California, to a close-knit family, both geographically and emotionally. Her personal and family experiences inspired her to write a "Remember When" column which ran in her San Jose Community Newspaper for more than fifteen years. With the hope of recording and sharing her family stories and personal experiences, she has written three unpublished books: *Things Your Grandma Never Told You, But Should Have, Willow Glen, Thanks for the Memories* and *Coping with the 21st Century (you can't warm your hands on a Styrofoam cup!)*. Rosalie is currently writing a column for FRA NOI newspapers, Chicago's Italian-American voice. E-mail her at: *RosaleeWright@aol.com*.

Youthful Promises. Reprinted by permission of Denise Fleming. ©2003 Denise Fleming.

Where the Heart Is. Reprinted by permission of Marie Dauphine Savino-Jones. ©2003 Marie Dauphine Savino-Jones.

Without You. Reprinted by permission of Alice Ann Knisely. ©2001 Alice Ann Knisely.

A Change of Seasons. Reprinted by permission of Diane Dean White. ©2002 Diane Dean White.

Taking It in Stride. Reprinted by permission of Cappy Tosetti. ©2001 Cappy Tosetti.

Love: A Novel Approach. Reprinted by permission of Deborah Shouse. ©2001 Deborah Shouse.

Freedom. Reprinted by permission of Bonnie West. ©1999 Bonnie West. Originally appeared in *Woman's Day,* Issue: September, 2000.

Life's Short. Reprinted by permission of Patricia A. Hoyt. ©2001 Patricia A. Hoyt.

His Hands. Reprinted by permission of Laurel A. Pilon-Weick. ©2000 Laurel A. Pilon-Weick.

How I Stopped Looking for Mr. Right. Reprinted by permission of Rosalie Wright. ©1989 Rosalie Wright.

The Change. Reprinted by permission of Paul Weller. ©1994 Paul Weller.

Bonfire of the Tampons. Reprinted by permission of Trisha Posner. ©2000 Trisha Posner.

Orchids and Corned-Beef Hash. Reprinted by permission of George M. Flynn. ©1999 George M. Flynn.

The Moment. Reprinted by permission of Beverly Matulis. ©2000 Beverly Matulis.

More Precious Than Gold. Reprinted by permission of Amy Ridgeway. ©2003 Amy Ridgeway.

What Mothers Teach. Reprinted by permission of Ferna Lary Mills. ©2002 Ferna Lary Mills.

Messy Rooms: A Neat Memory. Reprinted by permission of Karen McCowan. ©1998 Karen McCowan.

Sunshine. Reprinted by permission of Lauri Khodabandehloo. ©2002 Lauri Khodabandehloo.

A Scarf, Earrings, Necklace, Bottle of Perfume. Reprinted by permission of Andy Strasberg. ©2001 Andy Strasberg.

Middle-Aged Mommy. Reprinted by permission of Karen Brown. ©2002 Karen Brown.

Who Called the Sheriff? Reprinted by permission of Nancy B. Gibbs. ©2002 Nancy B. Gibbs.

A Perfect Moment. Reprinted by permission of Phyllis L. Nutkis. ©2003 Phyllis L. Nutkis.

The Reason. Reprinted by permission of Donald S. Verkow. ©1997 Donald S. Verkow.

The Gift of the Middle. Reprinted by permission of Sandra B. Smith. ©2002 Sandra B. Smith.

Crayons, Notebooks and Pencil Bags. Reprinted by permission of SuzAnne C. Cole. ©1998 SuzAnne C. Cole.

The Circle of Life. Reprinted by permission of Kelly Ann Salasin. ©2004 Kelly Ann Salasin.

I Worked Hard for That Furrowed Brow. By Ellen Goodman for *Boston Daily Globe.* ©2002 by Globe Newspaper Co. (MA). Reproduced with permission of Globe Newspaper Co. (MA) in the format Trade Book via Copyright Clearance Center.

Body Work. Reprinted by permission of Carol E. Ayer. ©2003 Carol E. Ayer.

The Leap. Reprinted by permission of Marjorie Woodall. ©1999 Marjorie Woodall.

I Never Saw My Mother Do a Sit-Up. Reprinted by permission of EllynAnne Geisel. ©2002 EllynAnne Geisel.

Life Lessons Well Learned. Reprinted by permission of Christina Abt. ©2000 Christina Abt.

Small Present, Huge Gift. Reprinted by permission of Jenna Cassell. ©2003 Jenna Cassell.

The Miracle. Reprinted by permission of Renette Meltebeke. ©2002 Renette Meltebeke.

Midlife Lessons Worth Learning. Reprinted by permission of Sheri Harney. ©2002 Sheri Harney.

Golf, Like Midlife, Is Absolutely Unfair. By Ellen Goodman for *Boston Daily Globe.* Copyright 2002 by Globe Newspaper Co. (MA). Reproduced with permission of Globe Newspaper Co. (MA) in the format Trade Book via Copyright Clearance Center.

Aging Gracefully. Reprinted by permission of Cyndy Salamanti. ©2002 Cyndy Salamanti.

Be Careful What You Ask For. Reprinted by permission of Kristi Meisenbach Boylan. ©2002 Kristi Meisenbach Boylan.

A Lesson in Surrender. From *If Not Now, When?* By Stephanie Marston. ©2001 Stephanie Marston. By permission of Warner Books, Inc.